ETERNAL WISDOM
Upadeshamritam

VOLUME 2

Compiled by
SWAMI JNANAMRITANANDA PURI

English translation from the orginal Malayalam
by
Dr. M.N. Namboodiri

Mata Amritanandamayi Center
San Ramon, California

ETERNAL WISDOM - UPADESHAMRITAM
Volume II

PUBLISHED BY:
Mata Amritanandamayi Center
P.O. Box 613
San Ramon, CA 94583-0613
Tel: (510) 537-9417

FIRST PRINTING 1999

ALSO AVAILABLE FROM:
Mata Amritanandamayi Mission Trust
Amritapuri P.O., Kollam Dt., Kerala
INDIA 690525

ISBN 1-879410-76-1

MOTHER...

Let my every action

Be a worship of You

With total self-surrender,

Let every sound falling from my lips

Be a chant of Your great mantra,

Let each movement of my hands

Be a mudra in worship of You,

Let every step I take

Be a circumambulation of You,

Let all my food and drink

Be offerings in Your sacred fire,

Let my repose

Be a prostration to You.

Mother, let each act of mine,

And every comfort,

Be a worship of You.

FOREWORD

Rare indeed are the mahatmas (great souls) endowed with the vision of seeing the entire universe within the Atman (Self), and the Atman within the universe. Even if they are recognized, they may not be inclined to communicate with us or counsel us, immersed as they are in the eternal silence of the Self. Therefore, it is our great fortune when a fully realized mahatma is ready to advise and discipline us with the tender love of a mother, and the inexplicable compassion of a guru. Throughout the world today, the *darshan* and the nectarous words of Sri Mata Amritanandamayi Devi are effecting transformations in the lives of hundreds of thousands of people. This book, though incomplete, is a precious collection of conversations between the Holy Mother and Her disciples, devotees, and inquiring visitors during the period from June 1985 to September 1986.

The wisdom of the mahatmas, who have come with the mission of uplifting the world, has both immediate and eternal meaning. Even though they elucidate values that are everlasting, they are attuned to the call of the times in which they live, and their words are in response to the heartbeat of their listeners.

Mother speaks Her immortal words, which transform society, at a time when man has lost his traditional values, nobler sentiments, and peace of mind in the frenzied attempt to reinforce the outer world of sensory pleasures, power, and prestige. Man's senseless pursuit of these distractions, while he remains oblivious of his own Self, has cost him the harmony and graciousness of his life. Lack of faith, fear, and a sense of competition has destroyed personal ties and family relations. Love has become no more than a mirage in a culture of excessive consumerism.

Selfless love of God gives way to a form of devotion that is driven entirely by desires. Man gives undue importance to an intellect that seeks the yield of immediate profit, while discarding the lasting glory promised by true wisdom. Lofty spiritual principles and noble experiences do not shine in the lives of the people, but are confined to mere words. It is at such a juncture that Mother speaks to us in a language of untainted devotion, a language of the heart, of wisdom, and of the love that is Her entire life. Her ambrosial words have both an immediate and eternal relevance.

The wisdom of Mother, who has personally listened to countless problems confided by hundreds of thousands of people, shows Her deep insight into the human condition. She recognizes their needs and descends to the level of the rationalist, the believer, the scientist, the ordinary man, the housewife, the businessman, the scholar, and the illiterate—man, woman, or child—and gives each one the appropriate answer, befitting their requirements.

Mother points at Her own life and declares, "As I see everything as the Truth, or Brahman, I bow to that Truth;

I bow to my Self. I serve everyone, seeing them as the Self."
She accepts *advaita* (non-duality) as the ultimate truth; yet
the path that She commonly prescribes is a harmonious
blend of *mantra japa*, meditation on a divine form, devotional singing, *archana*, *satsang*, and selfless service to the
world.

Her advice is not just theoretical, but highly practical
and rooted in daily living. Her instructions shed light on
the need for spiritual training and *sadhana* (spiritual practice) in the life of the individual and in society, the role of
selfless service in the search for the Self, the importance of
sincere prayer with devotion, and pure love. She also ad-
dresses issues concerning the code of conduct for the householder, the problems of daily life, the *dharma* of the
relationship between man and woman, and practical guide-
lines for spiritual seekers, sometimes offering riddles of a
philosophical nature.

We hear Her exhorting Her children to follow spirituality in their lives, to give up luxuries, to eliminate bad habits,
and to serve those who suffer: "Children, God-realization
is the real aim of life." Spirituality is not blind faith; it is
the ideal that eliminates darkness. It is the principle that
teaches us to face any adverse circumstance or obstacle with
a smile. It is a teaching for the mind. Mother points out
that we can effectively utilize all other learning only if we
acquire this knowledge.

Mother's infinite wisdom emerges as words of comfort
to those seeking solace from the problems of life, as an-

swers to questions posed by those who are inquisitive about spirituality, and as instructions given from time to time to Her disciples. She gives each answer according to the nature and circumstances of the questioner. Even when the questioner is unable to express his ideas fully, Mother, who knows the language of the heart, gives the appropriate answer. An answer from Mother, even before a doubt in the mind is expressed, is a common experience of those who come to Her.

In answer to a question explicitly put to Her by one person, it is Her practice to often include advice for a silent listener as well. Only the silent individual will understand that this was an answer for him. When one studies Mother's teachings, these special qualities should be kept in mind.

The words of a mahatma have many levels of meaning. We should absorb the meaning that is most appropriate for us. A well-known story in the *Upanishads* narrates that when Lord Brahma uttered the word 'da,' the demons interpreted it as advice to show compassion (*daya*), the humans as a call to give (*dana*), and the celestials as an injunction to practice restraint (*dama*).

Sweet is the experience of listening to Mother, and watching Her speak with vivid expressions and gestures, in a language that is simple, and at the same time, embellished with extremely appropriate stories and analogies drawn from life around Her. The love that shines in Mother's eyes, Her radiant, compassionate face, remain alive in the mirror of the listeners' mind as objects of meditation.

viii ETERNAL WISDOM—Upadeshamritam ❖ Volume 2

There is no scarcity of spiritual literature today, yet the sad fact remains that the highest ideals are confined to peoples' tongues, but are not found in their lives. Mother, however, speaks on the basis of Her daily life. She never gives advice that She Herself does not demonstrate in Her own life. She frequently reminds us that spiritual principles and mantras are not meant to remain on our lips, but are to be translated into our lives as well. The secret behind the deep spiritual principles flowing in a continuous stream from Mother, who has not studied the scriptures or taken instruction from a guru, is nothing but Her direct experience of the Self.

The lives of the mahatmas form the very foundation of the scriptures. Mother's sayings such as, "The whole world belongs to the one who knows Reality," "Kindness towards the poor is our duty to God," "If you take refuge in God, He will bring what you need when you need it," are mirrors of Her own life. In each of Her movements, there is the dance of compassion for the whole world, and love for God. Indeed, this unity of thought, word, and deed in Mother's life is the basis of Her statement that Her children do not need to study any other scripture if they analyze and study Her own life carefully. Mother shines in the midst of society as a living embodiment of *Vedanta*.

The mahatmas who sanctify the world through their presence are *tirthas*, holy places of pilgrimage, on the move. As regular pilgrimages and temple worship purify our minds when practiced for many years, so a single darshan, touch, or word from a mahatma sanctifies us and deposits in us seeds of exalted *samskara*.

The words of the mahatmas are not mere sounds. The mahatmas shower their grace along with their words. Their words are bound to awaken Consciousness, even in someone who listens without understanding their meaning. When these words appear in the form of a book, their study becomes the greatest satsang and meditation. Mahatmas like Mother, who have experienced Reality, transcend time and space. Reading or hearing Mother's immortal words enables us to maintain an unseen inner bond with Her and to become fit to receive Her blessings. That is the real greatness of the study of such books.

We humbly offer this collection of Mother's immortal words to the readers, with the prayer that it may inspire them to emulate the lofty spiritual ideals that shine throughout Her life, and to progress on the path of the ultimate Truth.

- The publishers

Eternal Wisdom
UPADESHAMRITAM
Volume 2

MOTHER LISTENS TO THE BHAGAVATAM

A discourse on the *Srimad Bhagavatam* was being given by Kavyakaustubham[1] Ottoor in front of the *kalari*.[2] A nectarous stream of devotion was gushing forth, about to break its banks. Everyone sat enraptured. Mother was in the audience, listening to the story of Krishna's childhood sports. Ottoor, who was well into his eighties, and whose mind always dwelt on Krishna, was telling the story as if he were witnessing it before his very eyes.

"...What antics is He up to now? Who knows? He broke the pot, and there was a deluge of curd everywhere—all

---

[1] "The *kaustubha* gem among poets." (The Kaustubha is a precious gem worn by Lord Vishnu on His chest.) This was the title Ottoor Unni Namboodiripad had been given as a distinguished poet. He was a famous poet and Sanskrit scholar, and the author of Mother's 108 Names. He spent his last few years living at the ashram.

[2] The little temple where the bhava darshan was held in the early days, which, before it was rebuilt into a temple, had been a cowshed when Mother was a child.

over Him as well. So it's easy to find out which way He went. There are a few footprints smeared with curd. But then, after a few steps, there's nothing… no footprints!

"Well, we are also in this predicament. We can take three or four steps towards the Lord, with the help of various signs—just a few steps, using all the *Upanishads* and *Puranas*—but that's all. After that, we have to discover Him through our own search.

"Yashoda is looking for Him. She knows very well where to look for Krishna. Just search wherever any butter or milk is stored! You can't miss Him! What a blessing it would be if we could see the Lord that easily! But that's how it was: whenever you wanted to see Him, you just had to go and look.

"So she keeps looking and then she sees Him, perched on top of a mortar which He has turned upside down. There is a veritable army around Him—Sri Rama's army![3] They're all holding out their hands and devouring the goodies. And Krishna is lamenting that He left two of His four arms in that prison, for a thousand arms would not have been enough to feed all those monkeys.[4] 'Quick, quick!' He says. 'You have to eat it all before Mother comes!'

---

[3] Ottoor is here referring to the gopas, the cowherd boys who were Krishna's companions, as "Sri Rama's army," that is, an army of "monkeys."

[4] When Krishna was born, his parents, Devaki and Vasudeva, were in prison, put there by Krishna's uncle, Kamsa. Krishna gave His parents a vision of His four-armed, glorious form as Lord Vishnu, and then reverted to the form of the human infant. The power of *maya* (illusion) made His parents instantly forget the vision they had experienced.

And every few moments, that all-seeing Witness glances around stealthily. Then He sees her!

"It is said that a crow and the wind will enter a space only if both the way in and the way out are open. Krishna has seen to that too. He has kept the escape door open, and just as He is a hair's breath away from His mother's grasp, He bolts.

"Why does He run? Well, Yashoda is holding a stick in her hand, and Krishna knows that she isn't old enough to need a walking stick... He knows that the rod is meant for Him. So He runs away."

> ...and His mother followed Him, whom even a yogi's mind, well conditioned by practice and austerity, fails to reach without His grace."
>
> Bhagavatam 10:9

As the *satsang* continued, Mother got up and walked towards the west side of the ashram. She stopped between the kalari and the *Vedanta* school, in front of some potted plants that hung from the beams of the school building. She gently caressed each creeper, and then, one by one, She held the flowing branches of each plant in Her hand, and kissed them. She touched the plants as lovingly as a mother caresses her new-born infant.

A girl approached Mother with a question, but Mother gestured for her to be quiet. When the girl reached out to touch a plant, Mother stopped her as if She was afraid the girl's grasp might hurt the plant. Mother continued to commune with the plants for a while. Perhaps they needed to share their sorrows with Mother, just like Her human children do. Who but Mother could console them?

By this time the discourse was over. Mother returned to the *kalari mandapam* (the open verandah of the little temple) and sat down.

TYAGA

A householder devotee: "Amma, you always talk about the importance of *tyaga* (renunciation). What is tyaga?"

Mother: "Son, every act that is done without regard for one's own comfort or interest is tyaga. Amma calls any action tyaga, if it is done as an offering to God for the benefit of the world, without any sense of 'I' or 'mine', and with no regard for your own comfort. The struggle a person undergoes for his own benefit cannot be considered tyaga."

Devotee: "Could you explain that, Amma?"

Mother: "When your child is sick, you take it to the hospital. You'll walk to the hospital, if necessary, even if it's a very long way. You are ready to fall at the feet of any number of people to get your child admitted to the hospital, and if the hospital rooms are full, you are ready to sleep on the dirty floor with the child. You'll take time off from work for several days to stay with the child. But because all this struggle is for the sake of your own child, it cannot be called tyaga.

"People are prepared to go up and down the court-house steps countless times just to fight for a tiny piece of land. But they are doing it for themselves. People work late and give up their sleep to get overtime pay. This is not tyaga. But if you sacrifice all of your comforts and come to the aid of another person, then you can call it tyaga. If you help a poor fellow human being with the money you have earned through hard work, that is tyaga. Say that your neighbor's child is sick, and there is no one to be with him in the hospital; if you stay with that child, expecting nothing in return from anyone, not even a smile, that qualifies as tyaga. If you reduce your expenses by foregoing some personal convenience, and use what you save from this for a benevolent purpose, that is tyaga.

"Through such acts of sacrifice, you knock on the door that leads to the realm of the Self. It is through such actions that you gain entry into that world. This is what is known as *karma yoga*. Other actions lead only to death. The actions you do with the attitude of 'I' and 'mine' can never be of any real benefit to you.

"When you visit a friend that you haven't seen for a long time, you may give her a bouquet of flowers. But you are the first to enjoy the beauty and fragrance of the flowers, and you also experience the gratification of giving. In the same way, you automatically derive happiness and contentment from your selfless acts of tyaga.

"Children, even if someone who is engaged in acts of tyaga doesn't find time for *japa* (repetition of a mantra), he will still attain the immortal state. His life will benefit others like nectar. A life filled with tyaga is the greatest form of satsang[5] because others can see and emulate it."

ADVICE ON JAPA

Br: "Amma, is it good to forgo sleep and stay up at night doing japa?"

Mother: "For years you have been in the habit of sleeping. Stopping it abruptly will cause disturbances. Sleep at least four or five hours, not less than four hours. Don't reduce sleep abruptly; do it gradually."

Br: "I often lose concentration while chanting my *mantra.*"

Mother: "The mantra should be chanted with great attention. Focus either on the sound of the mantra or on the meaning; or you can visualize each syllable of the mantra as you chant. You can also visualize the form of your Beloved Deity while chanting. Decide the total number of times you will chant the mantra each day. This will help you to do japa with determination. But do not chant heedlessly, just to reach a certain target number. The most important thing is that your mind is one-pointed. Using a *mala* (rosary) will help you to count and also to maintain your concentration.

"Concentration won't come easily in the beginning, so

---

[5] Sat = Truth, being; sanga = association with.

you should move your lips while chanting. In due course, you will be able to chant mentally, without moving your lips or tongue. Do japa with alertness, never mechanically. Each repetition should be like savoring a sweet. In the end, you will reach a state where even if you let go of the mantra, the mantra won't let go of you.

"Didn't Yashoda tie Krishna to a mortar? In the same way, imagine binding your Beloved Deity with the rope of love and then freeing Him. Picture in your mind, as vividly as in a movie, that you are playing with Him, talking to Him, and running after Him to catch Him. Once you are filled with love, no one need tell you to imagine those things, because thoughts about your Beloved One will be the only thoughts that spontaneously arise in your mind.

"Children, try to cultivate love within you, and develop the attitude, 'God is my All.'"

Friday, November 15, 1985

It was early evening. Mother and Her disciples had just arrived at the home of a devotee in Kayamkulam. He had invited Mother several times before, but She had only now accepted the invitation.

A small, temporary canopy had been raised in front of the house for the *bhajan* (devotional singing) program. There was a large crowd, most of whom were uneducated and had little spiritual understanding. The smell of alco-

hol hung in the air, and the family members made little
effort to control the crowd. In that atmosphere the
brahmacharis found it difficult to sing *kirtans* (hymns).
Perhaps it was because She had foreseen this that Mother
had not accepted the previous invitations. Mother often
said, "Amma is ready to go anywhere; She is ready to sing
in a bazaar and take insults from anyone that is not a
problem for Her. After all, isn't Amma singing God's name?
What shame could there possibly be in that? But Amma's
children won't tolerate anyone saying anything negative
about Her. Also, there are a few girls among us. They
can't just go and sing anywhere. They need to be protected. That is why Amma can't accept every invitation
indiscriminately."

THE SECRET OF KARMA

The return trip to the ashram in the van was a good
occasion for satsang with Mother. A brahmachari asked,
"Amma, is it unavoidable that we have to suffer for every
mistake we've made?"

Mother: "We have to accept punishment even for small
mistakes. Even Bhishma[6] had to suffer the consequences
of his mistake."

---

[6] Bhishma was the grandfather of the Pandavas and Kauravas. He was a
great warrior with great wisdom. Though his sympathies were with the
Pandavas, because of an oath he had made, he took the side of the
Kauravas in the Mahabharata war.

Br: "What did he do wrong? How was he punished?"

Mother: "He just stood there and watched while Draupadi was being disrobed, didn't he? Though he knew that Duryodhana and his brothers would never listen to reason, he should at least have reminded them of their *dharma*. But he didn't. He just kept quiet. He should have advised those evildoers about their dharma, regardless of whether or not his counsel would be heeded. Because he didn't utter a word against them, he became a partner in their wicked deed. It was because of this that he later had to lie on the bed of arrows.

"Watching an unrighteous act that you know is against dharma, while keeping your mouth shut, is the greatest form of unrighteousness. That is the conduct of a coward, not a person of courage. Let no one who commits such a sin think they can escape. Hell is meant for people like that."

Br: "Where is hell?"

Mother: "On earth itself."

Br: "But isn't it God who makes us do both right and wrong?"

Mother: "Son, that is true for someone who is convinced that everything is God's work. In that case, we should be able to see that everything is given to us by God, both when we enjoy the fruits of our good actions and when we suffer the punishment for our mistakes.

"God isn't responsible for our mistakes—we are. Say that a doctor prescribes for us a body-building tonic. He tells us how much to take and how often. If we ignore his instructions and drink the whole bottle at once, and if our health is ruined as a result, what is the point of blaming the doctor? Similarly, if we drive carelessly and then have an accident, can we blame the gasoline? How, then, can we blame God for the problems that are caused by our own ignorance? God has made it perfectly clear to us how we should live on this earth. It is useless to blame Him for the consequences of our not having followed His instructions."

Br: "The *Bhagavad Gita* tells us to act without any desire for the fruits of our actions. Amma, how can we possibly do this?"

Mother: "The Lord prescribed that in order to free us from suffering. We should perform our actions with *shraddha*,[7] without thinking or worrying about the results. Then we will certainly get the results our actions deserve. For instance, if you are a student, learn your lessons with great attention, without brooding over whether or not you will pass the exam. If you are constructing a building, build carefully according to the plan, without worrying about whether the building will stand or collapse.

"Good actions bring good results. If a farmer sells rice of good quality, people will buy it, and he will be properly rewarded for his work. But if he sells an adulterated prod-

---

[7] Shraddha in Sanskrit means faith rooted in wisdom and experience, whereas the same term in Malayalam means dedication to one's work and attentive awareness in every action. Mother uses the term in the latter sense.

uct hoping for extra profit, he will be punished either today or tomorrow, and he will lose his peace of mind. So do each action with alertness and an attitude of surrender to God. Each action will receive its result in full measure, whether you worry about it or not. So why waste time worrying about the fruits of your actions? Why not use the time to think about God?"

Br: "If the Self is all-pervading, shouldn't it remain in a dead body? In that case, how can death occur?"

Mother: "When a light bulb burns out or a fan stops turning, it doesn't mean that there is no electricity. When we stop fanning ourselves with a hand-held fan, the flow of air stops, but this doesn't mean that there's no air. Or when a balloon bursts, it doesn't mean that the air which was in the balloon ceases to exist. It is still there. In the same way, the Self is everywhere. God is everywhere. Death occurs, not because of the absence of the Self, but because of the destruction of the instrument known as the body. At the time of death, the body ceases to manifest the consciousness of the Self. So death marks the breakdown of the instrument, and not any imperfection in the Self."

Mother now began teaching two brahmacharis a bhajan. She sang one line at a time, and they repeated after Her:

Bhagavane, Bhagavane...

O Lord, O Lord!
O Lord, to whom the devotees are endearing,

O Pure One, Destroyer of sins,
There seems to be only sinners in this world.

Is there anyone who can show us the right path?
O Narayana, virtue has disappeared.
Man has lost all sense of truth and virtue.
Spiritual truths remain only in the pages of books.

All that is seen wears the vesture of hypocrisy.
Revive and protect dharma,
O Krishna!

Then Mother sang another song.

Amme kannu turakkule...

O Mother, won't you open your eyes and come?
Remove this darkness.
I shall repeat your countless names, again and
again,
With great reverence.

In this ignorant world
Who else is there but you
To remove my ignorance?
You are the Essence of Wisdom,
The Power behind this Universe.

O Mother, who adores Her devotees,
You are our very life-blood.

As we bow down at your feet,
Won't you graciously glance at us?

The seven sages are ever engaged
In singing your praises.
Now we afflicted ones are calling you—
O Great One, won't you come?

The van stopped at the Vallickavu boat jetty. The time had gone so quickly, everyone was amazed to realize they had almost reached the ashram.

At the ashram gate, a devotee eagerly awaited Mother. A young man was with him. The devotee prostrated fully when he saw Mother, while the young man casually stood by. Mother led them both to the kalari, and sat down with them on the open veranda of the little temple.

Mother: "Children, when did you come?"

Devotee: "A few hours ago. We were on the bus in Oachira, on our way here, when we saw your van go by in the opposite direction. We were afraid we wouldn't get to see you today at all. But when we arrived, we were told you were returning tonight, so we felt much better."

Mother: "Amma went to a son's house in Kayamkulam. They are very poor people, and had invited Amma for some time. Seeing how sad they were, Amma finally promised to go there today. How is your *sadhana* (spiritual practices) going, son?"

Devotee: "By Amma's grace, everything is going

smoothly. Amma, may I ask a question?"

Mother: "Of course, son."

RECEIVING MANTRA INITIATION
FROM A GURU

Devotee: "Amma, a friend of mine received a mantra from a *sannyasi* (monk). Recently, he tried to persuade me to get a mantra from that sannyasi as well. He kept insisting, even though I told him that I have already received a mantra from you. Finally, I managed to get away from him. Amma, when one has been given a mantra by a guru, is it right to accept a mantra from someone else?"

Mother: "Once you have chosen a guru, if you then look to someone else as your guru, it's like infidelity in a marriage. But if you haven't received a mantra from a guru, then it isn't a problem.

"Once you have received a mantra from a *satguru* (a Self-realized master), you don't need to go anywhere else. Your guru will look after you in every way. You can respect and honor other gurus, that is fine, but you are not going to gain anything if you don't stick to anything. Approaching another guru, while the satguru who has given you mantra initiation is still alive, is like a woman deceiving her husband and accepting another man. You accepted a mantra from your guru because you had complete faith in him. Choosing another person as your guru means that you have lost that faith."

Devotee: "What should a person do if they lose faith in the guru who has given them a mantra?"

Mother: "They should try as much as they can to keep their faith; but if they find it impossible, then it's useless to remain with the guru. Trying to revive lost faith is like trying to grow hair on a bald head. Once your faith is lost, it's extremely difficult to regain. So, before accepting a person as your guru, you should observe him carefully. It is best to receive a mantra from a satguru."

Devotee: "What is the advantage of receiving a mantra from a satguru?"

Mother: "Through his *sankalpa* (divine resolve), the satguru can awaken the spiritual power within you. If you pour milk into milk, you won't get any curd. But if you put a small amount of curd into a bowl of milk, all the milk will turn into curd. When a *mahatma* (great soul) gives you a mantra, his sankalpa is involved. His divine power enters into the disciple."

Devotee: "There are many who assume the role of a guru by giving mantras to people left and right. Is there any benefit to be had from the mantras they give?"

Mother: "There are those who give speeches just from book knowledge, or they may read the *Bhagavatam* and the *Ramayana* aloud as a livelihood. Such people cannot save themselves; how then can they possibly save others? If you have received a mantra from such a person, and you come across a satguru, then you should definitely ask to be reinitiated by the satguru.

"Only those who have done spiritual practices and have realized the Self are qualified to give mantras to others. Those who pretend to be gurus are like boats made of sponge. They cannot take anyone across to the other shore. If anyone gets into such a boat, the boat will sink and the passenger will go down with it. A satguru, on the other hand, is like a huge ship, and by boarding that ship, any amount of people can reach the other shore. Someone who accepts disciples and initiates others, without first having acquired the necessary power through sadhana, is like a baby snake that tries to swallow a big frog. The snake is unable to swallow the frog, but the frog can't get away."

Young man: "The scriptures recommend spending time in the company of the wise ones. What is the benefit of satsang with a mahatma?"

Mother: "Son, if we pass through an incense factory, the scent will remain on us afterwards. We don't have to work there, or buy any of the incense, or even touch anything—all we have to do is enter the place and the fragrance will linger on us, without any effort on our part. In the same way, when you are in the presence of a mahatma, a change takes place within you, without you even being aware of it. The time you spend with a mahatma is invaluable. The presence of a great soul will create positive *vasanas* (habits or tendencies), qualities, and *samskaras* (disposition) in us. Being in the company of dark-minded people, on the other hand, is like entering a room full of coal. Even if we don't touch the coal, our bodies will be black when we come out.

"One can easily find the opportunity to do *tapas* (austerities) for many years, but the chance to be with a mahatma is extremely rare and hard to come by. Such an opportunity should never be wasted. We should be extremely patient and try to get the most out of the experience. A mere touch or glance from a mahatma can benefit us far more than ten years of tapas. But to experience that benefit, we have to get rid of the ego and we need to have faith."

THE IMPORTANCE OF
DOING SADHANA IN SOLITUDE

Young man: "We walked through the ashram grounds today and looked around."

Mother: "What is there to see here, son?"

Young man: "I don't understand the need for the cave behind the kalari."

Mother: "In the beginning, solitude is essential for a seeker. It will prevent the mind from being distracted, and the mind will thus turn inward. If you follow the guru's instructions, you will be able to see God in everything.

"In this area there are no mountains, just houses everywhere. There is no solitude to be found here. We can't even dig deep in the ground to make a meditation cave because there is so much water. So the cave is only two or three feet deep. You can't really call it a cave.

"We have to prepare the field before we sow the seeds. We have to get rid of the weeds, plow the earth, make it smooth and even, and then, finally, we can plant. And as the crop begins to grow, we have to keep removing the weeds. But later, when the plants are fully grown, we no longer have to worry about the weeds, because then the plants will be strong enough to resist and the weeds cannot harm them. In the beginning, however, when the plants are young and fragile the weeds can easily destroy them. So in the beginning we should do our spiritual practices in solitude. We should immerse ourselves in japa and meditation, without mingling too much with others. Our field should be free from obstructing weeds. At a later stage, when we have been doing sadhana for some time, we'll have the strength to transcend all external obstacles.

"If you try to pump water to a higher level, you won't succeed if there is a leak at the bottom of the system. In the same way, we have to stop the leakage of the mental power that we have gathered, by giving up all our external interests. We need to spend time in solitude and purify our minds, by getting rid of the bad vasanas we have accumulated in the past. We should avoid interacting with too many people.

"A student can't sit and study in a noisy, crowded railway station, can he? He needs to be in an environment that is suitable for studying. Similarly, a *sadhak* (spiritual aspirant) needs solitude in the beginning. After a certain amount of practice you'll be able to meditate under any conditions. But for now, those special arrangements are needed.

"In addition to solitude, there is another reason for meditating in a cave. The vibrations below ground, and also in the mountains, have a unique quality which adds special power to one's sadhana. The mahatmas say that underground caves are especially suitable for spiritual practices. Their words are like the Vedas. We approach a doctor when we are sick and we accept what he tells us. Similarly, the words of the mahatmas are the authority we adhere to on the spiritual path.

"In the olden days, there were plenty of forests and caves where seekers could practice their austerities. They survived on fruits and roots and were immersed in tapas. But today the circumstances are different. If we need a cave, we have to make one. Though this cave is man-made, it's good enough for solitude and meditation."

Young man: "But does a seeker need a cave to do tapas? Don't we get cut off from the world if we stay in a cave? Isn't that a weakness?"

Mother: "Though there may be waves in the water of a dam, no water is lost. But if the dam breaks, all the water will be escape. Similarly, the sadhak loses his subtle energy when he talks and associates with others. To avoid this, it is good to be isolated in the beginning. That is the sadhak's period of practice. If you want to learn to ride a bicycle, you go to an open, empty place where you can practice without disturbing anyone. You don't consider this a weakness. The children[8] here (the ashram residents) need this cave and the solitude it provides. Later, they will go out and serve the world."

Young man: "But why don't they go to Mookambika[9] or the Himalayas to do tapas? There they would be in the proper environment."

Mother: "Son, being in the guru's presence takes the place of being in Mookambika or the Himalayas. The scriptures say that the guru's feet are the confluence of all holy waters. Also, the children here are sadhaks, and sadhaks need to be close to their guru so that they can be given the instructions they need. A disciple should never go far away from the guru without the guru's permission.

"A doctor doesn't just give a severely ill patient some medicine and send him home. He keeps the patient in the hospital for treatment. He examines the patient frequently and changes the dosage of the medicine depending on the stage of the illness. The same holds true for a disciple doing sadhana. He should always be under the guru's watchful eye. The guru should be close at hand to clear any doubts that may arise in the disciple, and to lead the disciple forward with the necessary advice during each step of his sadhana. Also, the guru should be someone who himself has traveled that path.

"If the sadhak is not guided properly, he can become

[8] Mother always refers to Her disciples and devotees as Her children.
[9] The hills near the famous Mookambika temple, which is an ideal place for doing sadhana in solitude.

mentally unstable. The body gets hot when you meditate a lot. If this happens, the sadhak needs to be given the proper advice on how to cool the body. At that stage his diet has to be changed, he needs solitude and shouldn't meditate too much. If a person who doesn't have the strength to lift more than forty kilos suddenly lifts a hundred kilos, he will stagger and fall. Similarly, if you meditate more than the body is able to bear, it can lead to a lot of problems. This is why the guru should be nearby, so that he can give the disciple the instructions he needs.

"If anything goes wrong with your meditation, you cannot blame it on God or on meditation per se. The fault lies in the particular meditation technique that is being used. At this stage, the children who are here need to have Amma close at hand, so that they can practice meditation properly and progress. The time has not yet come for them to do sadhana by themselves, so they shouldn't go far away from here. Later, however, that won't be a problem."

Young man: "What does one actually gain by doing tapas?"

Mother: "An ordinary person can be compared to a small candle, while a person doing tapas is like a power transformer, capable of distributing power over a wide area. Tapas gives the sadhak tremendous inner strength. When faced with obstacles, he doesn't weaken. He is extremely efficient in whatever he does. Tapas awakens detachment so that the sadhak acts without expecting the fruits of his actions. Through tapas, he acquires the ability to look upon everyone as equal. He doesn't feel any special attachment towards anyone, nor does he ever treat anyone with hostility. These qualities benefit both the sadhak and the world.

"It is easy to say, 'I am *Brahman*,' even when the mind is full of jealousy and hostility. Tapas is the training you do to transform the impure mind into a divine mind.

"Before you can pass an examination, you have to study. You can't expect to pass without studying at all, can you? And before you can drive a car, you have to learn how to drive. This can be compared to doing tapas. Having brought your mind under control, you can continue forward without weakening under any circumstances. Book learning alone cannot accomplish this; tapas is necessary. The result of doing tapas can be compared to the sun acquiring a wonderful fragrance. Those who do tapas are moving towards a state of wholeness. Their words are vibrant with life. People feel blissful in their presence. The *tapasvis* benefit the world because, through their tapas, they have gained the power to uplift others."

Young man: "What is meant by Self-realization or the supreme state of awakening?"

Mother: "Seeing God in all things, perceiving everything as one and the same, knowing all beings as your own Self—that is realization. When all thoughts have subsided and there are no more desires, when the mind is perfectly still, then you experience *samadhi*. In that state, the attitude of 'I' and 'mine' has vanished. You are then of service to everyone, and no longer a burden to others.

An ordinary person can be compared to a small, stagnant pond, while a realized soul is like a river, or a tree, giving comfort and coolness to those who come to him."

It was very late. Mother got up to leave. She said to the young man, "Why don't you stay here until tomorrow, son? If Amma continues to sit here now, these children will also sit here and they'll miss their routine in the morning. Amma will see you tomorrow."

Saturday, November 16, 1985

The next morning several of the brahmacharis missed *archana* because they had been up so late with Mother the night before. Later, when the meditation was about to begin, Mother came and asked them why they hadn't gone to archana. She said, "Those who have *vairagya* (detachment) will never break their daily routine, no matter how tired they are. Children, don't miss the daily archana. If you happen to miss it, then begin your meditation only after doing archana on your own."

Everyone stopped meditating and began chanting the *Lalita Sahasranama*, while Mother sat with them. When the archana was over, Mother got up and walked over to the courtyard on the northern side of the ashram. She was joined by a few brahmacharis and the young man who had arrived the day before.

BRAHMACHARYA

Young man: "Is celibacy compulsory here?"

Mother: "Amma has told Her children who are stay-ing here to transform their sexual energy into *ojas* (subtle energy), for then they will come to know their real na-ture, and that is true happiness. This is their way of life. Only those who can do this need to stay here. The others can leave and enter *grihasthashrama* (a spiritually oriented family life). The children who come here are told to prac-tice celibacy. Those who feel they will fail have the free-dom to leave at any time.

"The police department has its own rules, so does the military. Similarly, the brahmacharis and brahmacharinis here at the ashram have to follow the rules of *brahmacharya*. Observing celibacy is essential for those who have chosen to live here, and it applies not only in the sexual sense. They have to restrain all their senses: their eyes, nose, tongue, and ears as well. Amma doesn't force them. She just tells them that this is the path.

"In fact, Amma has advised them to get married, but they won't hear of it. So Amma has told them that here they have to live a certain way and follow certain rules, and if they can't do that, they are free to leave. No one is forced to live in this way. Not everyone can stick to this path. Amma tells them, 'Don't suppress anything. You can try this way of life, and if it doesn't work for you, get married.'

"If you dress up for a role, you should play it well, otherwise, don't even begin to play that role. If you want to reach the Supreme Goal, brahmacharya is essential. What did our mahatmas say about it?"

Young man: "Who are you referring to?"

Mother: "Buddha, Ramakrishna, Vivekananda, Ramana, Ramatirtha, Chattampi Swami, Narayana Guru. What did they all say? Why did Buddha, Ramatirtha, Tulsidas, and other mahatmas leave their wives and their homes? Why did Sri Shankaracharya[10] take sannyasa at such an early age? Do their actions imply that brahmacharya isn't necessary? Even after getting married, didn't Sri Ramakrishna practice brahmacharya to set an example for others to follow?

"Brahmacharya isn't just something external, it doesn't just mean foregoing marriage. Every step has to be taken in accordance with the highest principle. Not even a thought should violate that principle. Brahmacharya also includes refraining from harming others in any way, not listening to or looking at anything unnecessarily, and to speak only when it is needed. Only then can you call it true brahmacharya. On the spiritual path, brahmacharya is absolutely essential.

"Because it may be difficult to control your thoughts in the beginning, you can start by practicing brahmacharya outwardly. If brahmacharya isn't observed, you will lose all the strength you have gained through your sadhana.

---

[10] Sri Shankaracharya was a great mahatma and philosopher who lived in the eighth century. He was an exponent of Advaita philosophy.

Amma doesn't mean that you should suppress these things by force. For those who have *lakshya bodha* (constant intent on the spiritual goal), self-control isn't that difficult. People going to work in the Persian Gulf countries often return only after several years.[11] During that time they live far away from their wives and children. When it's a question of finding a job, you don't let your attachment to your family and country get in the way. Similarly, if your aim is Self-realization, you don't think about anything else. Other thoughts will fade automatically, without there being any need to forcibly control them.

"People believe that happiness can be found in external objects, and so they work hard for those things, wasting all their energy. We should reflect on this and understand the truth. Through our love for God and by practicing one-pointed tapas we will grow strong. This isn't difficult for those who understand that they only waste energy by looking for external happiness.

"Certain plants won't bear fruit if they have too many leaves. Only if they are pruned will they flower and bear fruit. In the same way, if we allow ourselves to be swayed by external pleasures, we won't be able to find the inner Truth. We have to get rid of our desires for worldly pleasures if we wish to reap the fruit of Self-realization."

Young man: "Does the spiritual culture of India completely negate worldly life?"

---

[11] Since the 1970's, a large number of people from India, especially from Kerala, have been going to work in the Gulf countries.

Mother: "No, not really. It only says that true happiness is not to be found in that way."

Young man: "Why can't we reach the Goal while at the same time enjoying worldly life?"

Mother: "Someone who truly yearns for realization doesn't even think about worldly life or physical pleasures. Those who live a family life can also reach the Goal, provided they recognize the limitations of worldly life, and are totally detached, leading a life of japa, meditation, and renunciation."

Young man: "Is it very difficult, then, to attain Self-realization while living a worldly life?"

Mother: "No matter how much you may try, it's not possible to taste the bliss of the Self while at the same time seeking worldly happiness. If you eat *payasam* (sweet rice pudding) from a vessel used for storing tamarind, how can you get the real taste of payasam?"

Young man: "Could you explain this a bit further?"

Mother: "When you partake of physical pleasures, you experience a certain amount of happiness, don't you? Without controlling this, you cannot ascend to the plane of spiritual bliss. You can get married and live with your wife and children—there is no problem with that—as long as you, at the same time, can keep your mind focused on the Supreme Self. How can anyone who is looking for happiness in the things of the world attain the joy that doesn't belong to this world?"

Young man: "But aren't worldly pleasures a part of life? For example, the very fact that we are sitting here now is the result of others having been involved in physical relations. If there were no relations between men and women, what would be the state of the world? So how can we negate that? Also, will ultimate bliss be withheld from someone because they are having a physical relationship?"

Mother: "Amma isn't saying that worldly pleasures should be completely rejected, but you should understand that true happiness is not to be found in such pleasures. The sweetness of a fruit lies not in the skin but in the inner part of the fruit. Knowing this, you don't give the skin more importance than it deserves. When you understand that sense pleasures are not the real aim in life, you will feel attached only to the *Paramatman* (The Supreme Spirit). Yes, it is possible to reach the Goal while living a family life, provided you remain completely detached, like a fish in the mud.[12]

"In the olden days, people followed the rules prescribed for different members of society. They lived according to the tenets of the scriptures. They didn't want mere sense pleasures; God was the goal of their lives. After a baby had been born, the husband treated his wife—who had given birth to his image in the form of the child—as his own mother. When their son became an adult, they handed all the responsibilities over to him and went off to live a

---

[12] In India there is a certain fish that lives in the mud. The fish is like Teflon: the mud doesn't stick to it.

life of seclusion in the forest. By that stage, the couple had attained a certain amount of maturity, having lived as householders. Their work, the task of raising children, and the struggle of meeting the various obstacles in life had ripened their characters. In the *vanaprastha* (forest-recluse stage), the wife continued to stay with her husband. But in the end, that tie was broken as well, when they became sannyasis—total renunciates. And finally they reached the Goal. This was the practice in those days. But today it is different. Because of people's attachment to their wealth and their families, and because of their selfishness, no one lives like that anymore. This has to change. We need to become aware of the real purpose of life and live accordingly."

Young man: "Don't some people say that the union of a man and a woman is the ultimate happiness? And that even the love of a mother for her children is sexual in origin?"

Mother: "That is how limited their knowledge is. That is all they are capable of seeing. Even in married life, lust shouldn't be the driving force. Real love should be the basis of the relationship between husband and wife. Love sustains everything. Love is the basis of the universe. If there were no love, no creation could take place. The real source of that love is God, not sexual impulse.

"Some couples tell Amma, 'Our sexual desire is weakening our minds. We can't maintain the attitude of being brother and sister. We don't know what to do.'

"What is the reason for that condition? Nowadays, man lives as a slave of lust. If that is encouraged even further, what will be the condition of the world? So Amma advises people to look within and to search for the source of real bliss. What should we do, encourage people to continue their erring ways on the path of thoughtless impulse, or turn them away from those errors to the path of discrimination?

"There are people who have made countless mistakes in the past, and yet, by doing sadhana they have managed to control their minds and have ended up benefiting the world. Those who used to look at even their own sisters with lust, have learned to look upon all women as their sisters.

"Suppose there are five brothers in a family. One is an alcoholic, the second brother chases after luxuries, the third one fights with everyone, and the fourth brother steals everything in sight. But the fifth brother is different from the others. He leads a simple life. He is good-natured, compassionate, and enjoys giving. He is a true *karma yogi*. This one brother maintains the harmony in the family. So whom should we choose to emulate among those five?

"Amma cannot hold any other view. It is not that She is turning Her back on the other people. Amma is praying that they will also come to this path, for only then will there be peace and contentment in the world."

Young man: "Amma, could you elaborate a little on the bliss of the Self, which you have been talking about?"

Mother: "That is something which has to be experienced. Can you explain the beauty of a flower, or describe the sweetness of honey? If someone hits you, you can say it is painful, but can you convey in words exactly how much pain you feel? So how can one describe the beauty of the Infinite?

"Spiritual bliss cannot be experienced by the intellect. The heart is needed. The intellect cuts things asunder like a pair of scissors, but the heart sews things together like a needle. Amma isn't saying that we don't need the intellect: both the heart and the intellect are needed. Like the two wings of a bird, each has its place. What if a dam in a river is about to break and a whole village will be flooded? A solution has to be found very quickly. In such situations, the intellect is required and you have to be strong. Some people break down and cry when faced with even small problems. We should be able to face any obstacles, without being weak-minded. We have to discover our inner strength. This will happen through spiritual practices."

Like a gentle breeze, Mother's words drove the clouds of ignorance from the minds of the intimate gathering of seekers, allowing them to bask in the light of Her wisdom.

Tuesday, January 7, 1986

At 9:45 in the morning. Mother joined the brahmacharis in the meditation room.

Mother: "Children, if you cling to Amma in the form of this person, you won't be able to progress. You should love the Mother of the Universe, not this physical body. You should be able to recognize the true principle behind Amma, and see Amma within yourselves, in every living thing, and in every object. When you are traveling in a bus, you don't get attached to the bus, do you? The bus is only the means you use to get to your destination."

A youth named Jayachandra Babu came forward and prostrated. He lived in Thiruvananthapuram, and had come for Mother's *darshan* for the first time the day before. Now he had come again after leaving a note at home informing his family that he was moving permanently to the ashram.

Mother said to him, "My son, if you stay here now, your family will raise a ruckus and blame Amma. They will say that Amma is keeping you here without their consent. So, for the time being, you have to go home."

At first Babu didn't want to leave, but when Mother insisted, he finally agreed to go home. He prostrated to Mother again and got up.

"Son, do you have enough money for the bus?" asked Mother.

"No, I didn't bring enough because I wasn't planning to go back."

Mother asked Br. Kunjumon to give him some money for the bus fare. Babu then left with Kunjumon, and Mother continued talking to the brahmacharis.[13]

WORSHIPPING A FORM

Mother: "Some people say, 'Don't meditate on a form. Brahman has no form, so you should meditate on the Formless.' What sort of logic is that? Normally, we imagine the object of our meditation, don't we? Even if we meditate on a flame or on a sound, it is still based on imagination. What is the difference between that type of meditation and meditation on a form? Those who meditate on the Formless also rely on imagination. Some think of Brahman as pure love, infinitude, or all-pervasiveness. Some repeat, 'I am Brahman,' or inquire, 'Who am I?' But these are still just mental concepts. Thus, it is not truly meditation on Brahman. What, then, is the difference between that and meditating on a form? To bring water to a thirsty man, a container is needed. To realize the formless Brahman, an instrument or a prop is necessary. Also, if we choose to meditate on the Formless, how can we do so without developing love for Brahman? It is therefore nothing but *bhakti* (devotion). The personal God is nothing but a personification of Brahman."

Br. Rao:[14] "It is that God that we see as Amma."

---

[13] Soon thereafter Babu joined the ashram and became a brahmachari.
[14] A few years later when he received sannyas initiation, Brahmachari Rao was given the name, Swami Amritatmananda.

Mother (laughing): "Picture Brahman with a head, two eyes, nose, and limbs! How does it look?"

A brahmachari: "What is the benefit of imagining such a being?"

Mother: "Worship becomes easy when we assign a specific form to Brahman. Then, through our *prema* (supreme love), we can easily realize the eternal Principle. All the water in a tank can flow out through a single faucet, which allows us to quench our thirst more easily."

Br. Venu[15] asked a different question: "Amma, it is said that Jarasandha made even Lord Krishna flee from battle. How could this be?"

Mother: "An *avatar* like Krishna would run away only to teach us something, and not out of fear."

Venu: "Jarasandha wasn't destined to have the good fortune to die at the hands of the Lord, so the Lord ran away. Isn't that true, Amma?"

Mother: "Yes, that is true. Also, Krishna would eradicate someone's pride only after bringing it out to the fullest extent. When a child puts on a scary face, the father will play along and pretend that he is scared, but of course he isn't really afraid of the child."

Another brahmachari asked a question: "Amma, lately I feel very sleepy during meditation. What should I do?"

Mother: "Run for a while in the morning, or do some type of work that will give you exercise. Let *rajas* (activ-

[15] Swami Pranavamritananda

ity) drive away *tamas* (inertia). Without doing any physical work, the *vata, pitta*, and *kapha* within you will go out of balance,[16] and you'll feel too sleepy to meditate." With a laugh Mother added, "In the end, God will give a lot of trouble to those who are too lazy to work."

MOTHER WITH A SCHOLAR

Mother emerged from the meditation room to find a *shastri* (religious scholar) waiting for Her. Seeing Mother, the elderly man tied his cotton shawl round his waist, as a sign of respect, prostrated fully, and placed some fruit he had brought at Mother's feet. He also held a copy of the *Brahma Sutras*, which he had carried wherever he went for the past forty years and had studied daily. Mother sat with him on the verandah of the meditation room.

Mother: "When did you arrive, son?"

Shastri: "I haven't been here long. I'm on my way back from Thiruvananthapuram. My son came here last month, and he told me about Amma. So I decided to stop and see you on my way back."

Mother closed Her eyes and sat in meditation for a while. When She opened Her eyes again, the shastri con-

[16] According to the ancient science of ayurveda, there are three primary life forces or biological humors, called vata, pitta and kapha, corresponding to the elements of air, fire, and water. These three elements determine the life processes of growth and decay, and are the causative forces in the disease process. The predominance of one or more of these elements in the individual determines his psycho-physical nature.

tinued, "Amma, I have been studying and speaking about Vedanta for the past forty years, but to this day, I haven't gained any peace of mind."

Mother: "Son, Vedanta has little to do with reading or giving speeches. Vedanta is a principle to be adopted in our lives. You may draw a neat, colorful plan of a house on a piece of paper, but you can't live in that sketch, can you? Even if you just want a small place to protect you from the rain and the sun, you have to transport bricks and lumber to the site and build the shelter. In the same way, you can't experience the Supreme without doing sadhana. If you haven't gained control over your mind, it's no use repeating the *Brahma Sutras*. A parrot or a tape recorder can do as much."

The scholar hadn't told Mother that he repeated the *Brahma Sutras* and the *Panchadashi* daily. He was amazed to hear Her hint at this. He then poured out all his troubles before Her. Mother caressed him and comforted him with words of solace. Making him sit close to Her, She then began giving darshan to others. The old man sat watching Mother with great concentration. Suddenly his eyes filled with tears and he began to weep. Mother turned to him and caressed him.

Shastri: "Amma, I feel a peace I haven't found in forty years! I don't need my learning or scholarship anymore. I just want you to bless me so that I don't lose this peace again."

Mother: "Namah Shivaya! It's not enough to read Vedanta and try to absorb it with the mind. It has to be brought into the heart. Only then can we experience the principles of Vedanta. Having heard that honey is sweet, you may put some in your hand, but unless you taste it with your tongue you cannot experience the sweetness. The knowledge you have accumulated with your intellect should be brought into your heart, because that is where the experience lies. A time will come when your heart and intellect become one. That stage cannot be described in words. It is a direct experience, a direct perception. Reading every book in existence won't give you that experience. You have to be convinced that only God is real, and then remember Him constantly. Purify your heart. See God in everything and love all beings. You don't have to do anything else. You will be given everything you need."

Shastri: "Amma, I have gone to many mahatmas and many ashrams, but only today has my heart opened up. I know that." With great tenderness, Mother wiped his tears as he continued: "It is your grace that has finally brought me to you. If Amma agrees, I would like to stay here for a few days."

"As you wish, son."

Mother asked a brahmachari to arrange for the shastri's stay, and then She went to Her room.

ABHYASA YOGA
The Yoga Of Practice

At three o'clock in the afternoon, Mother finished giving darshan. She went and sat down near the cowshed, on the northern side of the ashram, with the shastri and a few brahmacharis.

A brahmachari: "Amma, how can we always keep our minds on God?"

Mother: "For that you need constant practice. To constantly remember God is not your natural habit, so you have to cultivate it. Japa is the prescription. Don't stop doing japa for a moment, not even while eating or sleeping.

"Small children who are trying hard to learn arithmetic will recite, 'One plus one is two, one plus two is three,' and so on, while sitting and walking and going to the bathroom. They are afraid that if they don't memorize the sums, they'll be punished in class. So, no matter what they are doing, they continue to practice the sums mentally. That is what you need to do.

"Know that there is nothing in the world but God, that nothing has the power to function without Him. You should see God in everything you touch. When you pick up the clothes that you are going to wear, imagine they are God. And when you pick up your comb, see it as God.

"Think of God in the midst of every action you do. And pray, 'You are my only refuge. Nothing else is everlasting. No one else's love will last. Worldly love may make me feel good for a while, but ultimately it will only end up hurting me. It's like being caressed by someone with poisonous hands, because in the end such love brings only suffering. No salvation will come from that. Only you, God, can fulfill my yearning.' We should pray like this constantly. Without this kind of detachment, we cannot develop spiritually, nor can we help others. We should be firmly convinced that only God is everlasting.

"We have to get rid of all the vasanas which we have accumulated. But it is difficult to do this all at once. We need constant practice. We should chant our mantra continuously, while sitting, walking, and lying down. By chanting the mantra and visualizing God's form, our other thoughts will fade and our minds will be purified. To wash away the feeling of 'I', we need to use the soap of 'You.' When we perceive that everything is God, the 'I', that is, the ego, fades away and the supreme 'I' shines forth within us."

Br: "Isn't it difficult to visualize one's Beloved Deity while chanting?"

Mother: "Son, at this moment you are talking to Amma. Does seeing Amma make it difficult to talk to Her? You can talk to Amma and see Her at the same time, can't you? In the same way, we can visualize the form of our Beloved Deity and do japa at the same time. But even that isn't really needed if you can cry out and pray, 'O Mother, give me strength! Destroy my ignorance! Lift me onto your lap! Your lap is my only refuge; only there will I find peace. Mother, why are you pushing me into this world? I don't want to be without you for a moment. Aren't you the One who gives refuge to everyone? Please be mine! Make my mind your own!' Cry out in this way."

Br: "But I don't feel any devotion. And to be able to pray like that I need to feel devotion, don't I? Amma, you say that we should cry and call out to God, but I first have to feel like crying!"

Mother: "If you can't cry at first, say the words again and again and make yourself cry. A child will pester his mother to make her buy what he wants. He'll keep following her around and he won't stop crying until he has the desired object in his hand. We have to pester the Divine Mother like that. We have to sit there and cry. Don't give Her a moment of peace! We should cry out, 'Show yourself to me! Show yourself!' Son, when you say that you can't cry, it means that you have no real yearning. Anyone will cry when that longing comes to them. If you can't cry, *make* yourself cry, even if it takes some effort.

"Say that you are hungry but you don't have any food or money. You will go somewhere or do something to get food, won't you? Cry out to the Divine Mother and say, 'Why aren't you giving me tears?' Ask Her, 'Why don't you make me cry? Does it mean that you don't love me? How can I live if you don't love me?' Then She will give you strength, and you will be able to cry. Children, that is what Amma used to do. You can do the same.

"Such tears are not tears of sorrow. They are a form of inner bliss. Those tears will flow when the *jivatman* (individual soul) merges with the *Paramatman* (The Supreme Spirit). Our tears mark a moment of oneness with God. Those who are watching us may interpret it as sorrow. For us, however, it is bliss. But you have to do some creative imagination to reach that point. Give it a try, son!"

Br: "I used to meditate on the form of Bhagavan (referring to Krishna). But after meeting Amma that became impossible, because then I couldn't help meditating on Amma's form. Now I can't do that either. Amma, when I think of you, the Lord's form comes to my mind; and when I think of Him, your form appears. I'm unhappy because I can't decide who to meditate on. So now I am not meditating on any form. I meditate on the sound of the mantra."

Mother: "Focus your mind on what appeals to you. Understand that everything is contained in that, and is not separate from you. Whoever or whatever you encounter, know that all are different faces of that one form."

LOVE IS ALL IMPORTANT

Shastri: "Amma, what should we do to make the form of our Beloved Deity become clear during meditation?"

Mother: "The form becomes clear only when you develop pure love for the deity. As long as you cannot see God, you should be feeling a relentless sense of anguish.

"A sadhak should have the same attitude towards God as a lover towards his beloved. His love should be such that he cannot bear being separated from God, not even for a moment. If a lover last saw his beloved dressed in blue, then, whenever he sees just a hint of blue anywhere, he sees his beloved and is reminded of her form. While eating and even in his sleep, his mind rests only on her. When he gets up in the morning and brushes his teeth and drinks his coffee, he wonders what she is doing at that moment. This is the kind of love we should have for our Beloved Deity. We shouldn't be able to think about anything else but our object of worship. Even a bitter melon will lose its bitterness and become sweet if it is soaked in sugar for some time. Likewise, a negative mind will be purified if you surrender it to God and think of Him ceaselessly.

"Once, while walking in Vrindavan, a *gopi* saw a small depression in the ground beneath a tree. She began to imagine, 'Krishna must have come this way! The gopi who was with Him must have asked for a flower from this tree. He held her shoulder for support and then jumped up into the tree. This hole in the ground must be the mark made by His foot as He sprang up.' The gopi called the other gopis and showed them the Lord's footprint. Thinking of the Lord, they completely forgot everything else.

"In the eyes of this gopi, everyone was Krishna. If someone touched her shoulder, she imagined it was Krishna, and in her intense devotion she lost all external consciousness. Whenever the other gopis remembered Krishna, they also became oblivious of their surroundings and shed tears of bliss. We, too, should try to reach that state, associating everything we see with God. For us, there should be no world other than that of God. Then we need make no special effort to constantly see God in our meditation, because at no time will our minds be without Him.

"Our minds should cry out to everything we see, 'Dear trees and plants, where is my Mother? O birds and animals, have you seen Her? Dear ocean, where is the all-powerful Mother who gives you the power to move?' We can use our imagination in this way. As we persist like this, our minds will break through all obstacles; we will reach the Feet of the Supreme Being and cling to them. Use your imagination in this way. Then the form will definitely become clear in your mind."

Br: "Sometimes I feel that others are doing the wrong thing, and this destroys my peace of mind. How can we learn to forgive others?"

Mother: "Suppose you accidentally poke your eye with one of your hands. Your other hand doesn't slap the hand that hurt the eye, does it? There's no question of punishment. You simply forgive your hand. If your foot is hurt by accidentally stumbling into something, or if you cut your hand, you just bear it. You are ever so patient with your eyes, hands, and feet, because you know they are part of your own body. No matter how much pain they may cause you from time to time, you bear it. In the same way, we should look upon others as being part of ourselves. We should have the understanding, 'I am the cause of everything. I am in everything. No one is separate from me.' Then we won't look at the mistakes of others, and even if we do see their mistakes, we treat those errors as our own and we forgive them.

"We can also have the same attitude of surrender as Kuchela,[17] that whatever happens is God's will. We should think of ourselves as God's servants. Then we won't be capable of feeling angry with anyone, and we will develop humility.

"One way is to think of everyone as your own Self. The other way is to see everyone as God and to serve them.

"Live each moment with shraddha. Eat your food only

[17] Kuchela was a beloved friend and fellow student of the young Krishna. Later in life, Kuchela married and lived a simple life as a poor but self-controlled and contented brahmin. One day, weary of their poverty, Kuchela's wife asked her husband to go and see his old friend Krishna and appeal to Him for financial help. Kuchela decided to visit Krishna, not to ask for help, but simply to see his dear friend. Krishna gave Kuchela a loving welcome. Kuchela was filled with joy and peace, and didn't mention a word about his plight. Krishna, who knew Kuchela's heart, secretly decided to surprise his friend with great wealth. Unaware of this, Kuchela began the return journey home. His only regret was that he would have to tell his wife that he had failed to ask Krishna for help. When he reached home, he was astounded to find that where his poor hut had stood, there was now a palace with a beautiful garden, and his wife was adorned with costly gems and garments and surrounded by servants. Kuchela prayed never to become attached to the wealth he had been given, but to always love the Lord for love's sake only.

after chanting your mantra with the prayer, 'O God, did everyone else eat? Are they getting all they need? Please bless everyone so that they will be given whatever they need.' We should feel compassion for those who are struggling in life. Then our minds will become pure. Our compassion will bring us close to God."

Thus extolling universal love, Mother concluded Her discourse on the practice of devotion. Listening to Her nectarous words of advice, the shastri and the brahmacharis felt their hearts blossoming.

Wednesday, January 15, 1986

MOTHER WITH HER DEVOTEES

It was a little after eight in the morning. Mother was sitting in the meditation room with the brahmacharis.

Mother: "Children, if you just sit down thinking, 'I am going to start meditating now,' the form won't appear in your mind. You'll only sit there with your eyes closed, and after a while you'll remember, 'Oh! I'm supposed to be meditating!' So when you sit for meditation, begin by crying out to God, 'O God, won't you come into my heart? I cannot see you without your help. You are my only refuge!' Picture your Beloved Deity standing in front of you. Then, after a while, His or Her form will shine clearly in your mind."

Mother emerged from the meditation hall at nine-thirty. She was met by a married woman devotee, who had been staying at the ashram for a few days and was now refusing to go home. Mother tried to persuade her, but the woman said she didn't want to leave Mother. Mother turned to those standing nearby and said, "Amma has told her that she can stay here if she brings a letter from her husband. Without his consent, it wouldn't be correct to let her stay. If he were to come here and complain, what would Amma say? Also, others might try to follow her example. For several days she has been saying that her husband will come here in a day or two, but he hasn't come. She has a daughter at home as well." Turning to the woman, Mother said, "Amma can't wait any longer. You must leave tomorrow."

The woman was in tears. "Amma," she said, "if he doesn't come on Sunday, I promise I will leave on Monday."

Mother's heart melted at the woman's tearful request and She allowed her to stay.

As Mother walked towards the darshan hut, She looked in on a Vedanta class that was in progress. Seeing a brahmachari leaning against the wall as he listened to the discourse, She said to him, "My son, a spiritual person shouldn't lean against the wall like that in a place of learning. You should sit up straight, fully alert, without leaning on anything or moving your arms and legs; otherwise, it will only increase your tamas. A sadhak should abide within himself. He shouldn't depend on any external support.

Spiritual life doesn't mean sitting idly, fostering tamasic qualities. However difficult it may be, you should sit with your spine straight."

Mother continued to the darshan hut. She entered the hut and sat down on a simple wooden cot which was covered with a quilt made of tree bark. The people who had been waiting for Her came forward, one by one, and prostrated. One of them suffered from a neck injury. This was the second time he had come to see Mother. On his first visit he had not even been able to hold his head up and his shoulder had been paralyzed. Prior to that, he'd had an operation, but that didn't help. Mother had given him some *bhasma* (sacred ash) and had asked him to bring some ash collected from a funeral pyre.

Mother: "How are you now, my son?"

Devotee: "Much better. I can hold my head up. And I can travel without any difficulty. I couldn't do this before; I had to lie in bed all the time. It was very difficult to come and see you the first time, but today I had no trouble. I've brought the ash from a funeral pyre." He gave the packet to Mother.

Mother opened the packet and took a little of the ash in Her hand.

Mother: "Son, there's a lot of soil in this ash. You should bring pure ash without any soil in it. Be careful about that next time. This time Amma will give you some ordinary bhasma from here."

Mother took some sacred ash from a plate and rubbed his neck with it. She asked a brahmachari to fetch some paper to wrap the ash in. He brought a piece he had torn from a clean sheet of paper.

Mother: "Son, how could you tear such nice paper? A piece of newspaper would have been good enough to wrap the ash in. This white paper could be used for writing. Amma thinks about the usefulness of everything. Don't ever waste anything. Not to waste, that is shraddha, and only with shraddha can you progress."

A woman from Switzerland was sitting close to Mother. She had just arrived at the ashram and was meeting Mother for the first time. She had brought Mother some presents, which she now opened and showed Her.

Woman: "I spent a lot of time selecting these things. I didn't know what Mother would like."

Mother: "Amma knows how much you were thinking about Her when you bought these presents. But Amma doesn't need these things. She wants your mind.

"You brought these gifts out of love, but it won't always be possible to bring presents like this. If, at some point, you can't bring anything, don't feel unhappy about it, and don't stop coming just because you don't have anything to give Amma. All these things are perishable. But if you offer your mind, the benefit of that will last forever; your mind will be returned to you in a pure state."

Woman devotee: "Isn't it said that one shouldn't come

to the guru empty-handed, that one should always bring
something?"

Mother: "Yes, but not because the guru needs anything.
The devotees bring offerings as a symbol of the surrender
of their minds. In this way, they surrender their *prarabdha*
(fruits of past actions) at the guru's feet. If you don't have
anything else to give, a lemon is enough. If even that isn't
possible, it is said that a piece of firewood will do."

As Mother spoke, a woman came up to Her, put her
head in Mother's lap and burst into tears. Between sobs,
she said, "Amma, give me devotion! You have fooled me
until now, but that won't work anymore!" Affectionately,
Mother tried to console her, but the woman continued,
"This trick won't work any longer. Amma, who knows
everything, is asking me all these polite questions just to
fool me. Amma, don't ask me questions like that! What
can I tell you? You know me better than I know myself!"

The woman wished to donate her house to the ashram,
but Mother wouldn't accept it. The woman was crying
because she wanted Mother to agree. Still, Mother didn't
yield.

Not until half past three did Mother return to Her room
for lunch. Two brahmacharis were waiting for Her in the
room. She talked to them as She ate.

"My children, you should greet the people who come
here, and give them whatever help they need, but don't
waste a lot of time talking to them. It's no use trying to

strengthen their faith by talking. When you plant a sapling, it may have some leaves on it, but it's only by the new leaves that appear when the plant has put down its roots that you can estimate how the plant is actually growing. Only the faith that comes from one's own experience will be permanent, like the new leaves that sprout after the plant has taken root. Spend more time talking only to those who have a real desire to know."

The day before, one of the brahmacharis had been talking for a long time to a devotee who had come for darshan. From Mother's words, the brahmachari now realized that Mother, who dwells within us all and knows everything, was aware of this.

Br: "Amma, what should we do if people follow us around asking a lot of questions?"

Mother: "Tell them just enough to clear their doubts."

THE CONCERNS OF
THE COMPASSIONATE ONE

It was five in the afternoon. A teen-age boy had been staying at the ashram for a few days. His relatives had now come to take him home. They stood in front of the building on the north side of the ashram, talking to him for a long time, but he didn't want to leave. His mother was upset. Finally, Mother came. She lead the woman to the verandah of the building, sat down with her, and talked to her for awhile. The woman wept and asked Mother to send her son home. Mother agreed. The youth accepted Mother's words and left with his family. Afterwards, Mother sat on the doorstep of the building with a few brahmacharis.

Mother: "What can Amma do? How many mothers tasting such bitter tears does She have to see? Amma can foresee that many brahmacharis will come here. From the signs we see now, it looks as if they will arrive soon. The other day, a son came from Nagercoil, but he was sent back to get his father's permission. The last time the son, who just left a moment ago, came here, Amma told him to come back to the ashram only after some time. She told him then that he could come back only after he had received his parents' consent, but he didn't listen.

"Where will everyone live here? Amma is considering having some rules about admitting brahmacharis."

Now the conversation turned to another subject.

Mother: "A daughter came for *bhava darshan* from Pandalam. She didn't take the *tirtham* (holy water) which Amma gave her. She has suffered a great deal, but her sorrows have not ended. Amma offered her the tirtham with total compassion, but what can Amma do if it isn't accepted? That girl doesn't believe in Amma, but the son who is going to marry her is a devotee. He brought her here hoping that his future wife would feel some devotion for Amma.

"Amma took pity on them. Isn't that girl going to marry Amma's son? Amma's mind and all Her compassion flowed to them through the tirtham and the *prasad* (consecrated offerings) they were given. After they had left, Amma called that son's brother who was at the ashram and said to him, 'Amma sees a lot of suffering in their future. A terrible danger lies ahead. Ask them to pray sincerely.' Amma said to him, 'When they didn't accept the tirtham, Amma didn't take it back. Instead, She poured it on the floor. Because of this, they won't have to suffer so much.'

"That daughter will definitely come back. After all, she is going to be the wife of Amma's son. Amma won't let her distance herself. But only by working very hard can she escape her prarabdha. Had she accepted the tirtham Amma gave her, she wouldn't have to suffer much."

Fortunate, indeed, are those who are able to receive and hold Mother's grace, for Mother is the embodiment of Compassion. But how can we receive the rays of Her grace if we neglect to open up our hearts? That is why Mother advises us to follow Her words to the letter—not for Her sake, but for ours.

Friday, January 17, 1986

MOTHER, THE RIVER OF COMPASSION

In the morning Mother and the brahmacharis set out for Ampalappara in northern Kerala. When they reached the banks of the Bharata River, Mother decided to stop for a swim. The water level was low and most of the sandy riverbed was dry. Water flowed only in a narrow stream near the opposite bank. The van had just started crossing the bridge to the other side when Mother suddenly asked the driver to stop. She told him to go back and turn into a narrow road just before the beginning of the bridge. The little road led to the front porch of a large house. Mother told the driver to stop a short distance from the house. Everyone wondered why Mother had led them to that spot, because the river wasn't easily accessible from there.

As soon as the van stopped, Mother asked for some hot *kanji* (rice gruel) water to drink. But there was only cold water in the van. A brahmachari asked Mother if he could fetch Her something to drink from the house nearby. She readily agreed. This was surprising because on such trips Mother usually never accepted anything from the houses along the way; they would only drink what they had brought with them.

The brahmachari hurried to the house. A few minutes later an old woman, followed by a small boy, came running out of the house towards the van. The brahmachari came trailing behind with a glass of kanji water. As the woman approached the van, Mother stretched out Her arms through the open window and took hold of her hands. The old grandmother wept and chanted, 'Narayana, Narayana...' over and over again. But she was so breathless from her running that she couldn't say the divine name properly. Her devotion was something to behold.

When she was finally able to speak, she said in a faltering voice, "Ottoor Unni Namboodiripad told me about Amma. Ever since, I have been longing to see you. But I am very old and it's hard for me to travel. It has made me feel so sad that I couldn't go and see you. Not a day goes by without me thinking about you. I heard that you visited the *kovilakam*[18] in Tripunittura. I am a member of that family. I was hoping that, somehow, by your grace, I would get to see you in this life. That wish has been fulfilled today. I never expected that I would get to see you so soon! It's all because of your grace. A young man came and asked for some *kanji*. He said it was for Mother. 'What Mother?' I asked. When he said your name, I knew it was the same Mother I was longing to see. I gave him some kanji and pickled mangoes and then I ran here with my grandson." Her voice faltered.

"Alas, apart from this kanji, I have nothing else to give you! Forgive me, Amma!" Tears were streaming down the old woman's face.

Mother wiped the woman's tears with Her sacred hands and said softly, "My daughter, Amma doesn't need anything. She wants only your heart."

Mother drank almost all of the kanji water and ate some of the pickled mangoes. The old woman told Mother

---

[18] Residence of members belonging to the royal family.

how to get to the river, and as Mother began to walk with the others along the path, the woman said, "Amma, when you've finished swimming, please bless me by stepping into my house!"

When Mother came back from the river, She fulfilled the woman's wish and entered the house, where the woman and her husband were waiting. The old lady led Mother to a chair on the verandah, and was so overwhelmed with joy that she forgot everything. Her husband went inside and fetched some water. Together they washed Mother's feet. In response to their unblemished devotion, Mother went into a state of *samadhi*. As it would have taken time to go inside and fetch a nice cloth, the woman wiped Mother's feet with the end of the sari she was wearing. As she bent down to do this, tears fell from her eyes onto Mother's feet.

After spending a little more time with them, Mother and Her children resumed their journey. As they crossed the bridge, Shashi, one of Mother's householder devotees, was waiting for Her with his car. On Shashi's insistence, Mother traveled in his car the rest of the way.

At about two-thirty in the afternoon, Mother and Her children reached the house of Narayanan Nair in Ampalappara, a small village about 250 kilometers northeast of the ashram. The natural beauty of Kerala's rural villages, which has been destroyed in most places, was still evident here. Surrounded by forested hills, the village of thatched huts lay nestled in a lush, tropical garden of coconut palms and flowering trees and bushes. Many people were awaiting Mother's arrival.

As Mother entered the house, the family, who were devoted to Mother, made Her sit on a *peetham* (sacred seat). They washed Her feet and decorated them with red *kumkum* and sandal paste. Then they did *arati* with camphor. The room resonated with the sound of Vedic mantras which were being chanted by the brahmacharis. Everyone was deeply moved as their eyes feasted on Mother's divine form. After the *pada puja*,[19] Mother moved to the adjoining room where She received the devotees for darshan.

The family gave the brahmacharis cups of *jappy*. Everyone liked the hot, sweet milk drink.

Mother noticed a woman devotee helping a brahmachari to wash his hands by pouring water on them. Later She remarked, "As sadhaks, you shouldn't seek anyone's help, because then you will lose the power you have gained by your tapas. We shouldn't make anyone pick up even a leaf for us. Instead, we, ourselves, should serve others as much as possible."

A brahmachari was arranging the oil lamps and some other items on the spot where the bhajan singing was going to take place. As he was about to light the lamps, Mother stopped him and said, "Son, face north when you light the lamps." The brahmachari didn't understand what

---

[19] The ceremonial washing of Mother's feet.

She meant, so Mother took the small lamp that he was using to light the other lamps. She arranged the lamps carefully, and covered the *kindi*,[20] which was full of water, with a leaf. Then She placed the kindi in front of the lamps, put flower petals on the leaf, and lit the lamps. To the brahmachari She said, "Don't face south when you light the lamps. Also, when you light the wicks of a lamp, do it clockwise round the lamp, just as you do *pradakshina* (circumambulation) in the temple."

Mother pays great attention to such details, especially when giving instructions to the brahmacharis. She says, "Tomorrow they will have to go out into the world, so they have to be very alert in everything they do."

The bhajan program began. Before long a little child came crawling towards Mother. Mother lifted the infant onto Her lap. She gave it a hand bell to hold, and while She continued to sing the kirtan, She helped the child's little hands to sound the bell, keeping the time of the music.

Gopivallabha Gopalakrishna...

> *O Gopala Krishna,*
> *Beloved of the Gopis,*
> *Uplifter of the Govardhana Hill,*
> *Lotus-eyed one,*

---

[20] A traditional bronze or brass container with a spout.

Who lives in Radha's mind—
You are the color of a blue lotus.

O Krishna, who moves about in Vrindavan,
Whose eyes are like the petals of a red lotus,
O Son of Nanda,
Rid me of all bondage.

O Beautiful Child,
O Krishna,
Bestower of liberation...

Wednesday, January 22, 1986

Two western women were meditating in the meditation room. A little girl, who was the daughter of one of the women, sat nearby filling in a coloring book. Her mother had given her the task of coloring so that she wouldn't disturb the meditation. Mother came into the room, followed by a few disciples, and watched the little girl quietly coloring in the pictures.

When the meditation was over, Mother pointed to the child and said to the others, "We should turn the children's attention to positive activities like drawing and singing when they are very young. Could this child paint pictures without having a lot of patience? Painting and drawing teaches her patience and she will also develop concentration. On the other hand, if we just leave the children to themselves, they will run around wasting their time and do mischief. It will then be difficult to teach them discipline later."

There were hardly any visitors at the ashram that day, except for a small group of westerners, who had arrived a few days earlier. They spent their time helping with the ashram chores and reading books from the library. The yearning for Truth was intense in these devotees, who had already known life's material comforts and pleasures. Being tired of a hostile, competitive world, they saw in Mother the fountainhead of pure, selfless Love, and they had crossed the oceans to drink from that Love.

A brahmachari told Mother that a youth was waiting to see Her. She asked him to call the young man. She sat down on the western side of the meditation room and motioned for the youth to sit next to Her.

Mother: "Have you been here for long, son?"

Youth: "No, I just arrived."

Mother: "How did you hear about the ashram?"

Youth: "I've been going to different ashrams for some time. Last month a friend of mine came here. He told me that I should definitely go and see Amma."

Mother: "Have you finished your studies?"

Youth: "I've got an M.A. degree and I've been trying to get a job. Meanwhile, I've got a temporary job at a private college, so I'm earning some money. But I've decided not to look for another job. I have a sister. As soon as she's married, I'd like to join an ashram."[21]

[21] In India it is traditionally the responsibility of the parents and older brothers of the family to see that the girls are given away in marriage, and thus making sure that their future is taken care of.

Mother: "Won't your family object to that?"

Youth: "Why should they?"

Mother: "Won't it hurt your parents?"

Youth: "They get what they need from their pension. They also have land."

Mother: "Who will look after them when they get older? Aren't you the one who should do that?"

Youth: "What guarantee is there that I'll be anywhere near them when they are old? I could be working somewhere abroad, and then I won't be able to come running to help them, will I? And what if I die before them?"

Mother laughed and said, "Smart young man!"

Youth: "My friend wanted me to ask you to arrange a job for me. But I told him that if I saw Amma, I would ask Her only for my spiritual upliftment."

THE SADHAK AND THE SCIENTIST

Youth: "Amma, how is the life of a sadhak superior to that of a scientist? For the sadhak to reach his goal and for the scientist to succeed in his research, both need one-pointed concentration. So what is the difference between them? Isn't the life of a scientist also a type of sadhana?"

Mother: "Yes, it is sadhana. But a researcher thinks about an object. If he, for example, studies a computer, his object of meditation is only the computer. He thinks about it a lot and gets to know it. But his mind is concentrated only for as long as he is engaged in his research. At other times, his mind runs in all directions and gets involved in ordinary things. This is why the infinite power doesn't awaken in him. A tapasvi, on the other hand, is quite different. As he does his spiritual practices, he begins to perceive everything as one. A sadhak strives to realize That which is latent in everything. Once he has attained realization, he has acquired all powers. For him, there is nothing left to know.

"Think of a pool with brackish water. If you pour a little water into one side of the pool, you reduce the amount of salt in that area for a while. If it rains, on the other hand, the entire pool will be affected. In the same way, by doing tapas with an expansive mind, an infinite power awakens in the sadhak, and he realizes everything. This doesn't happen to a scientist, because his approach is quite different."

Youth: "The scriptures say that everything is the same Self. In that case, if one person attains the state of realization, shouldn't everyone else get it at that moment as well?"

Mother: "Son, if you turn on the main switch, electricity is available throughout the house. But for there to be light in your own room, you still have to turn on the switch in that particular room, don't you? Turning on the light in one room doesn't automatically light up all the other rooms. Everything is the same Self, but only the person who purifies his mind through sadhana realizes that Self.

"Think of a lake covered with duckweed. If you clear

the weed on one side of the lake, that side will be clean and you can see the water, but that doesn't mean that the entire lake becomes clean."

QUESTIONS ABOUT SADHANA

Youth: "Many people say that a seeker should strictly obey the *yamas* and *niyamas* (the do's and don'ts on the path of yoga). Is it really important? Isn't it enough just to know the principles? After all, acquiring knowledge is the important thing, isn't it?"

Mother: "Son, the earth attracts everything to itself, doesn't it? If you sleep on the black sands of the seashore,[22] you'll feel exhausted when you wake up in the morning, because the sand absorbs your strength. At this stage, you are under nature's control, so you have to obey certain laws and limits. Right now, those laws and limits are essential. But once you reach the stage where you are beyond the control of nature, there is no problem. Then your strength cannot be lost, because nature will be under your control. Until then, however, certain restraints and regulations are necessary.

"When you plant a seed, you have to put a fence around it to protect it from being scratched up and eaten by a chicken. Later, when the seed has grown into a tree, it will provide shelter for birds, human beings, and every-

[22] In some parts of Kerala, including the area where the ashram is located, the sand on the beaches is black because of a high metal content.

thing else. In the beginning, however, the seed has to be protected even from the little chicken. Similarly, being weak-minded to start with, we need rules and limits until we have gained enough mental strength."

Youth: "To develop that strength, doesn't the mind have to enjoy the discipline of serious sadhana?"

Mother: "Yes, you have to love discipline as much as you love God. Those who love God also love discipline. We should love discipline more than anything.

"Those who have the habit of drinking tea at a regular time will get a headache and feel other discomforts if they don't get their tea. Those who smoke *ganja* regularly will feel restless if they don't smoke it at the usual time. The habit that they had yesterday will automatically make itself known at a certain time today. Similarly, if we make a schedule for all our activities and strictly observe it, it will develop into a habit; it will even remind us at the right time of whatever we have to do. It is highly beneficial to follow such a routine in one's sadhana."

A householder devotee who had been listening to Mother said, "Amma, I have been meditating every day, but I don't seem to be making any progress."

Mother: "Son, your mind is tied up with many different things. Spiritual life requires a great deal of discipline and self-control, without which it is difficult to benefit from the sadhana as much as you would like. It may be true that you are doing sadhana, but do you know what it can be compared to? It is like taking an ounce of oil and pouring it into a hundred containers, one after the other. In the end there is no oil left—only a thin film sticking to the insides of all the containers. Son, you do your spiritual practices, but then you get involved in a variety of things. All the power you have gained through concentration is lost by your diversions. If you could only see the unity in all diversity, you wouldn't lose much. If you can perceive everything as the essence of God, you won't lose your spiritual strength."

Devotee: "At home everyone's afraid of me. I get very angry if the others don't live according to my regimen."

Mother: "Son, you won't really benefit from your sadhana if you do your spiritual practices while at the same time harboring anger and pride. It is like putting sugar on one side and ants on the other: the ants will eat all the sugar. And you're not even noticing what's happening! Whatever you have gained by your sadhana, you lose through your anger. A flashlight running on batteries loses all its power after you have turned it on a number of times, doesn't it? In the same way, whenever you get angry, you lose your energy through your eyes, nose, mouth, ears, and through every pore of your body. Only by practicing mental restraint can you preserve the energy you have gained from your sadhana."

Devotee: "Are you saying that someone who gets angry can't experience the bliss arising from sadhana?"

Mother: "Suppose you lower a bucket into a well to draw water, and the bucket is full of holes. With great effort you manage to pull up the bucket, but by the time it reaches the top, there's no water left in it. All the water has leaked out through the holes. Son, that is what your sadhana is like. Your mind is enmeshed in anger and desire. From time to time, all that you have gained through great effort in your sadhana is allowed to drain away. Though you are doing spiritual practices, you are not enjoying the benefit, nor do you appreciate its real value. Spend some time in solitude now and then, calm your mind, and try to do sadhana. Stay away from situations that awaken any feelings of anger or desire. Then you will certainly come to know the source of all power."

Devotee: "Amma, at times I can't control my desires. If I try to control them, they only get stronger."

Mother: "Desires are very difficult to control. Still, certain restrictions should be observed, otherwise it isn't possible to subdue the mind. Foods like meat, eggs, and fish produce more semen, which increases sexual desire. Then the senses will act in certain ways to fulfill those desires, and you'll lose your energy. Eating sattvic food in moderate quantities won't cause any harm. Diet control is essential when doing sadhana, especially for people whose minds are not strong, because they are easily affected. But for someone who has a lot of mental strength, some changes in the diet won't have any significant effect."

Youth: "Does a person's nature change according to his diet?"

Mother: "Yes, definitely. Each type of food has its own

quality; and each flavor, such as hot, sour, and sweet, has its own influence. Even sattvic food should be eaten in moderation. For example, milk and ghee are sattvic, but you shouldn't eat too much of them. Each type of food has a different effect on us. Eating meat will make the mind unsteady. For those who are doing sadhana with an intense yearning to conserve energy and realize the Self, discipline regarding food is absolutely essential in the beginning.

"When you plant a seed, it needs to be protected from the sun. But once it has grown into a tree, it will have the strength to withstand the sun. Just as it is necessary for someone who is recovering from an illness to be on a wholesome, suitable diet, a person who is doing sadhana should be careful about the food he eats. Later, when you've made some progress in your sadhana, food restrictions are no longer crucial."

Youth: "It is often said that a sadhak should be modest and humble, but it seems to me that those are really signs of weakness."

Mother: "Son, if you wish to develop a good samskara, you have to be humble in your relationship with others. Humbleness is not a weakness. If, out of a feeling of self-importance, you get angry or behave with an attitude of superiority towards others, you lose your energy, and you lose your awareness of God.

"Hardly anyone wishes to be humble. People don't have any humility because they are proud of what isn't real.

The body is a form filled with nothing but ego, the sense of 'I.' The body[23] is polluted by the ego and by anger and desires. To be purified, you need to cultivate such qualities as humility and modesty. By perpetuating the ego, your pride in the body increases. For the ego to be eliminated, you have to be willing to have the attitude of humbleness and of bowing down to others.

"It is no use pouring water into a dirty bucket, because all the water will get dirty. If you mix something sour with payasam, you won't be able to enjoy the taste of the payasam. In the same way, if you maintain the ego while doing sadhana, you cannot take total refuge in God, or experience and enjoy the benefits of your sadhana. When you destroy the sense of 'I' through your humbleness, your good qualities emerge, and your jivatman is elevated to the Paramatman.

"At this point, you are like a small table lamp that gives just enough light to read a book, if the book is held close to the lamp. But if you do tapas and eliminate the ego, you will shine like the sun."

SURRENDERING TO THE GURU

Youth: "Amma, these days many people consider obedience towards a guru to be a weakness. They think it is beneath their dignity to prostrate to a great soul."

Mother: "In the olden days, the front door of a house

---

[23] When Mother refers to the body here, the mind is included.

was very low. One reason for this was to cultivate humble-ness. To avoid hitting their heads on the door post, people had to lower their heads when they entered. Likewise, when we lower our heads in front of the guru, we are avoiding the dangers of the ego and thus allowing the Self to be awakened.

"Today each of us is an image of the eight forms of pride or sense of 'I.' If we wish to change and bring out our true form, we have to assume the role of a disciple and obey the guru's words with humility. If we adhere to the guru's words today, then tomorrow we can become a refuge for the whole world. Through our proximity to the guru, the *shakti* (divine power) within us will awaken, and our sadhana will make it blossom."

Youth: "Amma, don't the scriptures say that God is within us and not separate from us? What, then, is the need for a guru?"

Mother: "Yes, son, God is definitely within you. There is a treasure chest full of diamonds within you; but not being aware of this, you have been searching for them outside of yourself. The key to that chest is in your pos-session, but because it hasn't been used for a long time, it has become rusty. You have to polish it to remove the rust and open the treasure chest. It is for this that we approach the guru. If you wish to know God, you have to eliminate the ego by taking refuge in a guru, and by obeying the guru with humility and surrender.

"A tree can give fruit to countless people. At this stage,

however, you are just a seed; you haven't yet grown into a tree. By doing tapas the guru has become *purnam* (complete). So you need to approach a guru and do sadhana according to his or her instructions.

"If you dig a well on top of a mountain, you may not find any water, even if you dig hundreds of feet. But if you dig only a small hole next to a river, you will soon find water. In the same way, your close proximity to a satguru will quickly bring out your good qualities, and your spiritual practices will soon bear fruit. Now you are the slave of your senses, but if you live in accordance with the guru's will, the senses will become your slaves.

"Those who live with their guru need only strive for the guru's grace. Through that grace, the power of the guru's tapas will come to them. If you were to directly touch something carrying an electric current, the electricity would enter into you, wouldn't it? If you take refuge in the guru, his or her power will flow into you.

"The guru is selfless. The guru is a repository of good qualities, such as truth, dharma, love, and compassion. Words like 'truth' and 'dharma' have no life in themselves, but a satguru is the living embodiment of these qualities. The world receives only goodness from such beings. If we make friends with someone who has bad qualities, he will be a bad influence on us; but if we have a friend with good qualities, our nature will change accordingly. Similarly, those who are with the guru become fertile fields in which good qualities are cultivated.

"If you don't remove the weeds from a farm field, the weeds will destroy the seeds you have sown. If you do sadhana without eradicating the ego, your sadhana will be fruitless. When concrete is made, the broken stones that are used for making it first have to be washed. Similarly, the thought of God will become firm only in a pure mind. By doing your sadhana selflessly, without any sense of ego, you will experience the truth: that you are God."

Mother's nectarous words of wisdom ceased to flow for the moment. She turned to some visiting devotees and said, "The area around the kitchen is dirty. Amma came down to clean it, but on the way She saw this little girl drawing pictures and stopped to watch her. Then this son came, and Amma sat down and talked with him. You children aren't leaving until after darshan tomorrow, are you? Amma will see you later." Having said this, She walked towards the kitchen.

Friday, February 7, 1986

After the morning *puja* and *arati* (ritual worship) in the kalari, Br. Unnikrishnan[24] brought the burning camphor outside where the devotees were waiting. They touched the flame and then touched their foreheads. Some of them also took a little bhasma from the plate on which the camphor burned and put it on their foreheads. A few minutes later Mother came to the kalari, and everyone prostrated.

[24] Swami Turiyamritananda

Following their meditation, Rao and Kunjumon also came. They prostrated to Mother and sat down next to Her.

THE REMOVER OF DOUBTS

Rao: "Amma, you say we should grieve with longing to see God. But you are right here with us, so when we meditate on your form, how can we be sad?"

Mother: "You should feel the pain of separation from God. That is the grief you should feel!"

Rao: "If we have a real master as our guru, will he not give us that grief?"

Mother: "Namah Shivaya! It isn't enough to have a guru with the highest credentials—the disciple also has to be qualified."

Kunjumon: "We have reached Amma, so we have nothing to worry about! We are saved!"

Mother: "That faith is good, children. But don't limit yourself to the external Amma whom you see as this body. If you do, you will lose your strength and falter. Try to see the real Amma, the real Principle. Try to see this Amma in everyone. Amma has come to help you children do this."

Kunjumon: "Yesterday someone asked what Amma's intention is in starting this ashram."

Mother: "To enhance people's faith in God, to inspire them to do good deeds and to take to the path of truth and righteousness. That is our aim."

A woman devotee: "Amma, those who call out to God

seem to experience a lot of sorrow in their lives."

Mother: "Children, the tears that flow when one prays to God with love are not tears of sorrow; they are tears of bliss. Nowadays, people pray to God only during times of distress. If you pray to God in times of both happiness and sadness, you will no longer have to experience any suffering. Even if some suffering should come to you, it won't appear as suffering. God will look after you. If you can pray to Him with an open heart and shed a few tears out of love for Him, then you are saved."

As She talked about loving God, Mother entered a sublime mood of devotion. She began describing the days She had spent immersed in *prema bhakti* (supreme love and devotion).

"Oh, what struggles Amma had to go through in those days! She couldn't step on the street without being jeered at by people. She was an object of ridicule. No one would give Her even one meal. She wished She had at least one spiritual book to read, but there were none. Nor did She have a guru. Children, a spiritual life without a guru is like the life of a child without a mother. Amma grew up like a motherless child. The people around Her knew nothing about spirituality. When She sat in meditation, someone would come and pour cold water over Her, or they would slap Her. They threw Her out of the house. This was the kind of treatment Amma got! But even so, She didn't think of it as suffering, because She believed that God would never forsake Her. In spite of everything

She had to bear, She forgot it all the moment She uttered Devi's name. Whenever She felt sad, She revealed Her sadness only to Devi. Through Her tears She communicated with Devi."

Mother sat in silence for a while. Then She sang in a tremulous voice:

Oru tulli sneham…

> *O Mother, give a drop of your Love*
> *To my burning heart,*
> *So that my life will be fulfilled.*
> *Why do you give burning fire*
> *As a fertilizer for this scorched creeper?*
>
> *I keep bursting into tears.*
> *How many hot tears do I have to give*
> *As an offering to you?*
> *Don't you hear the pounding of my heart*
> *And all my agony coming out in suppressed sighs?*
>
> *Don't let the fire enter and dance*
> *Through the sandalwood forest.*
> *Don't let this furnace of sadness reveal its intensity*
> *And burst forth like shattering tiles.*
>
> *O Devi,*
> *Chanting, "Durga, Durga,"*
> *My mind has forgotten all other paths.*
> *I want neither heaven nor liberation—*

I want only pure devotion to you.
I want neither heaven nor liberation—
I want only pure devotion to you...

Mother sang the last two lines again and again. Tears welled up in Her eyes. She wiped Her eyes and said, "In those days, Amma used to sing these lines spontaneously whenever She felt overwhelmed with grief, and She wept as She sang each line. Sometimes, when She uttered God's name, She would burst out laughing over and over again. Watching this, Sugunachan (Amma's father) would think, 'It's all over! The child has gone mad!' He would come running and hit Her on the head. People believed that if they hit Her on the head on such occasions, Her mind would be all right again. When She didn't show any signs of change, he would call Her mother, 'Damayanti, the girl has gone crazy! Get some water and pour it on Her head. Quick!' Then the *dhara*[25] would start, and they'd pour pot after pot of water on Amma's head. When She cried for God, they brought Her medicine, thinking She was sick.

"Younger children came and asked, 'Why are you crying, *chechi* (elder sister)? Do you have a headache?' They sat close to Her and started crying as well. After some time, they figured out the reason why chechi was crying:

---

[25] A continuous stream of liquid. The term is used to denote a form of medical treatment by which a medicinal liquid is poured continuously over the patient. It is also a form of ceremonial bathing of the icon of a deity.

it was because chechi couldn't see 'Mother Devi.' So the little girls put on saris and came to Her, pretending they were Mother Devi. Amma hugged them when She saw them dressed like that. She didn't see them as children— to Her they were the Goddess Herself.

"Sometimes when Amma wept uncontrollably, Her father picked Her up and held Her against his shoulder. He consoled Her saying, 'Don't cry, my dear. I will show you Devi in a moment.' She was so innocent that She believed him and stopped crying.

"In those days, Amma didn't like to talk to anyone. Whenever someone came to talk to Her, She drew a triangle on the ground and imagined Devi sitting within it. The person soon realized that She was in another world, so they got up and left. She pictured everyone as Devi. Because of this, sometimes when the village girls were passing by, She tried to embrace them."

Rao: "Why don't we experience that kind of innocent devotion?"

Mother: "Isn't it because of your devotion that you have come here, leaving your home and family?"

Rao: "Amma, when we see you in front of us, to whom should we call out, and for whom should we cry?"

Mother laughed and changed the subject: "Isn't it time for your class? Don't waste your time sitting with Amma. Go!"

Mother picked up a baby sitting next to Her and got up. With the baby in Her arms, She walked to the darshan hut calling, "Come, my children!" The devotees followed Her inside.

THE EMBODIMENT OF THE SCRIPTURES

Mother was standing outside Ottoor's room. She stood listening for a little while, quietly hiding beside the door. Lord Krishna's name, uttered in a quivering voice, rose from within the dark room.

"Narayana, Narayana, Narayana…"

Finally, Mother entered Ottoor's room. Seeing Mother's beautiful form standing in front of him, the old man sprang to his feet and prostrated, in spite of Mother's objections. Even before She had sat down on his bed, he knelt down and put his head in Her lap, with the freedom of a little child.

Mother: "My son, Amma couldn't help standing there when She heard you reciting the Lord's name with so much devotion!"

Ottoor: "I don't think I really have any devotion for the Lord. Otherwise, wouldn't the all-compassionate Kanna have given me darshan?"

A brahmachari who had been listening said, "But aren't you seeing Amma now?"

Ottoor: "It seems Sharada Devi once said to Ramakrishna Deva, 'You know, I don't have the patience to wait for as long as you do. I can't bear to see my children suffer.' I believe it is that same person who has given me darshan today. Amma always talks about devotion, just like Sharada Devi."

Mother: "Do you know why Amma talks about devotion? Because that is Her own experience. There are so many scholars and sannyasis today. They talk about *advaita* (non-duality) but they don't live it. Their minds are full of anger and desires. Advaita isn't something to talk about; it is to be experienced.

"There's a story in the *Upanishads.* A father sent his son to learn the scriptures. When the son returned, the father saw how proud he was and realized that the boy hadn't imbibed the essence of what he had learned. He decided to teach his son the true principle. He asked him to bring some milk and sugar. He then made him dissolve the sugar into the milk. Then he fed his son portions of the milk from different parts of the container and asked how it tasted. The son said it was sweet. 'How sweet?' asked the father. But the son couldn't describe it. He just stood there in silence. Suddenly, he understood the truth. The young man who had made so much noise about the Self, learned that the Self is something that has to be experienced, and that it cannot be described in words.

"No one can describe Brahman. Brahman can't be known through the intellect. It is an experience. Anyone can say, 'I am Brahman,' but they still experience nothing but the pains and pleasures of life. Those who have experienced Brahman are different. Neither fire nor water can hurt them. Did anything happen to Sita when she jumped into the fire? Nothing. Some people say they are Brahman, but if you were to hold that 'Brahman' under water, they would gasp for breath, desperately afraid for their lives. And if they were thrown into fire, they would burn. They have no experience of Brahman beyond worldly pleasures and suffering. Without doing disciplined sadhana, you cannot possibly experience that you are Brahman."

Pointing to a cow grazing nearby, Mother continued, "Do you see that cow? Will you get any milk by pressing her ears? Can you say there is milk in all parts of her body? Only her udder contains milk for us to drink, and we will get that only if we milk her.

"It is true that God is everywhere, but to actually experience Him we have to do sadhana under the guidance of a guru, with a one-pointed mind and with lakshya bodha."

Br: "Amma says that She hasn't learned the scriptures, and yet, whatever Amma says comes straight from the scriptures!"

Mother: "Son, the scriptures were written from experience, weren't they? Amma is talking about things that She has seen and heard and experienced, so it must be in the scriptures."

Br: "Amma, will Ramarajya (the kingdom of Rama) ever return?"

Mother: "Ramarajya will come, but there will also be at least one Ravana. Dwaraka will return, too, but Kamsa and Jarasandha will also be there."

Br: "Amma, people say there is such a thing as reincarnation. Is it true?"

Mother: "Last month, some of us learned a song together. Because we can't remember it now, can we say that we didn't learn the song? There are many witnesses to the fact that we did learn it. It may be impossible for you to recall your previous lives, but a tapasvi can do it. It becomes possible when the mind is made subtle through sadhana."

Later in the afternoon, Puthumana Damodaran Namboodiri, a famous Tantric priest from Kerala, accompanied by a group of people, came for Mother's darshan. This was Puthumana's first visit to Mother. Mother didn't say much. Most of the time, She sat with Her eyes closed, looking inward. She appeared to be in meditation.

Puthumana read aloud a Sanskrit poem he had written about Mother and offered it to Her. He said, "I know it is wrong to wish for wealth, but the mind desires it. I know it is wrong to desire the fruit of one's actions, but if we can't achieve desirelessness in action, what is to be done?"

Mother didn't reply. She just looked at him and smiled. Her silence is often more expressive than Her words.

Puthumana (referring to Mother and Ottoor, who was sitting beside Her): "I'm so happy to see you two together like Krishna and Kuchela!"

Ottoor: "How true! But, on the other hand, such a sight as this has probably never been seen before. Darkness flees when the sun appears, but here you can see with your own eyes, darkness (pointing at himself) in solid form!"

Everyone laughed. Fortunate is the devotee who turns into the embodiment of helplessness in the presence of the Mother of the Universe, who is the abode of compassion! What can stop Her flow of grace then?

Sunday, February 16, 1986

HER SANKALPA IS TRUTH ITSELF

Mother returned from Alappuzha this morning. She had spent two days there with Her children. A Ramayana *yajna* (a discourse on the Ramayana lasting for several days) was being held there. Most of the brahmacharis wouldn't return until later that night, after taking part in the procession of lights at the conclusion of the yajna.

On the way back, Mother had said to a brahmacharini, "Daughter, cook some rice as soon as you get back to the ashram." But when they got back, rice and vegetables had already been cooked. The brahmacharini couldn't decide what to do. She said to the others, "Why did Mother ask me to cook? Everything has already been prepared. If I cook more food, we'll have to throw it away, won't we? There isn't even the usual crowd here today. But, then, if I don't cook, I'll be disobeying Mother." Though the others told her not to cook anything because it would be a waste, she decided to ignore their advice and simply obey

Mother's instruction. So she cooked the rice, thinking that any leftover food could be used for the dinner that night.

By the time lunch was served, it was apparent that everyone's calculations had been wrong—except Mother's. The crowd of devotees had grown considerably, and when lunch was finished, nothing was left over. There had been just enough. Had the young woman not followed Mother's instruction, everyone would have felt bad not being able to feed all the devotees. Every word of Mother's is meaningful. It may seem meaningless or unimportant at first, but that is only because of our inability to understand it at a deeper level.

In the evening, as Mother was walking over to the kalari for bhajans and bhava darshan, a brahmachari asked Her, "Since the ashram doesn't have the money to continue the construction of the new building, why not make a plea for help through *Matruvani*?"[26]

In a serious tone Mother said, "Is that really you saying this, son? It seems that you haven't learned anything from your experiences so far. Those who have surrendered to God don't have to worry about anything. We should never approach anyone with a desire in mind, for that will only bring us suffering. Let us take refuge in God alone. He will bring us everything we need. Where there are tapasvis, there is no shortage of anything; everything comes automatically when needed.

---

[26] The ashram's monthly magazine.

"Did we start this construction with any cash in hand? Did we start with some source of help in mind? Not really. We have taken refuge only in God so far, and because of this, He has not allowed there to be any obstructions to the work—and He will continue to look after us."

When the foundation stone had been laid for the large building now being built, everyone had wondered about this. The ashram had no funds to speak of. However, the ashram did own two houses in Tiruvannamalai near Ramanashram, and the idea of selling them had come up. But when Mother had visited the place, so many devotees had come to Her for darshan that some people didn't like the idea of selling the house. When Mother heard about this after having returned home, She said, "If we are located that close to another ashram, there is likely to be some competition. So let's not have an ashram near Ramanashram. We'll sell the houses and do something here. An ashram should always be in a place where it can be of some service to others. Our ashram isn't needed at that place, because Ramana Bhagavan's ashram is already there."

The two houses in Tiruvannamalai were sold, and a date was set for laying the foundation stone of an ashram building in Amritapuri. Simultaneously, the owners of some land adjoining the ashram put their property up for sale. The ashram bought that land with the money earmarked for the new building. At the time, a brahmachari had remarked that there was no point in laying the foundation of a main ashram building as they no longer had any money for the construction. Mother had replied, "Let us nevertheless proceed with our plan. God will look after everything. He will make it happen."

The foundation had been laid as scheduled and the work had begun. Ever since, the construction had progressed without any obstacles. Somehow, whatever was needed always arrived on time. And Mother insisted that they shouldn't seek help when anything was needed for the building.

Mother now said as She was walking to the kalari, "When we accept everything as God's will, all our burdens are taken away, and we won't experience any difficulties with anything. There is a little daughter who loves Amma very much. She calls Amma 'Mataji.' One day she fell from a swing, but she wasn't hurt. She got up from the ground and said, 'Because of Mataji's power, I sat on the swing; then Mataji pushed me off the swing, and Mataji made sure I wasn't hurt.' We should be like that. While others may see their joy or suffering as their prarabdha, we should accept all our joy and suffering as God's will."

Mother turned to a young man, who had expressed a desire to live at the ashram, and said, "Spiritual life is like standing in the middle of a fire without getting burnt." Mother reached the kalari, and sat down for bhajans. The sacred music began to flow, laden with devotion.

Gajanana he Gajanana…

O elephant-faced One
O Son of Parvati
Abode of Compassion
Supreme Cause…

Tuesday, February 25, 1986

THE HOLDER OF UNSEEN STRINGS

A middle-aged woman from Bombay and a young woman who had just arrived from Germany came to Mother together, prostrated, and offered a plate of fruit at Her feet. Mother embraced them. This was the young woman's first visit to the ashram. Her eyes were overflowing with tears.

Mother: "Where do you come from, daughter?"

But the young woman was crying so much that she couldn't reply. Mother held her and stroked her back. Her companion finally told Mother about the circumstances that had brought the young woman to the ashram.

She came from Germany and was a devotee of Sharada Devi. She had read many books on Sharada Devi, and her devotion had grown steadily. She couldn't bear the grief of not being able to see the Goddess who was the object of her worship. One morning, when she was meditating, she clearly saw in her mind a smiling woman, wearing pure white, with her head covered with the end of her garment. The young woman wondered who this could be, for she had never seen her before, not even in a picture. She was convinced that this must be another form of Sharada Devi, whom she loved so much. She felt she was seeing Sharada Devi in person, and was overcome with bliss.

Three days later, she received a letter from a friend. Inside was a photo of the same woman she had seen in her meditation. Her joy knew no bounds. She wrote to her friend asking for more details about the woman in the picture. But he knew nothing about her. A friend of his had gone to India and had sent him the picture from there. Since he, himself, was not spiritually inclined, he had sent it to her because he knew she was interested in spirituality. The only clue as to where she might find the woman was an address on the back of the photo.

She wasted no time. She immediately made arrangements to go to India, and then she flew to Mumbai (Bombay). In Mumbai, she boarded a plane to Cochin, holding the photo in her hand. Even on the plane, she kept looking at the picture. An older Indian woman sitting next to her noticed this and asked about the picture. The young woman started talking to her. She showed her the address written on the back of the photo, and told her that she had just arrived in India for the first time and that she didn't know the way. To her great surprise the woman told her that she, herself, was on her way to that same ashram and would take her there! She was one of

Mother's devotees! Thus the young woman reached the ashram without difficulty.

It is worth noting here that a mahatma will help seekers on the spiritual path by attracting them in a manner appropriate to each person's samskara, and by guiding them along the way. Many people believe that Mother is Krishna, Shiva, Ramakrishna Paramahansa, Kali, Durga, Mookambika, or Ramana Maharshi. Mother has even given darshan to people in their forms. But it is impossible to guess what Mother's previous incarnation may have been.

Mother instructed a brahmacharini to make arrangements for the two women to stay. Then Mother went behind the brahmacharis' huts, where a lot of rubbish was lying around, and started cleaning the area. The brahmacharis felt embarrassed and came running to help. Some of the devotees also came forward to help Mother. Mother talked to the devotees as She worked, suggesting solutions to their problems.

BRINGING UP CHILDREN

A family from northern Kerala, who had arrived at the ashram the day before, was working next to Mother. The father took the opportunity to tell Mother about his daughter's studies. "Amma, she doesn't study at all. Please talk some sense into her. My wife just spoils her."

Wife: "But Amma, she's still a child! I don't spank her or anything like that because my husband punishes her, and that is enough. I don't want both of us to punish her!"

A devotee: "These days, it's usually the mother who spoils the children."

Mother: "Why blame just the mothers? The fathers also have a role in bringing up their children. Nowadays, parents think only of sending their children to school at an early age, making them study as much as possible, and then arranging a job for them. They don't pay any attention to the children's spiritual development or to the purity of their character. The first thing parents should attend to is the character of their children. They should teach them good behavior, and this means instructing them in spiritual matters. The parents should tell their children stories that teach moral principles, and they should train them to do japa and meditation. By doing sadhana, the intelligence and memory of the child will greatly improve. Just by glancing at a textbook, they'll be able to recall everything they have studied during the year. And when they hear a question, the answer will appear in their minds just like a computer. They will also be well behaved. They will progress spiritually and will also be materially successful in life."

When the work was finished, Mother sat down under a nearby coconut tree. The devotees gathered around Her. One of them introduced a young man who was new to the ashram.

Devotee: "He is from Malappuram. He spends all his time working for nature conservation. He and some of his friends are trying to preserve temples and temple tanks (pools)."

The young man smiled shyly and bowed to Mother with joined palms.

Mother: "All the ashram land here has been reclaimed from the backwaters. The children have planted coconut palms, banana trees, and flowering plants wherever they could."

Mother washed Her hands and walked over to the kalari, with the devotees following close behind.

WHERE TO LOOK FOR HAPPINESS

Mother sat down on the verandah of the kalari. The devotees prostrated and sat down with Her. The newcomer asked, "Even though so many material comforts are available, people are unhappy. Why is it so, Amma?"

Mother: "Yes, that is true. Nowadays, most people fail to find peace and contentment. They build large palatial homes and end up committing suicide inside! If luxurious homes, riches, physical comforts, and alcohol were sources of happiness, would there be any need to die of depression like that? So real happiness is not to be found in such things. Peace and contentment depend entirely on the mind.

"What is the mind? From where does it arise? And what is the purpose of life? How are we meant to live our lives? We don't try to understand these things. If we understood them and lived accordingly, we wouldn't need to wander anywhere looking for peace of mind. But, instead, everyone searches for peace outside of themselves.

"This reminds Amma of a story. An old woman was searching very intently for something in front of her house. A passerby asked, 'What are you looking for, grandma?' 'I'm looking for one of my earrings that I lost,' she replied. The man joined her in the search. They searched and searched but couldn't find the earring. Finally, the man said to the old woman, 'Try to remember exactly where it could have fallen.' She said, 'Actually, it fell somewhere inside the house.' The man was annoyed by this and said, 'Then, why on earth are you looking for it out here, when you've known all the time that you lost it in the house?' The old woman replied, 'Because it's so dark inside. I thought I'd look for it out here because there is some light from the street lamp.'

"Children, we are like that old woman. If we wish to enjoy peace in our lives, we have to find its real source and search for it there. We will never get any real peace or happiness from the external world."

THE BENEFITS OF YAGAS

Young man: "A *yaga* (elaborate Vedic sacrificial rite) took place recently. Many people were against it, complaining that money was being spent unnecessarily."

Mother: "Yes, the question was asked why we should spend money on God. Son, God doesn't need any yagas; it is man who benefits from them. Yagas purify the atmosphere. Just as we remove the phlegm from inside the body through *nasyam* (an ayurvedic treatment), the smoke rising from the *homa* (sacrificial fire) cleanses the atmosphere. Amma isn't suggesting that we spend an excessive amount of money on homas, yagas, and the like. There is no need to offer gold or silver to the fire. There is, however, a principle behind these ceremonies. When we offer something that we are attached to into the sacrificial fire, it is equal to severing that attachment. The biggest yaga takes place when we sacrifice our ego for the love of God. That is what real *jnana* (supreme wisdom) is all about. We should discard the idea of 'I' and 'mine', and see everything as the one Truth, as God. We should understand that nothing is separate from ourselves. By offering our ego into the homa fire, we become complete.

"Homas benefit not only those who perform them, but all the people in the surrounding area as well. If we cannot perform such ceremonies, we should grow plenty of trees and medicinal plants, because they also cleanse the air. Many diseases will be prevented if we breath in the air that has come into contact with medicinal plants.

"Man has become very materialistic. He is in a hurry to cut down trees and turn them into money. He clears forest land and turns it into farms. These acts have changed nature. No longer does the rain fall or the sun shine at the right time, and the atmosphere has become terribly polluted. Man lives without knowing himself. He lives only for his body, while he forgets the *Atman* which gives the body life.

"People ask, 'Why should we waste money on yagas and homas? Surely God doesn't need such things.' But those same people don't complain about the millions spent on bringing a handful of soil from the moon. The people themselves actually benefit from ceremonies like yagas and homas.

"Today people laugh at the practice of lighting an oil lamp at home. But the smoke from the lamp purifies the atmosphere. During the twilight hours, impure vibrations permeate the atmosphere. This is the reason why we chant the divine names or sing bhajans during that particular time. If we fail to do japa at that time, our worldly tendencies will grow stronger. Also, we shouldn't eat at sundown. Eating at that time of day will lead to illness, because at twilight the air is poisonous. It is said that the demon king Hiranyakasipu was killed during *sandhya*, the twilight hour. At that time the ego is most predominant. Only by taking refuge in God, can we destroy the ego. But these days people watch TV or listen to film songs[27] at that hour.

"How many homes have puja rooms? In the olden days, the puja room was given prime consideration when building a house. Today God is usually relegated a place under

---

[27] The Indian equivalent to western pop music.

the staircase. To God, who dwells in our hearts, we should give the heart of the house. That is how we express our relationship with Him. God, however, doesn't need anything.

"God needs nothing from us. Does the sun need the light of a candle? It is we, who are living in the dark, who are in need of light. Do we need to give water to a river to quench its thirst? By taking refuge in God, it is we who gain purity of heart, and with a pure heart, we can constantly enjoy the state of bliss. By surrendering to God, it is we who are given peace, yet we tend to worship God in a way which suggests that God is in need of something!

"Although God has infinite power and is present everywhere, He can be seen only by those who are pure in heart. It is difficult to see the sun's reflection in muddy water, but in clear water the image can easily be seen.

"When we make God a part of our lives, our lives, and also the lives of others, will be sanctified. We then begin to experience peace and contentment. Think of a river that is full and pure. We are the ones that benefit from it. With the water from that river we can clean our dirty gutters and canals. A stagnant, putrid pond can be purified by connecting it to the river. God is like a pure river. By cultivating a relationship with God, our mind becomes so expansive that it encompasses the whole world. In this way we come closer to the Self and we benefit others as well."

MORE QUESTIONS FROM DEVOTEES

A woman devotee: "Amma, did the ashram residents move here because you asked them to?"

Mother: "Amma hasn't asked anyone to stay here. A householder takes care of only one family, but a sannyasi has to bear the burden of the whole world. We have to consider all the problems that may arise later if we allow everyone to stay here who comes here wanting to be a sannyasi, because most of them are unable to sustain their initial sense of detachment. In fact, Amma told all the children that She didn't want to keep them here, but they didn't want to leave. In the end, Amma told them She'd let them stay if they brought a letter of consent from home. Several of them came back with permission from their families. That's how most of the children became residents. One can see that they have real detachment.

"Some of them, however, didn't get permission, but they stayed here anyway because their longing and detachment was so strong. Big problems broke out at home. Their parents tried to stop them by going to court. They came with the police and dragged the children away, and even took them to the mental hospital! (Laughing) Do you know why? Because some of the children who had been drinking alcohol, stopped drinking when they met Amma! Their parents refused to let their children become sannyasis and serve the world, even if it meant sending them to their graves!"[28]

Young man: "Has anyone later regretted that they chose ashram life?"

Mother: "None of those who had a true sense of their goal have regretted that they chose this life. Their journey is one of great bliss. They don't even fear death. If a light bulb burns out, it doesn't mean that there's no electricity. Even though the body dies, the Atman doesn't perish. They know that. They have surrendered their lives to God. They don't think about the past, nor do they think about tomorrow or worry about it. They aren't like a person who goes for a job interview; they are like someone who has already found a stable job. A person who goes for an interview is anxious about the result; he is worried about whether or not he will get the job. But he who has been given the job goes away in peace. Most of the children here have absolute faith that their guru will lead them to the Goal."

Young man: "Amma, what should a spiritual person pray for?"

Mother: "They should pray, 'O God, countless people are suffering. Give me the power to love them! Make me love them selflessly!' This should be the aim of a spiritual person. Tapas should be done for the sake of acquiring the strength to save others. A true tapasvi is like an in-

---

[28] By Mother's grace and their determination, these youths finally managed to come and settle at the ashram.

cense stick that allows itself to burn out while giving its fragrance to others. A spiritual person finds happiness in being loving and compassionate towards everyone, even towards those who are against him. He is like a tree that gives shade even to those who are in the act of cutting it down.

"A real tapasvi wishes to serve others through self-sacrifice, just like a candle gives light to others while it melts and burns down. Their aim is to give happiness to others while forgetting their own struggles. This is what they pray for. This attitude awakens the love for God within them. Mother is waiting for such individuals. Liberation will come searching for them, and will wait on them like a servant maid. Liberation will come flying to them like leaves in the wake of a whirlwind. Others, whose minds are not as expansive, will not attain realization, no matter for how long they may be doing tapas. This place is not for those who come seeking only their own liberation.

"Children, sadhana doesn't mean just praying and doing japa. Real prayer includes being compassionate and humble towards others, smiling at someone and saying a kind word. We should learn to forgive the mistakes of others and to be deeply compassionate—just as our one hand automatically caresses the other hand if it is in pain. By developing love, understanding, and broadmindedness, we can ease the pain of so many people. Our selflessness will also enable us to enjoy the peace and bliss that is within us.

"When Amma was young, She used to pray, 'O God, all you need to give me is your heart! Make me love the whole world in the same selfless way as you do!' That is what Amma is telling Her children to do now; they should long for God in this way."

Mother stopped speaking and sat for a while with Her eyes closed. Then She opened Her eyes and asked a brahmachari to sing a kirtan. As he sang, everyone repeated each line after him in the traditional way:

Vannalum Ambike, taye manohari...

> *Come, O Mother, Enchantress of the mind!*
> *O Ambika, let me see you!*
> *Let your beautiful form shine*
> *In the lotus of my heart.*
> *When will that blessed day dawn*
> *When my heart will be filled with devotion for you?*

Mother raised both Her arms in an ecstatic mood and continued to sing:

Namam japichu samtruptanayennu...

> *When will I bathe in the tears of joy*
> *That come from chanting the divine name?*
> *Will the day ever dawn*
> *When my mind and heart are made pure?*

*Will the day arrive when I give up my pride and
shame,
My rituals and toils?
When will I drink that intoxicating devotion
And lose my mind to Love?
When will I burst into tears
In the midst of blissful laughter?*

Mother sang the lines again and again. When the hymn
came to an end, She remained in an elevated mood, with
tears trickling down Her face. Everyone present bowed to
Her quietly within their hearts.

It was time for the regular bhajans. Mother and the
others went to the kalari and the singing began.

Kezhunnen manasam, Amma...

*O Mother, my mind is crying.
O Mother, my Mother, can you hear me?
With an aching heart, I have wandered all over the
land,
Searching for you.
What am I to do now, O Mother?*

*What sin has this helpless one committed
For you to show her such indifference?
O Mother, I will wash your flower-like feet
With my hot tears.*

O Mother, I am weakening
From the unbearable burden of past deeds.
O Mother, don't delay giving refuge
To this humble servant,
Who is utterly exhausted.

Mother, who had described service as being synonymous with devotion just a few moments ago, was now weeping with love for the Mother of the Universe. Watching this play of moods, who could help but marvel at Mother's inscrutable and quickly changing bhavas?

Wednesday, February 26, 1986

THE MOTHER WHO DISCIPLINES
WITH THE ROD

Manju, a girl who lived at the ashram, and who hadn't been able to be with Mother for several days, stayed home from school today, hoping to spend some time with Mother. When Mother found out the reason for Manju's truancy, She threatened the girl with a cane and escorted her to the ferry. Returning to the hut to give darshan, Mother was greeted by a small boy and his father.

Boy's father: "My son insisted on seeing you, Amma. So I had to bring him here. I even let him skip school. He wouldn't agree when I told him to wait till Sunday when there's no school."

Mother (laughing): "Just a moment ago, Amma drove a girl off to school with a cane! Don't you want to go to school, son?"

Boy: "No, I want to be with Amma!"

Mother (laughing): "If you stay here, Amma's mood will suddenly change. You know that tree out in front with many little branches? We're growing that tree just for spanking children! So don't skip school for the sake of coming here, son. You're Amma's child, aren't you? Then go to school and pass your exams, and then of course Amma will let you stay here."

The boy melted before Mother's affection, especially when Mother's kiss put a seal of love on his cheek.

SANNYASA IS ONLY FOR THE BRAVE

A devotee came forward and prostrated to Mother. He told Mother that one of his friends, who was married and had two children, had just left his family. He had lived a life of luxury, even though he didn't have a steady income, and had gone deep into debt. With creditors harassing him at home, and unable to find a way out of his troubles, he had finally left home saying he was going to become a sannyasi. The devotee asked Mother, "For many people, isn't ashram life an escape from real life? When they face unbearable difficulties and struggles, people take up sannyasa."

Mother: "Such people won't be able to stick to it. They won't be able to persevere in spiritual life. Spiritual life is for those who are strong and brave. Some people put on the ochre robe at the spur of the moment, without thinking it over carefully. Their lives will be full of disappointment.

"A householder takes care of only his wife and children; he only has to pay attention to their problems. But a spiritual person must carry the burden of the whole world. He mustn't falter in any situation. He must be firm in his faith and spiritual wisdom. He cannot be weak. Even if someone beats him, or if a woman tries to touch him, he shouldn't waver an inch. His life should never be influenced by anyone else's words or deeds.

"But today people are not like that. If someone utters a few insulting words out of anger, they are ready to kill that person, right there and then. If they can't take revenge immediately, they'll constantly be thinking of a way to get back at him. The balance of their lives rests on a few words from the lips of others. A real spiritual being isn't like that at all. He trains himself to stand firmly centered within himself. He learns what life is really about. Spiritual life is impossible without real discrimination and detachment.

"Once there was a wife who was never satisfied with what her husband earned. She berated him constantly. All the husband ever heard from her was the cry for more and more, until he finally became weary of life itself. He thought of committing suicide, but couldn't bring himself to do it. He decided to leave home to become a sannyasi. He traveled for a while, until he found a guru. Before accepting him as a disciple, the guru asked, 'Did you leave home because of some discord in your family or because you have gained true detachment?'

"The man said, 'I left home with the hope of becoming a sannyasi.'

'Don't you have any desires?'

'No, I have no desires.'

'So you have no desire for wealth or power?'

'No, I don't want anything. I'm not interested in anything.'

"After asking some more questions, the guru accepted the man as his disciple and gave him a *kamandalu*[29] and a staff.

"A few days later, the guru and disciple started on a pilgrimage. When they felt tired, they rested on the bank of a river. The disciple put down his kamandalu and staff and went and bathed in the river. When he returned, he couldn't find his kamandalu. He searched everywhere, and when he couldn't find, it he got very upset.

"The guru said, 'You told me that you're not attached to anything. Then why are you making such a fuss over a kamandalu? Let it go. And let us continue on our way.'

---

[29] A vessel made of the shell of a coconut with a handle and bent nozzle, used by monks for collecting water and food.

"The disciple said, 'But without it I can't drink any-thing! I have no container to keep water in!'

"The guru said, 'You are supposed to be desireless, and yet you cling to such a small desire? See everything as God's will.'

"The disciple, however, remained distraught. Seeing this, the guru gave him his kamandalu back. The guru had hidden it to test him.

"They continued their journey. As lunchtime approached, the disciple became very hungry, but the guru gave him nothing to eat. When the disciple complained, the guru said, 'A spiritual person needs patience and endurance. He should be able to go on without faltering, even if he doesn't get any food for a day. How can you be so weak from hunger already? It's only noon! Indulging in food should be one of the first things a spiritual seeker gives up. The stomach is what should shrink first in spiritual life.'

"The guru gave the disciple an herbal powder to be mixed with water to suppress his hunger. The disciple couldn't stand the bitter taste and he vomited. With that, he decided he'd had enough, that he preferred to suffer his wife's tirades at home rather than continue the life of a sannyasi. So he asked for the guru's permission to go home.

"The guru said, 'What did you have in mind when you set out to become a sannyasi?'

"The disciple answered, 'I never imagined it would be anything like this. I thought I'd simply have to take a bath every day, wear sacred ash, and sit somewhere with my eyes closed. I thought people would come and prostrate and give me *bhiksha* (alms), and that I would have plenty to eat at regular mealtimes, without having to do any work.' And thus, he went home to his wife.

"This is what will happen if one enters sannyasa because of some quarrel with others, or out of spite, or if one is simply trying to run away from life, without having developed any real *vairagya* (detachment).

"We shouldn't adopt the life of a renunciate without first learning to discriminate between the everlasting and the evanescent, and without first developing detachment. Our aim on the spiritual path should be to feel empathy for those who are sick and poor, or who are suffering in any way, and to live a life of selfless service, dedicated to the welfare of others. Every breath the spiritual person takes should be a breath of sympathy for those who are suffering in this world, and not for his own comfort. At the same time, he should constantly be developing inner strength by ceaselessly praying, 'O God, where are you? Where are you?'

"Whereas an ordinary person is like a candle, a sannyasi shines like the sun, giving light to thousands. He isn't even concerned about his own liberation. The meaning of renunciation is to be willing to offer the world all the power you have gained through your sadhana. That is the sannyasi's only aim. A spiritual being is one who wants nothing else than to live a life of true renunciation.

"Only after testing them in different ways, did Amma allow the children who came here to stay. She fed them only once a day, and gave them tasteless food without any salt or spices. But they gladly accepted it. They had self-control. Amma tested them to see if they would try to get hold of some tasty food for themselves after entering the life of service. She also watched them to see if they'd just sit in the name of meditation, without doing any work. No matter how much tapas they do, they also have to help with the necessary ashram work. If they're not prepared to do that, they'll become lazy and will only be of harm to society.

"Amma told them that if they didn't have any specific task to do, they could at least till the soil around a few coconut trees. They did every kind of work, and they are hanging on, in spite of having gone through all kinds of tests.

"Amma has seen that same alertness in all the children who have come here so far. Those who don't have it won't be able to stay, and will eventually have to return to worldly life."

It was three o'clock when Mother went to Her room.

Friday, February 28, 1986

THE PRINCIPLE OF AHIMSA

The *Matruvani* magazines were to be sent out the next day. Much work remained to be done, and it was already late in the afternoon. Mother and the brahmacharis sat on the verandah outside the meditation room, putting the magazines into envelopes and gluing on stamps. Peter, who was from Holland, approached the verandah. In an angry tone, he asked Br. Nealu,[30] "Who decided that insecticide should be sprayed on the rose bushes? Those poor defenseless insects shouldn't be killed like that!" Nealu translated his words to Mother, but Mother continued to work without commenting. She only glanced at Peter.

With a sad expression on his face, Peter stood by himself at a distance from the group.

After a little while, Mother called him. "Peter, my son, get some water from Gayatri[31] for Amma to drink."

Peter was still looking sad when he brought the water to Mother.

Mother took the glass and said, "This is boiled water, isn't it? Fresh water is enough for Amma."

Peter: "I will bring filtered water, Amma. Or do you want some coconut water?"

Mother: "Amma wants plain unboiled water."

---

[30] Swami Paramatmananda
[31] Swamini Amritaprana

Peter: "Better not drink unboiled water, Amma. You may get sick."

Mother: "But so many living things die when we boil water. Isn't that a sin, son?"

Peter had no answer.

Mother: "Think of how many lives perish when we walk, crushed by our feet. How many organisms die when we breathe! How can it be avoided?"

Peter: "I admit this is beyond our control, but we can at least avoid spraying the plants."

Mother: "All right. Suppose either your child or Amma gets sick. Won't you insist that we take medicine?"

Peter: "Yes, of course. The most important thing is that you get well."

Mother: "But think of how many millions of germs will die when we take the medicine?"

Again Peter had no answer.

Mother: "So it won't do to feel compassion for the germs of the disease, will it? To whom will the rose plant tell its grief when it is attacked by worms? Shouldn't we protect it, we who are its guardians?"

The shadow left Peter's face.

THE MARKS OF REMEMBRANCE

A group of young men came to see Mother. Standing at a distance, they watched Her for awhile, until they finally came over and joined the work. They seemed to want to ask Mother some questions, but something held them back. One had smeared bhasma all over his forehead, and at the point between and just above the eyebrows, he had put a mark of sandalwood paste with a dot of kumkum in the center. He nudged the person sitting next to him and said, "See, Amma is also wearing bhasma."

"What are you children talking about?" Mother inquired.

Young man: "Amma, my friends think it's silly that I put these marks on. They make fun of me, saying that I'm painted like a tiger."

The other young men looked embarrassed. One of them asked, "Why do people apply all that ash and sandalwood paste on their foreheads? What is the reason?"

Mother: "Children, we wear sandal paste and sacred ash, but do we think about the meaning behind it? When we take ash in our hands, we should think of the perishable nature of this life. Today or tomorrow we will turn into a handful of ashes. It is to raise our awareness of this that we wear bhasma. When the lover catches sight of just the hem of his beloved's sari, he is reminded of her. In the same way, the sacred ash, sandal paste, and *rudraksha* beads are meant to remind us of God, to kindle within us the remembrance of the Self. No matter how important or ordinary we are, we may die at any moment. Therefore, we should live without being attached to anyone except God. The people we are attached to will not come with us in the end."

A youth: "What about sandal paste marks?"

"Sandalwood has great medicinal qualities. By putting sandal paste on particular parts of the body, the nerves and the body are cooled, and they become more healthy. There is also a symbolic principle behind the practice of wearing sandal paste. Sandalwood is fragrant. That fragrance is found in the wood, and nowhere else. In the same way, we should realize that infinite bliss is to be found within ourselves, and we should live according to this truth.

"If a piece of sandalwood lies out in the mud, the outer part of it will rot and smell badly. But what a wonderful fragrance we can get from that same piece of sandalwood if we wash it clean and rub it on a stone! In the same way, as long as we are immersed in worldliness, we cannot enjoy the fragrance of the inner Self. We destroy the Consciousness within us by going after trivial sense pleasures. Without realizing it, we waste our body and senses on pleasures that last only for a few moments. This is what the sandal paste reminds us of. If we utilize this life for the sake of knowing the Self, we can live in bliss forever."

Youth: "Why do people wear rudraksha beads?"

Mother: "The rudraksha seed symbolizes total surrender. The beads are strung on a thread, which forms a mala. The beads are held by that thread. Each of us is a pearl strung on the thread of the Self. A rudraksha mala reminds us of this truth and teaches us to completely surrender to God."

TEMPLE WORSHIP

Youth: "Amma, if we tell people we are going to the ashram, they'll make fun of us. They say that temples and ashrams are meant for old people."

Mother: "Nowadays people criticize the temples, but the temples are meant to enhance spiritual thoughts and to develop good qualities in people.

"We see political workers marching with their flags. Suppose someone tears up one of those flags or burns it or spits on it. They'll beat him to death! But what's in a flag? It's just a piece of cloth. If you lose it, you can buy any number of new ones. But a flag is more than a piece of material. It symbolizes an ideal, and this is why people won't tolerate any disrespect shown towards it. In the same way, a temple is a symbol of God. We see God in its images. When we enter the temple and receive darshan, good thoughts blossom in our minds and we remember the true ideal. The atmosphere in a temple is very different from that of a butcher shop or a bar. The atmosphere has been purified by the sacred thoughts of countless worshippers. Such a place of devotion gives solace to those who are suffering, like the cooling shade of a tree in the hot sun, or like a warm blanket in the cold. We can progress spiritually by worshipping God in the temple and by imbibing the good samskara of such a place.

"There ought to be at least one temple in each village. Today everyone is preoccupied with selfish thoughts. The temple can remove the bad vibrations which those thoughts create. The atmosphere will be purified even by just two seconds of the one-pointedness we experience while worshipping in a temple.

"People ask, 'How can God live in an image? Shouldn't we be worshipping the sculptor who made the statue?' But if you look at a painting of your father, is it your father or the painter that you see? God is everywhere. You cannot see Him with your eyes, but when you see the image in the temple, you remember God. That remembrance will bless you and purify your mind."

A young man: "Amma, you have cleared our doubts. I usually wear a sandal-paste mark, but I had no idea of its significance. My parents were doing it, so I did the same. Whenever my friends asked about it, I didn't know what to say. Many people who believed in God when they were children have lost their faith. They have become slaves of alcohol and tobacco. Had there been someone who could have explained things logically to them, they wouldn't have ruined themselves. I might have gone that way, too, but I couldn't turn away from God entirely due to some fear I felt. I'll come back here with some of my friends, Amma. Only you can bring them to the right path."

Mother (laughing): "Namah Shivaya! Son, a person who believes in God and follows the divine principles as his ideal cannot become a slave of bad habits. Because he abides within himself, he seeks his happiness within, and not outside of himself. He derives bliss from God who resides within him. Nothing external can bind him. Amma doesn't insist that everyone should accept God in their lives, but why become a slave of bad habits? Why become a burden to your family and society? Today it is fashionable to drink, smoke, and squander money. It's a pity that the politicians and other influential people don't make an effort to turn young people away from these things. If they fail to set an example, how will others ever learn and absorb spiritual ideals?"

Mother opened a copy of *Matruvani*. Seeing that one of the pages hadn't been printed properly because it had a fold in it, She said, "Children, before putting the magazines in the envelopes, you should go through the copies and check each page. Don't you think the ashram residents ought to be alert and pay careful attention to everything?"

A brahmachari brought bhasma packets and sweets on a plate. Mother motioned for the young visitors to come close to Her. "Come, my children!" She said. The young men who were meeting Her for the first time received prasad from Her sacred hands and then took leave of Her, gratified that some of the doubts that had been bothering them had been cleared up at last.

Monday, March 10, 1986

DOING SADHANA WITH THE GURU

The pipeline bringing water to the ashram was broken. It would take a few days for it to be repaired. For the
past several nights the residents had been bringing water
from the other side of the backwaters, where there was a
single public water tap. The local residents used the tap
for their needs during the day, and so the ashram residents went for water at night. Having crossed the canal
in a boat, the brahmacharis filled their containers, and
then returned to the ashram jetty, where Mother and the
other brahmacharis joined them in carrying water from
the boat to the ashram. The work usually went on until
four or five in the morning.

It was now midnight. One load of water had just been
delivered to the ashram. The brahmacharis had crossed
the canal to fetch the next load. Mother was lying on the
sand at the edge of the backwaters. Someone had spread
a sheet for Her to lie on, but She had rolled over onto the
sand. In a fire nearby, dry leaves and rubbish were burning, making smoke to drive away the swarms of mosqui-
toes.

While waiting for the next load of water, the brahmacharis
sat around Mother and meditated. The flow of water from
the tap on the other side of the canal was so slow that it

would take at least two hours before the boat would return with the next load. After some time, Mother got up from the sand and threw more leaves into the fire, which flared into a roaring blaze.

Mother: "Children, imagine the form of your Beloved Deity standing in this fire. Meditate on that."

A brahmachari kept the fire going. The surrounding landscape and the still backwaters glowed in the moonlight, making it appear as if the land and water were covered by a blanket woven with glistening silver. A deep peace pervaded the night. The quiet was broken only by the occasional whining of a few dogs on the other shore. Then Mother's sweet voice filled the air as She sang:

Ambike Devi Jagannayike Namaskaram...

> *O Mother, Goddess of the Universe,*
> *I bow to you.*
> *O Giver of joy,*
> *I bow to you.*
>
> *O Mother, whose nature is peace,*
> *And who is all-powerful,*
> *You are the Great Deluder,*
> *Without beginning or end—*
> *O Mother, who is the innermost Self,*
> *I bow to you.*

Knowledge, speech, and intelligence—
Everything is you alone.
O Devi, it is you who controls my mind.
This being so, O Auspicious One,
How could I ever describe your greatness?
I do not know the seed mantras required
For worshipping you—
All I can do
Is bow down to you.

O Mother, you pour out your great compassion
On the devotee who constantly remembers you—
Your glory is beyond all imagination.

As the kirtan ended, Mother chanted "Aum" three times. The divine syllable resounded from everyone.

Mother: "Children, visualize a still, bright fire like this one in your heart or between your eyebrows. Night is the ideal time for meditation."

The boat returned with water and the work started again. When the boat went back again with empty containers for more water, Mother asked everyone to resume their meditation. Thus the night passed with a combination of work and meditation until five in the morning. As it was a darshan day, the flow of devotees would soon begin. When would Mother get a little rest? For Her there seemed to be no such thing as rest.

Wednesday, March 12, 1986

WORK DONE WITH SHRADDHA
IS MEDITATION

All work associated with the ashram was done by the residents, and their job assignments were frequently changed. As Mother often said, "The brahmacharis shouldn't be lacking in any skill. They should be able to do any kind of work."

This morning, Mother began patrolling the ashram at seven o'clock, picking up pieces of paper and toffee wrappers lying on the ground. As She reached the cowshed on the north side of the ashram, the cows raised their heads and looked at Her. She caressed their foreheads with the affection of a mother for her children. The floor in front of one of the cows was covered with spilled *pinnak*[32] mixed with water. The cow had pushed the bucket over while drinking from it. Mother cleaned the bucket, and then fetched some water and washed the floor. The brahmacharini who was with Her wanted to help, but Mother wouldn't allow it. The expression on Mother's face made it clear that She was pained to see that the cow was not being given its drink with proper attention. When Mother had finished cleaning the floor, She went straight

---

[32] The pulp left after extracting oil from coconuts or other seeds.

to the hut where the brahmachari who was in charge of the cows was staying.

"My son," She said to him, "aren't you the one who gives the cows their drink every morning?"

From Mother's question, the brahmachari knew he had made some mistake, but he couldn't figure out what it was. He stood in silence.

Mother continued, "Son, the first quality a sadhak should have is shraddha. Is this how you give the cows their drink? One of the cows toppled everything onto the floor. Didn't this happen because of your lack of attention? You were told that you should stay with the cows until they have finished drinking. The cow spilled the pinnak because you failed to obey your instruction, isn't that so? If you can't stay on the job until it's done, Amma will do it Herself. You should look upon the cow as a mother. Looking after the cows is a way of worshipping God. Son, that cow had to go hungry because of your carelessness. And because you left it unattended, a lot of pinnak was wasted."

The brahmachari realized his mistake. He tried to explain why he had left the cowshed. "I left early because it was time for meditation."

His reply didn't satisfy Mother. "If you were really devoted to meditation, you would have fed the cows a little earlier so that you would have been ready for meditation on time. It's a sin to let the poor animals go hungry in the name of meditation. What is meditation? Does it just mean that you sit with your eyes closed and nothing else? Any work you do with japa and constant remembrance of God is also meditation."

Br: "Amma, the other day you fasted, without even drinking any water, because two brahmacharis were late for meditation. I didn't want that to happen again because of me." His eyes filled with tears as he spoke.

Mother wiped his tears and said soothingly, "What did Amma say that upset you like this, son? She just wants you to pay attention from now on. Amma was very serious the other day because those two sons deliberately avoided the meditation. They could have done their reading and writing later. But your case is different. You were doing a job, one that Amma had given you. That is not different from meditation, because dedication to your work is a form of meditation. Your commitment to the work entrusted to you shows your level of surrender and the intensity with which you are focused on the Goal. Working merely to escape meditation, or meditating to escape work—both have to be avoided "

Mother wouldn't tolerate any breach of the ashram rules. Everything had to be done on time. There was not to be any lapses or lateness in attending the meditation or the Vedanta and Sanskrit classes. She would scold the brahmacharis a couple of times. If that didn't help, She would take the punishment Herself by fasting, sometimes foregoing even water. The severest punishment for the brahmacharis was to know that Mother wasn't eating on their account.

Mother and the brahmachari walked over to the kalari mandapam where everyone was meditating. Mother sat down in a lotus posture near the wall, facing east. The brahmachari who had come with Her sat close to Her. After the meditation, everyone came up to Mother, prostrated, and gathered around Her.

ONE-POINTEDNESS

One of the brahmacharis took the opportunity to tell Her about a problem he was experiencing. "Amma, I can't get any concentration when I meditate. I feel very bad about it," he said.

Mother smiled and said, "Children, you don't achieve *ekagrata* (one-pointedness) all of a sudden. It takes constant effort. Don't break the discipline of sadhana just because your mind isn't getting one-pointed. You have to do your sadhana with strict regularity. You need unwavering enthusiasm. You should remember during every second that you are a spiritual aspirant.

"There was once a man who went to the backwaters to fish. He spotted a school of large fish close to the shore. He decided to build a mud dam around that spot and then to empty the water in the dam to catch the fish. He built the dam, and then, having no container with him, he began to scoop up the water with his hands. The dam broke from time to time, but he refused to give up. He continued the task with great patience and absolute faith in what he was doing, without thinking of anything else. By evening, he had emptied the dam and caught plenty of fish. He went home happily, amply rewarded for the hard work he had done with so much confidence, patience, and unswerving dedication.

"Children, don't be disheartened if you don't see any results in spite of all your effort. Each chant of the mantra has an effect, you are just not aware of it. And even if you are not achieving one-pointed concentration, you will still benefit by meditating at a regular time. Through constant japa, the impurities in your mind will disappear, without you even being aware of it, and your concentration will increase during meditation.

"It is not difficult for you to think about your parents, relatives, friends, or your favorite food. You can see them in your mind's eye the moment you remember them, and you can hold them there for as long as you wish. This is possible because of your long association with them. You don't have to teach or train the mind to think about worldly things, because the mind is used to them. You have to build a similar attachment to God. That is the purpose of japa, meditation, and satsang. Constant effort is needed however; and with that effort, the form of your Beloved Deity, and the mantra pertaining to that form, will appear in your mind just as naturally as worldly thoughts do. No matter what you are thinking or seeing, you will constantly retain your awareness of God. For you, there will be no world apart from God.

"Children, don't be disheartened if you are not getting any real concentration in the beginning. If you try constantly, you will definitely succeed. You should always have the attitude, 'Only God is eternal. If I don't get to know Him, this life will be fruitless. I must see Him as soon as possible!' Then you will automatically get concentration. Children, there are no obstacles on the path of a person who is constantly aware of the Goal. For him, all situations are regarded as favorable."

Br: "I can't meditate in the morning because I feel so sleepy."

Mother: "Son, if you feel sleepy during meditation, chant your mantra, moving your lips as you do so. If you have a mala, hold it close to your heart and chant. This will make you more alert. When you sit for meditation, your spine should be straight. Only laziness makes you want to slouch. If you feel sleepy in spite of all this, stand up and chant the mantra. And don't lean on anything when you stand. When you lean on something, your mind gets attached to that comfort. If you still cannot overcome your sleepiness, run for a while and then resume your meditation. Drive away the tamas with rajas. Doing hatha yoga is also beneficial.

"Only if you have real lakshya bodha will your drowsiness be dispelled. Some people working night shifts in factories may not sleep for two or three nights in a row. Still, they don't fall asleep in front of the machines, because if they lose their concentration even for a moment, their hands could get caught in the machines—they could lose their hands and their jobs as well. Knowing this, they manage to chase sleep away, however strong it may be. We should have the same alertness and wakefulness when sitting for meditation. We should understand that we are wasting our lives if we succumb to sleep and waste the time of meditation. Then we won't give in to sleep."

THE SELFISHNESS OF
WORLDLY RELATIONSHIPS

Mother came out of the meditation room and found that some devotees were waiting to see Her. They prostrated to Her. She led them to the kalari mandapam and sat down with them. One of the devotees offered Mother a plate of fruit.

Mother: "How are you now, son?"

The man lowered his head without saying anything. His wife had left him for another man, and out of sheer despair he had started drinking. Four months ago, a friend had brought him to Mother. When he had gone up to Mother for darshan, he had been so drunk that he was out of his senses. Mother hadn't let him leave immediately; She had kept him at the ashram for three days, and he never again touched another drop of alcohol. Since then, he came to see Her whenever he had any free time. But it still clearly pained him that his wife had left him.

Mother: "Son, no one loves anyone more than they

love themselves. Behind everyone's love is a selfish search for their own happiness. When we don't get the happiness we expect from a friend, our friend becomes our enemy. This is what can be seen in the world. Only God loves us selflessly. And it is only through loving Him that we can love and serve others selflessly. Only God's world is free from selfishness. We should focus all our love and attachment on Him alone. Then we won't despair if we are abandoned or wronged by anyone. Hold on to God. He is all you need. Why think about the past and grieve?"

Devotee: "I'm not as troubled as I was before, because now I have Amma to protect me in every way. Amma, your mantra is my support whenever I feel troubled." Mother gave him some bhasma and he rose to leave.

When he had left, Mother said to the others, "Look at the experiences people have! They are lessons for us. Does a husband truly love his wife? And is her love for him real love? Also, why do parents love their children? They love them only because they came from their own blood and seed! Otherwise, wouldn't they love all children equally?

"How many people are ready to die for their children or spouses? Even if that son was ready to die when his wife left him, it was not out of love for her, but for himself. It was out of the disappointment of losing his own happiness. If he had truly loved his wife, he would have accepted that she was happier with someone else. Her happiness would have been more important to him than anything else. That is selfless love. And if his wife had truly loved him, she wouldn't even have looked at another man's face.

"We say that we love our children, but how many people are ready to give up their life to save their child from drowning? A daughter came to Amma with her story. Her child had fallen into a deep well. She saw her child fall but couldn't do anything. By the time some divers arrived, the child was dead. Why didn't the mother think of jumping into the well to save her child? Ninety-nine percent of people are like this. Very rarely will anyone risk their life to save someone else. That is why Amma says that no one but God loves you selflessly. Hold on tightly to Him. This doesn't mean that you shouldn't love others. See God in everyone and love that God. Then you won't succumb to grief if anyone's love disappears."

A young man who was visiting the ashram for the first time was sitting behind the others, listening to Mother. But he listened without any sign of respect or reverence on his face. When Mother stopped talking, he pointed to a picture of Mother in Krishna bhava and asked, "Isn't that you wearing a crown and peacock feathers and things? Why are you dressed like that? Is it some sort of play?"

Hearing such an unexpected question, all the devotees turned round and stared at him.

PLAYING A ROLE FOR SOCIETY

Mother: "Son, how do you know that this world itself

isn't a play? Everyone is acting in a play without realizing it. It is a play that is meant to wake people up from another play, it is a play that is meant to remove their ignorance.

"Son, you were born naked. Why are you wearing clothes when you know that your real form is naked?"

Young man: "I am a social being. I have to obey the norms of society, otherwise society will criticize me."

Mother: "So you are wearing clothes for the sake of society. Amma's costume is also worn for that same society. Those who reach the Goal through the path of jnana can be counted on the fingers of your hand. Amma can't ignore all the others who can advance only through the path of devotion. Sri Shankaracharya, who was an exponent of Advaita, founded temples, didn't he? He said that God is consciousness, but didn't he show that a mere stone is also God? And didn't he write the *Saundarya Lahari*, describing the Divine Mother's form? The same Vyasa who wrote the *Brahma Sutras* also wrote the *Srimad Bhagavatam*. Realizing that the philosophy of non-duality and Vedanta cannot be digested by ordinary minds, they tried to strengthen the devotion in people.

"Son, Amma knows Her own nature and real form very well, but the people of today need some instruments to realize that Supreme Principle. Images of God are needed to increase people's faith and devotion. It is easier to catch a chicken by offering it food than by chasing it. When it sees the food it will come close, and then you can catch it.

In order to uplift ordinary people to the spiritual plane, we first have to come down to their level. Their minds are only able to grasp names and forms, so it is only through names and forms that we can help them to elevate their minds. Think of the uniform of a lawyer or a policeman. When the policeman appears in his uniform, there is order and discipline. But people will have quite a different attitude if he's wearing his off-duty clothes, won't they? This is the significance of costumes and ornaments.

"Those who are able to see the stone in the idol, the gold in the earring, the cane in the chair—the Substratum of everything, the real Essence of everything—do not need any of this. They have already attained the vision of Advaita. But most people haven't reached that level. This is why they need all those things."

The young man asked no more questions. Mother closed Her eyes and meditated for awhile.

THE SECRET OF KARMA YOGA

When Mother opened Her eyes again a devotee asked, "Will the actions of a *karma yogi*, who serves the world, cease as he advances spiritually?"

Mother: "Not necessarily. Actions may continue till the very end."

Devotee: "Amma, which is superior, bhakti or karma yoga?"

Mother: "We can't really say that bhakti yoga and karma

yoga differ from each other, because a true karma yogi is
a real devotee, and a true devotee is a real karma yogi.

"Every action isn't necessarily karma yoga. Only those
actions performed selflessly, as an offering to God, can be
called karma yoga. Neither does doing four
circumambulations, raising your arms, and offering salutations to the deity qualify as bhakti. Our minds should
dwell on God, and our every action should be a form of
worship. We should see our Beloved Deity in everyone,
and offer them our love and service. We should surrender
to God with all our heart. Only then we can say we have
bhakti.

"A true karma yogi keeps his mind on God while engaged in each action. We should have the attitude that
everything is God. Then it is bhakti. On the other hand,
if we think about other things while we are doing puja
(ritual worship), then the puja cannot be considered bhakti
yoga, because it is just an external action and not real
worship. But even if our job is cleaning lavatories, if we
chant the mantra while working, with the attitude that it
is God's work, then it is both bhakti yoga and karma yoga.

"There was once a poor woman who used to utter the
words, '*Krishnarpanam astu*' ('Let this be an offering to
Krishna') before doing anything. Whether she was clean-
ing her front yard or bathing her child, she always said,
'Krishnarpanam astu.' There was a temple next to her house.
The priest in that temple didn't like the woman's prayer.
He couldn't bear the thought of her saying, 'Krishnarpanam

astu,' while throwing out rubbish. He used to chastise the woman for this, but she never said anything in reply.

"One day she picked up some cow dung that was lying in her front yard and threw it out. As usual, she didn't forget to say, 'Krishnarpanam astu.' The cow dung landed in front of the temple. The priest saw this and began to tremble with rage. He dragged the woman to the temple and made her remove the cow dung. Then he beat her and chased her away.

"The next day the priest couldn't move his arm; it was completely paralyzed. He cried out to the Lord. That night the Lord came to him in a dream and said, 'I enjoyed the cow dung my devotee offered me far more than the sweet payasam you gave me. What you do cannot be called worship, whereas every one of her actions is a form of worship. I will not tolerate you harming such a devotee of mine. Only if you touch her feet and beg her forgiveness will you be cured.' The priest realized his error. He asked the woman to forgive him, and was soon cured."

TURN TO GOD RIGHT NOW

Devotee: "I am very busy with my work and can't find any time for meditation. Also, when I try to do japa, I don't get any concentration. Amma, wouldn't it be best for me to wait with japa and meditation until I am no longer so busy and have some peace of mind?"

Mother: "Son, you may think you will turn to God when

your workload is lighter, or after you have had enough of worldly pleasures—but that won't happen. You should turn to Him right now, in the midst of all your difficulties; He will certainly show you a way.

"Amma will give you an example. Suppose a young woman has a mental disorder. A young man comes with a marriage proposal, but finding out about her illness, he says that he will only marry her when she is cured. The doctor's opinion, however, is that she will recover from her illness only if she gets married. So for her, waiting to be cured before getting married is useless!

"Or imagine the water saying, 'You may come to me only after you have learned how to swim.' How would that be possible? You have to get into the water to learn how to swim! In the same way, only through God can you purify your mind. If you remember God while you work, you will be able to do your work well. Any obstacles will disappear, and above all, your mind will be purified.

"If you think you will begin to keep your mind on God when all your difficulties are over and your mind has become peaceful, you are mistaken, because that is never going to happen. You will never reach God that way. It's useless waiting for your mind to improve. Perseverance is the only way to better yourself. At any moment you may lose your health or mental abilities, and then your life will have been wasted. So let us follow the path to God right now. This is what is needed."

A visitor: "Amma, a number of young people have left their homes and have come here searching for God. But aren't they at an age when they are meant to enjoy life? Can't they think of God and take up sannyasa later?"

Mother: "Son, we have been given this human body for the purpose of realizing God. Each day we come closer to death. We lose our strength through worldly pleasures. But by constantly remembering God, our minds will grow stronger. This strengthens the positive samskara in us and we can even transcend death. So we should try to conquer our weaknesses while we are still healthy and full of vitality. Then there is no need to fear about tomorrow.

"Amma remembers a story. In a certain country anyone could become king, but each king could rule for only five years. After that, he was taken to a deserted island and left there to die. There were no human beings on the island; there were only beasts of prey that would immediately kill and devour the king. Even though they knew this, many people came forward wanting to be king out of a desire to enjoy the power and pleasures of that position. As each one ascended the throne, they were elated. But from then on, there was only sorrow, for they feared the day they would be torn to pieces and eaten by the beasts on the island. Because of this, each king was filled with turmoil and never smiled. Though every luxury imaginable was available to them—delicious food, servants, dance, and music—they weren't interested in any of it. They weren't able to enjoy anything. From the moment they assumed power, they saw only death in front of them. They had come for happiness, but not a moment was free of sorrow.

"The tenth king was taken to the island when his allotted time was over and, like all the previous kings, he was consumed by the wild beasts. The next person who came forward to be crowned as king was a young man. But he wasn't at all like the other kings. He wasn't the least unhappy after assuming power. He laughed with everyone, he danced, he went on hunting trips, and often rode around inquiring about the welfare of the people. Everyone noticed that he was always joyful.

"Finally, his days in power were coming to an end, but there was no change in his demeanor. Everyone was amazed. They said to him, 'Your Majesty, the time for you to leave for the island is drawing near, but you don't seem sad at all. Usually, the agony starts as soon as someone ascends the throne, but you are joyful even now!'

"The king replied, 'Why should I be sorry? I'm ready to go to the island. There are no longer any dangerous animals there. When I first became king, I learned how to hunt. I then went to the island with my troops and we hunted and killed all the beasts of prey. I cleared the forest on the island and turned it into farmland. I dug wells and built some houses. Now I shall go and live there. Having given up this throne, I shall continue to live like a king, because everything I need is on the island.'

"We should be like that king. We should discover the world of bliss while we are in this physical world. Instead, almost everyone can be compared to those earlier kings. They don't have a moment free from anxiety and anguish about tomorrow. Because of this, they are unable to do even today's work properly. There is sorrow today and sorrow tomorrow. There is no freedom from tears until the last moment. But if we spend each moment today with shraddha, we won't have to suffer tomorrow—all our to-morrows will be days of bliss.

"Children, don't think you can enjoy the world of the senses now, and think of God later. The sensory world can never give us any real satisfaction. After eating some payasam, we may feel satisfied for a while, but a little later we'll want twice as much! So don't ever think of enjoying the physical world first and then seeking God later! We will never be able to satisfy the senses. Desires do not die that easily. Only someone who has discarded all desires is complete. Children, perform your actions with your mind surrendered to God. Then you can conquer even death, and bliss will be yours forever."

Wednesday, April 16, 1986

"YET I ENGAGE IN ACTION"[33]

---

[33] From the *Bhagavad Gita* Chapter 3, verse 22

The work of pouring concrete for the new building began this morning. Because it was rough work, everyone asked Mother not to join in.

Br. Balu:[34] "Amma, we're making concrete. The cement and gravel will spill on you, and the cement causes burns."

Mother: "Will it burn only Amma's body, and not you children?"

Balu: "But there's no need for you to help. We're here to do the work."

Mother: "Son, Amma doesn't mind working. She didn't grow up sitting in Her room. She's used to hard work."

When Mother said this, everyone knew they were defeated. Mother joined the line of people who were carrying buckets with cement.

A bucket full of concrete mixture suddenly slipped from a brahmachari's hand and fell to the ground. He moved back quickly so that it missed his feet, but some of it splashed on Mother's face. She cleaned Her face with a towel that a brahmachari offered Her, and then tied the towel around Her head, jokingly assuming a pose that created ripples of laughter in the middle of the hard work.

As the sun grew hotter, pearls of sweat began to trickle from Mother's forehead. Seeing Her toiling under the hot sun, a devotee came with an umbrella to hold over Her head, but She wouldn't even let him open it. "When so

---

[34] Swami Amritaswarupananda

many of Amma's children are struggling in the sun, is Amma to seek comfort under an umbrella?"

As the work continued, Mother reminded Her children, "Imagine that the person next to you is your Beloved Deity, and imagine that you are passing the bucket to Him or Her. Then it won't be a waste of time."

Immersed in Mother's words and Her laughter, no one was aware of how difficult the work was, or the passage of time. Whenever She noticed that the mantra was slipping away from Her children's minds, Mother would sing the divine names.

"Om Namah Shivaya, Om Namah Shivaya…"

The work continued until evening. Being unaccustomed to such hard physical labor, most of the brahmacharis developed blisters on their hands. But when the work was over, there was no time to rest. They bathed and prepared to depart for Thiruvananthapuram, where a bhajan program was going to be held.

One of the brahmacharis had not taken part in the work. He had spent the whole day studying Sanskrit. Seeing him at the ferry, Mother went up to him and said, "My son, a person who has no compassion for the suffering of others isn't spiritual at all. Such a person will never see God. Amma can't just stand aside and watch Her children work. Her body weakens if She even thinks about the children working all by themselves. But as soon as

She joins them, She forgets everything. Even if Amma is too weak to work, She will go and keep them company, thinking that She can at least take their fatigue upon Herself. How could you be so lacking in compassion, son? When so many people were working, where did you get the strength of mind to stay away?"

The brahmachari couldn't answer. Seeing him standing there with his head bowed in remorse, Mother said, "Amma didn't say this to make you feel sorry, son. It was to make sure you'll be more mindful next time. It doesn't help to just stuff the intellect with knowledge—you have to become loving and compassionate. Your heart has to expand along with the intellect. That is what sadhana is for. No one can experience the Self until his heart is filled with compassion."

The ferry arrived. By the time Mother and the brahmacharis reached the other shore, Br. Ramakrishnan[35] was ready with the van. He had gone to Kollam in the morning to get the van repaired, and had returned just in time to drive Mother and the others to the program. As a result, he hadn't had time to eat anything all day. Mother got into the van and called him to come and sit next to Her.

Ramakrishnan: "My clothes are dirty and I'm stinking with sweat. If I sit next to you, your clothes will get dirty and you will also smell, Amma."

---

[35] Swami Ramakrishnananda

Mother: "That isn't a problem for Amma. Come here, son! Amma is calling you. It's the sweat of one of my children, the sweat of hard work. It's like rose water!"

On Mother's insistence, Ramakrishnan finally came and sat down next to Her, while Br. Pai[36] drove the van. On the way, Mother made them stop to pick up some food for Ramakrishnan from a devotee's house.

SATSANG EN ROUTE

The group traveling with Mother included a young man, about the same age as the brahmacharis, who had arrived at the ashram that day for the first time. His eyes were full of wonder as he sat watching the scene of Mother and Her children traveling together, laughing and making a lot of joyous noise.

"Come here, son," Mother called, making room for him beside Her.

Mother: "Is it hard for you to travel in this way, having to squeeze like this?"

Young man: "No, Amma. When I was in college, I often used to travel standing on the step outside the bus, because the busses were so full. So it's no problem for me."

Mother: "In the beginning, Amma used to travel by bus on Her way to bhajan programs and to visit the homes

---

[36] Swami Amritamayananda

of devotees. Then the number of children increased, and
it wasn't always possible for us all to get into the same
bus.[37] It was also difficult to carry the tabla and harmonium
on the bus, and not always possible for us to reach the
destination on time. So everyone persuaded Amma to buy
a van, and finally She consented. But by now the repairs
have cost more than the price of the van! Isn't that right,
Ramakrishnan?"

Everyone laughed. Loud conversation was coming from
the back of the van. Mother turned around and called,
"Balu, my son!"

"Yes, Amma!"

"Sing a bhajan!"

Br. Srikumar lifted the harmonium onto his lap.

"Manasa bhajare guru charanam..."
(O Mind, worship the Guru's feet)

Mother and the others sang several more songs. Then
everyone was silent for a few minutes, savoring the sweetness
of the holy names they had just celebrated in song. Mother
leaned on Gayatri's shoulder, with half-closed eyes.

When the newcomer saw that Mother was smiling at
him, he decided to ask a question. "Amma, isn't it said
that sadhaks shouldn't associate with women? Then how
can a woman guide them as their guru?"

---

[37] Indian buses are usually extremely crowded.

Mother: "Son, is there man or woman on the plane of Truth? For a man, it is much better to have a woman as his guru than having a male guru. My children are very fortunate in this way. Those who have a man as their guru have to transcend all women, but those who have a woman as their guru, transcend all the women in the world by transcending just the one woman in their guru."

Young man: "Didn't Ramakrishna Deva prescribe strict control concerning women and gold?"

Mother: "Yes, what he said is certainly true; a sadhak shouldn't even look at the picture of a woman. But those who have a guru have someone to show them the proper path and to guide them along that path. All they have to do is follow the guru.

"The poison of a snake can kill you; and yet the antidote is made from that same poison, isn't it? A real guru will put all kinds of obstacles in the path of the disciple, because only in that way can the disciple develop the strength to transcend all obstacles. But those who are not under a guru's direct supervision certainly have to be very careful.

"Pai, my son, look straight ahead when you drive!" Mother said, laughing. "He is looking at Amma in the mirror while he's driving!"

Young man: "Amma, you don't seem tired even after having worked all day without a moment's rest? To us it seems that the body is a bag of suffering!"

Mother: "Yes, the body is said to be a bag of suffering. And yet, the sages, who have experienced the Truth, say

that this is a world of bliss. To those who live in ignorance, the body is indeed a bag of suffering. But through
constant effort, a solution can be found. Suffering can be
eliminated by knowing what is everlasting and what is
transitory.

"Look at a black crow sitting in the middle of a flock of
white cranes. That blackness accentuates the beauty of
the whiteness. Only because black is present can we appreciate the beauty of the white. In the same way, suffering teaches us the value of joy. Once we have experienced
suffering, we will be more careful.

"A man was out walking when his foot was pricked by
a thorn. After that he stepped forward very carefully and
thus avoided falling into a deep pit nearby. If the thorn
hadn't pricked him, he wouldn't have paid as much attention and would have fallen into the pit. So a small amount
of suffering can save us from great danger. Those who go
forward with perfect attention will transcend all suffering
and attain everlasting bliss. Those who know the Infinite,
those who have realized the Truth, do not suffer—they
experience only bliss. Suffering comes when you think you
are the body, but if you look upon that same body as the
vehicle you use to reach eternal bliss, then there is no
problem."

Young man: "However joyful this life is said to be, it
seems filled with sorrow in actual experience."

Mother: "Son, why fall into the pit knowingly? Why
continue to suffer, when there is a way to avoid it? Like

the warmth of the sun and the coolness of water, joy and sorrow is the nature of life. So why lose all your strength by grieving? Why work for no wages? But if you think you will benefit from being sad, then be sad by all means!

"If there is a wound on your body, you don't just sit and cry—you apply some medicine and dress the wound, otherwise it may become infected and make you weak. When you understand the essence of spiritual life, you won't be weakened by trivial things. If you know that a firecracker is about to go off at any moment, you won't be startled when it explodes. But if you are unprepared, the sound may give you such a fright that it could even affect your health. The way to avoid sorrow is to keep the mind on the Self. It is true that the mind cannot easily be brought under control, nor can it be done in an instant. It is difficult to cross the ocean, but those who make the effort and learn the method are able to get across.

"The mahatmas have told us the way to cross this ocean of *samsara*. The scriptures are the instructions they have given us. We only have to follow them. We need to absorb the essential principles by studying the scriptures and listening to satsangs. We should never waste the opportunity to be near a mahatma. We should apply their advice in our lives and do sadhana regularly. We need the company of great souls. We should have an attitude of surrender to the guru. If we move forward with shraddha, we will be free of all sorrow."

The van swerved violently. Pai had barely avoided colliding with a lorry that was coming head on.

"Son, drive carefully!"

"Amma, that lorry was on the wrong side of the road!"

Mother noticed that the hands of one of the brahmacharis were bandaged. With great tenderness, She took his hands and placed them in Her own. "Oh, your hands are all cracked! Does it hurt, son?"

Br: "No, Amma. Just the skin came off. I put the bandage on to keep the dirt out, that's all."

Mother lovingly kissed his work-torn hands.

The program ended late, and they drove back in the middle of the night. Inside the van, sleepy heads knocked against each other. Mother lay with Her head in Gayatri's lap. Through the open window, a cool wind caressed the locks that fell from Mother's forehead, which was shaped like a half moon. In the light of the passing street lamps, Her nose ornament glittered like a star.

Saturday, April 19, 1986

LAWYERS IN SEARCH OF JUSTICE

It was four in the afternoon and Mother had not yet finished giving darshan to the devotees. A lawyer, who was a regular visitor at the ashram, entered the darshan hut with a friend who had never seen Mother before. After prostrating to Mother, the two young men sat down on a straw mat.

Lawyer: "Amma, this is my friend who works with me. He has some family problems and has decided to divorce his wife. But she doesn't want them to separate. She is planning to sue him for support for herself and their child."

Mother: "Son, why are you thinking of abandoning her?"

Friend: "Her behavior isn't good. Several times I have seen her do some really bad things."

Mother: "Did you see it yourself, son?"

Friend: "Yes."

Mother: "You shouldn't do anything without you, yourself, having seen it, son. Because that would be a great sin. The sin of causing tears in an innocent person is more harmful than any evil deed. If you forsake her, your child will have to grow up without a father; and if your wife remarries, the child won't have a real mother either.[38] Having brought a child into this world, wouldn't it be a shame to make that innocent child's life a never-ending misery? If your wife's bad behavior is something you could tolerate, wouldn't it be better to try to live with her in harmony?"

Friend: "No Amma, it isn't possible—not in this life anyway. Just thinking about her makes me feel hatred. My trust is totally gone."

Mother: "Firmness comes from trust. If that is gone,

[38] It should be noted that Mother is referring to this woman in particular, and not to all women in that situation.

everything is gone. Amma says this only because you say that you, yourself, have witnessed her bad behavior, and that you can no longer be with her. It would have been better if you could have been reconciled somehow. But Amma will not try to force you to stay with your wife. Give it some thought and then make a decision, son. Even if you end your relationship, you will have to provide your wife with some living expenses. Many people have come here with similar problems, and in most cases, the wife was innocent. It was the husband's suspicion that caused all the problems."

Friend: "I have forgiven her many times, Amma. It isn't possible anymore. I've even thought of suicide."

Mother: "You shouldn't think like that. Does your life rest on the words and actions of someone else? All your problems arise because you don't stand firm within yourself. Son, don't waste your time brooding over this. Whenever you can, read spiritual books instead. You can avoid feeling troubled if you have some spiritual understanding."

Friend: "We consulted an astrologer who said it was all right for me to do japa, but that I shouldn't meditate as it would do much harm."

Mother (laughing): "That's interesting! No meditation? Of course, there is one thing: When you buy a new car, you shouldn't drive it too fast in the beginning. Also, after driving it for some time, you should give it a little rest; otherwise, the engine will get overheated. Similarly, you shouldn't meditate for too long in the beginning, or the body will get hot. Some people, in their initial surge of vairagya, meditate too much, and that is not good.

"When you do japa, try to do it with concentration. When you chant the mantra, visualize your Beloved Deity, or concentrate on the letters of the mantra. Meditation will not cause you any harm, son. Once you clearly see the form of your Beloved Deity, just concentrate on it. Without concentration, there is no benefit."

Friend: "The astrologer suggested that wearing rings with certain stones would remove the bad effects of planetary positions."

Mother: "It is true that certain stones are prescribed for each planet, but nothing can give you as much benefit as meditation. Son, chanting your mantra will protect you from all dangers, like an armor."

The two men prostrated and got up. The lawyer asked his friend to wait outside for a moment. He then said to Mother in private, "He came only because I insisted. When I think of their little girl, I pray that the family doesn't fall apart. Amma, please find a way to make them come to their senses."

Mother: "There's only anger in that son's heart towards his wife. At this stage, whatever we say won't enter into his heart. But Amma will nevertheless make a sankalpa."

The lawyer knew from experience the significance of the words, 'Amma will make a sankalpa.' His face brightened with relief. He felt as if a big load had been removed. Mother's compassionate glance followed the two friends as they walked away together.

Saturday, May 10, 1986

UNEXPECTED TRIALS

It was two in the morning. Sand was being carried into the grounds for the foundation of the main ashram building. Along with the brahmacharis, some devotees had also joined Mother in this late-night task. Everyone wanted to take advantage of the rare opportunity to work alongside Mother and to later receive Her prasad.[39]

Many people had tried in vain to stop Mother when She had joined the work after bhajans and had begun hauling sand. She had said, "Can Amma just sit and watch Her children work? That would be twice as heavy a load for Amma! Amma's prayer in the old days was for the opportunity to serve God's devotees. God is the servant of those who render selfless service.

"But let's stop now, children. You've been working since morning." Mother called Gayatri and asked, "Daughter, are there any *vadas* (a savory snack made of lentils) to give the children?"

Gayatri looked up at the stars. They seemed to smile

---

[39] Usually when Mother had finished working with Her disciples and devotees late at night, She would distribute some snacks and a hot drink to everyone as prasad.

back with a twinkle saying, "Good luck finding vadas at this time of night!"

Mother said, "Go and grind some split peas. We'll make vadas in an instant."

Gayatri went to make the dough and a fire was started. When Gayatri returned a little later, Mother began frying the vadas Herself. She put the fried snacks in a container, and gave some of them to a brahmachari saying, "Go and divide the vadas equally among everyone, son."

He distributed them to everyone nearby and then walked away to give to some people who were in another part of the ashram. Mother gave one more vada each to those around Her. Soon, the brahmachari returned. After taking a vada for himself, there was one left.

Mother: "Didn't Amma ask you to give them equally to everyone?"

Br: "I gave one to everybody. There is one left. We can break it into pieces and give it to everyone."

Mother: "No, you take it. Amma gave everyone a second one and you got only one. Amma was watching to see whether you would eat the last one without bringing it back.

"A sadhak's goodness can be seen in his willingness to selflessly give to others whatever he has. Also, he proves his maturity by passing tests that come unexpectedly. In school, some tests are given without any advanced warning; you find out about them only when you arrive in the morning. Passing those tests shows the student's real ability.

Everyone knows the dates of the other tests and has time
to study for them. What use is there in telling you in advance
that Amma is going to test your nature? If She warns you
beforehand and then tests you, it's as if you rehearse for
a role and then play it. No, you have to pass the surprise
tests. That will show how alert you are.

"Every word and act of a true seeker is accompanied by
great alertness and discrimination. The seeker won't utter
a single word unnecessarily. He'll gladly carry out the guru's
every command, because he knows that his guru's every
word is for his own good. A disciple should feel bliss in
following each word of the guru. You have to be ready to
do any kind of work, with the view that it is leading you
to the Goal."

A firm resolve arose in everyone's mind to implement
Mother's words in their lives.

Brahmacharini Leela[40] asked a question: "Amma, was
Ravana a real person, or does he just represent a principle?"

A brahmachari: "If Ravana wasn't a real person but
only a symbol, then we would have to say that Rama is
also a mere symbol."

Mother: "Rama and Ravana were both real personali-
ties who really lived. But the description of Ravana as

[40] Swamini Atmaprana

having ten heads was meant to depict a human being who was a slave of all the ten senses."[41]

Br. Shakti Prasad: "If goats and human babies can be born with two heads, why not a Ravana with ten heads?"

Mother: "If God wills it, nothing is impossible. Children, go to bed now. You have to get up in the morning."

Sunday, May 18, 1986

Sundays are usually crowded at the ashram, especially if it's a weekend holiday. This was such a Sunday and the darshan hut was packed. The electricity wasn't working, and without the fans, the hut was very hot. Nevertheless, the large crowd seemed to make Mother even more cheerful. She insisted that the hand-held fans be used to fan the devotees instead of Her, and She instructed the brahmacharis to provide chairs for the sick and the elderly, and to bring them water if needed. She was particularly concerned about the people waiting outside in the sun. Because it was so crowded, it was difficult for Mother to hear everything in detail or to respond to the sorrows and complaints of the devotees. So before many of them had even begun to speak about their problems, Mother, who could read their thoughts, suggested solutions and consoled them with assurances of Her blessings.

---

[41] This refers to the five instruments of perception: eyes, nose, ears, skin, and tongue; and the five instruments of action: hands, legs, mouth, genitals, and excretory organ.

"Children, come quickly! Don't worry about prostrating or anything!" She said to them. For only if the people inside the hut moved out, could those who were waiting outside in the sun come in and sit down.

EMPATHY FOR THE POOR

A woman devotee, with tears streaming down her face, told Mother about her problem: "Amma, all the chickens in our area are sick. Our hen is also starting to get sick. Amma, won't you please save her?"

A brahmachari standing nearby felt disdain for this woman who, instead of quickly leaving after having received Mother's darshan, bothered Mother with such a trivial matter on a crowded day like this. But the very next instant, Mother cast him a glance that was so severe it made him squirm. Mother lovingly consoled the woman and gave her some bhasma to put on the hen. The woman left happily.

As the woman moved on, Mother called the brahmachari over to Her. "Son, you don't understand her suffering. Do you know how much grief there is in this world? If you did, you wouldn't have viewed her with contempt. By God's grace, you have everything you need. You can live without any worries. The only income that woman has is from the eggs that her hen provides. Her family will starve if the hen dies. When Amma thinks about that woman's life, She doesn't see her suffering as trivial. That woman spends part of her meager savings from the sale of the eggs to come here. Knowing how she struggles, Amma gives her money for the bus fare now and then. Look at her attitude of surrender, even in the midst of so much misery! Amma gets tears in Her eyes when She thinks of this! One who eats to his heart's content doesn't know the pain of hunger. You have to starve to know that pain.

"Always listen very carefully to what everyone has to say. Don't compare one person to another. We should think from their level; only then can we understand their concerns and respond appropriately and console them."

A young man had been watching Mother intently from the moment he had stepped into the hut. He was a college teacher from Nagpur who had arrived several days earlier. The day he arrived, he had said that he had to return immediately after seeing Mother, because he had to get back to his hometown urgently. But that was several days ago—he had yet to leave. Mother now said to those around Her, "This son has been here for a few days. Amma has told him several times to go home and come back later, but he doesn't want to listen. He hasn't left so far."

The young man didn't know what Mother was saying because he didn't understand Malayalam. But when everyone turned around and looked at him, he knew Mother was talking about him. A man sitting next to him translated Mother's words. The young man responded, "I am not going in the first place, so why talk about coming back?"

Mother (laughing): "Amma knows the trick to send you running!"

Everyone laughed at this.

BEGGING FOR THE SAKE OF HER CHILDREN

O Annapurna, who is always filled
With the elements that sustain life,
O Beloved of Shankara,
Grant me the alms of wisdom and renunciation!
                                    —Sri Shankaracharya

The lunch bell had rung some time ago, but many people had not yet eaten because they couldn't tear themselves away from Mother. It was getting late and an ashram resident came and told Mother that those who were serving lunch were waiting. On Mother's insistence, some more people went to eat. But several devotees wouldn't get up until Mother was ready to leave the darshan hut. They were unconcerned about food. Their fulfillment lay in not wasting a single moment that they could spend in Mother's presence. The ashram residents bore the inconvenience of this, because they had to wait until three or four in the afternoon to serve them their lunch.

It was past three in the afternoon when Mother finally got up. The devotees crowded around Her, prostrating to

Her, and in so doing inadvertently blocked Her way. Taking hold of them and making them stand up, She patted and caressed some of them as She made Her way towards the kitchen.

In the kitchen Mother found that those who were serving lunch were having a problem. As on other bhava darshan days, more food had been cooked than appeared necessary, and it had all finished very quickly. More rice had been cooked, but that, too, had been consumed in no time. All afternoon, people had continued to arrive at the ashram unexpectedly. A third batch of rice had been cooked, and that was now almost gone, with many hungry mouths still to feed. More rice was burning on the fire, but there were no vegetables to go with it. The kitchen workers were wondering what to do, when Mother walked in.

Unflustered by all this, Mother opened some jars containing tamarind, mustard seeds, and curry leaves. Within minutes some *rasam* (tamarind boiled with water, salt, chili, onion, etc.) was ready. A woman devotee had brought a container full of curd in the morning. Some onions, tomatoes, and green chilies were chopped and added to the curd. Soon everything, including the rice, was ready. Mother, Herself, served Her children the lunch. The devotees ate the prasad from Mother's sacred hands with more relish and satisfaction than had it been a sumptuous feast.

A last round of devotees now came for lunch, and Mother served them as well. After making sure that all of the householder devotees had eaten, the ashram residents sat down to eat. Only rice and rasam was left. Three brahmacharis served the others, and by the time they had finished serving, all the rice was gone. Mother couldn't bear the thought that three of Her children had to go hungry after working continuously for several hours. Nothing was left in the kitchen but uncooked rice, and it would take time to cook that for them.

Seeing that Mother was worried about them, the three brahmacharis said firmly that they weren't hungry and didn't want anything. But Mother didn't agree. "Children, wait for ten minutes," She said. "Amma will be right back!" And then She went out carrying a container. Was She going to Sugunachan's house? Or perhaps She had gone to Her room to see if there was any food there that the devotees might have offered. As they waited, the brahmacharis washed all the dishes and cleaned the kitchen.

Soon Mother came back, Her face beaming with a smile as bright as the full moon. She must have found some food for Her children. The brahmacharis couldn't suppress their curiosity. Looking into Her container, they saw that it was full of different kinds of cooked rice mixed together.

The brahmacharis' eyes filled with tears. "Amma!" one of them cried out. Mother had gone around to the neighboring huts, begging for food for Her children. She was now back with the *bhiksha*. This was the cause of the joy on Her face.

All the neighbors were poor fisherfolk who had barely enough to eat. Knowing this, Mother had taken only a handful of rice from each hut.

The brahmacharis glanced at a picture on the wall depicting Lord Shiva as a mendicant begging for food from Devi Annapurneshwari who was sitting on a throne.[42] Now Devi, Herself, had knocked on the doors of the fishermen for bhiksha for Her children. Mother sat down on the floor, leaning against the door, while the brahmacharis sat around Her. Making balls from the rice and a little *sambar* that was in the container, She fed Her children with Her own hands.

"One more ball!" Mother said.

"No, Amma, there won't be anything left for you."

"Children, when you've had enough food, Amma's hunger will be gone!" She fed one of them with one more rice ball. There were barely two handfuls of rice left, and a piece of potato from the sambar. Mother ate that and got up, fully contented.

Thursday, May 25, 1986

Ramakrishnan lay in bed with fever. Mother was sitting beside him. A brahmachari came into Ramakrishnan's hut bringing coffee made with basil leaves, black pepper, and ginger.

---

[42] The Goddess of Plenty, a form of Durga.

On the wall hung an old photo of Mother wearing a colored sari and blouse. Noticing it, Mother said, "In those days Damayanti had to force Amma to wear a sari. Once, as Amma was getting ready to go somewhere, She got a sound thrashing for not wearing a sari. So She put one on, but as soon as She was on the boat, She took it off and held it in Her hands, all rolled up." Mother laughed.

THE FIRST FEEDING

A woman had brought her baby for Mother's darshan. For years she had longed for a child, but hadn't been able to conceive. Finally, after meeting Mother, she had given birth to a boy, through Mother's sankalpa. Now she had come with her relatives for the baby's *anna prasana*, the first feeding of solid food. They were in a hurry to get the ceremony over with, so that they could return home.

The woman said, "Ammachi, please give my baby the food right away. We can't stay here tonight with the baby, because he won't sleep without a crib. I haven't brought any milk for him, either. If we leave now, we can reach home before evening."

Mother: "My daughter, don't talk like that! You received this baby through God's blessing. You have come to a place of God. It is only when people come to a place like this that they are suddenly in a hurry! They want to rush back as soon as they reach the temple or the *gurukula*.

When you take a sick child to the hospital, do you say to the doctor, 'I'm in a hurry! Please let me go soon'? Do you say, 'Doctor, I haven't brought the baby's crib or his milk, and he's sleepy, so you have to look at him right away'? When we come to a temple or an ashram, we should have an attitude of surrender. Daughter, by doing good deeds, going to temples and ashrams, and engaging in thoughts of God, our prarabdha becomes much lighter. Don't you realize that?

"You rush away from here, and if the bus breaks down on the way, to whom will you complain? It saddens Amma that you, who have been coming here for years, are speaking like this. You should never talk like this, daughter. Leave it to God's will. Why didn't you rather think, 'Amma will feed the baby when She likes'? That is surrender. If you go now, you will have a lot of trouble on the way, so Amma won't let you go back yet."

It was the first time the woman had heard Mother speak in such a serious way, and her face turned pale. Seeing this, Mother motioned for her to come close to Her and said, "Amma was speaking out of the sense of freedom She feels with you, daughter. Don't feel bad!"

The woman's face brightened when she heard this.

Even though Mother had objected at first, She gave the baby his first feeding of rice without delay, and sent them off so that they could reach home before nightfall.

Friday, May 30, 1986

It was almost noon. Mother was talking to the devotees in the darshan hut. Among them was a brahmachari
visiting from another ashram in Kidangoor. She said to
him, "Son, there's a difference between buying medicine
for a wound on one's own hand, and going out to get
medicine for someone else's pain. The latter shows that
one has a loving heart. This is what a spiritual seeker
needs; it is what his spiritual practices are for. Sadhana
shouldn't be done for one's own liberation, but for the
sake of becoming loving, compassionate, and understanding enough to remove the suffering of the world. There's
no benefit to be derived from just sitting somewhere with
our eyes closed and doing nothing else. We have to become so large-hearted that we experience the suffering of
others as our own, and work to alleviate their suffering."

TREATMENT FOR MOTHER

Mother had been coughing severely since morning. A
brahmachari went to call Dr. Leela.

The previous week a devotee had come to the ashram
suffering from a bad cough. The sound of his coughing
had echoed throughout the ashram. He had been hacking
and coughing as he came to the kalari and prostrated to
Mother. But when he came out of the little temple after
receiving Mother's darshan, his cough was gone. It had

vanished the moment he drank the holy water Mother had given him. He had stayed at the ashram for a week and had gone home happily this morning.

Once, when Mother was in Tiruvannamalai, She had been ill. Nealu had decided that She needed to see a doctor without delay. Even though there were a few doctors in Tiruvannamalai who were Mother's devotees, She was taken to a new doctor. Without waiting for anyone's permission, Mother had innocently walked straight into the doctor's consulting room. The doctor had been furious and had told Her to get out. Mother used to recall this with a laugh, saying, "There's no reason to blame him. He was examining someone else when Amma suddenly barged in! He must have lost his concentration!" As She had walked out of the doctor's office, both the doctor and the nurse had called Her back. They had no idea who She was or why She had come. Afterwards, Mother had said, "Amma will never again go to see a doctor. If She must see a doctor, one of Her doctor children has to come to the ashram."

Mother's words came true. The first doctor taking up permanent residence at the ashram was Bri. Leela. When she met Mother she was working at a hospital run by the Sri Ramakrishna Math in Thiruvananthapuram. In Mother, Leela saw the ultimate goal of her life. Soon afterwards, she gave up her job and came to live at the ashram. Now she was in charge of whatever treatment Mother needed.

Since Leela knew that Mother's ailments could not be cured by medicines alone, she wasn't the least bit perturbed when Mother got sick—even when She appeared to be very weak. She saw Mother's illnesses as the *leela* (play) of the beloved consort of Lord Shiva who once brought death to the Lord of death himself. In other words, she saw Mother's illnesses as the mere play of the Divine Mother.

"Should I get you some pills, Amma?" Leela asked. Putting her hand on Mother's forehead, she said, "You don't have a fever. It's nothing serious. You'll be fine in a little while."

Mother laughed and said, "Even if Amma is dead, my daughter Leela will examine the body and say, 'It's nothing serious. You'll be all right in a little while!'" Everyone joined in the laughter.

Saturday, May 31, 1986

SADHANA SHOULD COME FROM THE HEART

A brahmachari came to Mother and asked for practical suggestions for his sadhana. Mother gave him instructions on meditation: "Son, concentrate on the point between the eyebrows. See your Beloved Deity there, just as you watch your own image in the mirror." Placing Her finger between his eyebrows, She added, "Imagine that you have a shrine here and visualize your Beloved Deity sitting in it.

"Those who meditate only according to a timetable, as if it were a duty, will never see God. You have to cry for God, day and night, with no thought of food or sleep. Only those who have done this have realized God. You have to develop that kind of detachment. If someone smeared chili paste all over your body, think of how you would struggle to escape the burning! You should pine to see God with the same intensity. You should cry for that vision, without wasting even an instant. Only then will all other thoughts disappear, as in deep sleep, and you will reach the plane of divine experience.

"When fishermen put a boat out to sea, they close their eyes, and with loud cries they push hard to get past the waves. Everyone rows hard without stopping, making a lot of noise as they row, until they get beyond the waves. After that, they can set the oars aside and rest. It's the same ocean in both places, but one part is restless from the waves, while the other is still. To begin with, we shouldn't rest even for an instant. We have to be alert. Only then can we reach that stillness beyond.

"Totapuri[43] was established in Advaita. Still, he stood at the center of a ring of fire and did tapas. Ramakrishna Deva attained realization through incessant remembrance of God. To attain realization, you have to constantly keep God in your thoughts. A real sadhak doesn't do japa and meditation just according to some schedule. His love for

---

[43] A great ascetic following the path of jnana (supreme wisdom), who initiated Sri Ramakrishna into sannyasa.

God is beyond all rules. In the beginning, a sadhak has to adopt certain rules, but the spiritual practices shouldn't be considered a mere duty. We should cry and pray for God. It isn't a weakness to cry for God. We should cry for God alone, and for nothing else. Isn't that what Ramakrishna did? And what Mira did?"

THE SAME TRUTH BY DIFFERENT NAMES

Br: "Is it wrong if someone who meditates on Krishna, chants a Devi mantra or Devi's thousand names?"

Mother: "That's not a problem. Whatever mantra or holy name you chant, your thoughts should be directed towards your favorite deity."

Br: "How is that possible? Aren't there special *bijaksharas* (seed letters) for each deity? How can it then be proper to chant a different one?"

Mother: "By whatever name you call it, the Divine Power is one and the same. Whether you call a coconut 'tenga'[44] or 'coconut,' its identity doesn't change, does it? Likewise, people cherish different pictures of God in their hearts, each according to their samskara. They know God by different names, but the all-pervading Consciousness is beyond all names. God is not someone who responds only if He hears the sound of a certain call—He dwells in our hearts, and He knows our hearts. God has an infinite amount of names. Every name is His.

---

[44] Malayalam for coconut.

"When you perform a puja, you should direct it towards the particular deity to whom the puja pertains, and with the appropriate mantras. But when your aim is to attain the Self, it doesn't really matter if the form you meditate on is different from the deity of the mantra you are repeating; because we are seeing everything as different forms of the Supreme Self. We should see that everything is contained in That, and that this one Principle exists within all of us. It is the same Consciousness that permeates everything, that permeates all forms, including ourselves. Though initially it is better to fix the mind on one particular name and form, as you advance on the path you should be able to perceive the one Supreme Principle in all names and forms.

"The purpose of mantra japa is to lead us to the ultimate silence of the Self, from where all sounds and forms arise. Mantra japa, done with the proper understanding of this principle, will ultimately take us to the Source, at which point the seeker realizes that the form he has been meditating on, as well as all other forms, exist within himself, and are the manifestations of the one Self.

"When Krishna was living with the gopis in Vrindavan, the gopis wanted to see Him and to be in His company every moment. They adored Him so much that they referred to Him as their *Hridayesha*, the Lord of their hearts. Then one day Krishna left for Mathura and never came back. Some people went to the gopis and teased them, saying, 'Where is your Hridayesha now? It seems that

Krishna is not Hridayesha but *hridayasunya* (heartless).' The gopis replied, 'No, He is still our Hridayesha. We used to see Krishna only in His physical form, and we could hear His voice only with our ears. But now we see Him in all forms: our very eyes have become Krishna Himself. Now we hear Him in all sounds: our ears have become Krishna. Verily, we, ourselves, have become Krishna!'

"Similarly, though we initially see God in a particular deity, and call Him by a particular name, when our devotion matures and blossoms fully, we come to see God in all forms and names, and within ourselves."

The evening bhajans were over. *Doshas* were being served for dinner. As an unexpectedly large crowd had arrived, the dosha-making continued until ten-thirty. Each fresh pancake was served as soon as it was ready. Mother went into the kitchen and sent a brahmachari to get another dosha pan from Her parents' house. As soon as it was brought, She put it on another burner and started making doshas. Isn't it said that God appears as bread before those who are hungry, be that hunger physical or spiritual?

PERFORMING EACH ACTION AS A FORM OF WORSHIP

After dinner, Mother joined the brahmacharis in carrying gravel, which was to be used for making concrete.

They made a chain and were passing the gravel in round steel pans from one person to another. Those who had been reluctant to even wash their own clothes before coming to the ashram, took part in this festival of hard work along with Mother. They were about to learn some practical lessons of spirituality.

In the middle of the work, Mother said, "Children, this is also sadhana. Even when you work, your thoughts should be on God. Any work you do while focusing your mind on God is karma yoga. When you pass the gravel to each other, imagine that you are handing it to your Beloved Deity, and when you take it from the person next to you, imagine you are receiving it from the Deity."

Mother sang a kirtan, and everyone joined in the singing while they continued to work.

Tirukathakal patam…

> *O Goddess Durga,*
> *O Kali,*
> *Remove my sad fate.*
> *Each day I beg for a vision of your form.*
>
> *Please give me a boon.*
> *Let me sing, glorifying your sacred deeds;*
> *And when I sing your praises,*
> *Please come into my heart.*

O Essence of the Vedas,
I don't know the method of meditation,
And my music lacks a melody.
Have mercy on me—
Let me be immersed in bliss.

You are Gayatri,
You are fame and Liberation,
Kartyayani, Haimavati, and Dakshayani—
You are the very Soul of realization,
My sole refuge.

O Devi,
Give me the power to speak on the essential prin-
ciples.
I understand that without you—
who are the embodiment of the Universe—
Shiva, the Causative Principle,
Would not exist.

It was well after midnight. With threads of silver light, the moon wove a delicate, glittering veil over the expanse of coconut treetops. In those silent hours of the night, a mother and her children were immersed in the work of erecting a mansion of peace, one that tomorrow would serve as the refuge of countless thousands. The scene called to mind the nectarous wisdom of the *Bhagavad Gita*: "When it is night for all beings, the self-controlled one stays awake." This was being played out here. As the whole world slept, the Mother of the Universe toiled without rest to build a world of eternal light. The moments shared with this great architect of a new age were precious gems that Her children stored in the treasure chests of their hearts, to be remembered later, enriching their lives immeasurably.

Monday, June 9, 1986

The traditional rites for initiating Anish into brahmacharya began this morning. A priest had come from Alleppy for the homa and other rites for the initiation. The sacred fire blazed in the kalari and Vedic chanting resounded in the air, while Mother's divine presence filled everyone with bliss.

Mother was in a childlike mood. Each of Her words and actions spread joy to everyone. She was amused at the sight of Anish who had shaved off all his hair except for the traditional tuft at the back, in preparation for receiving the yellow robe. She took a hibiscus flower and tied it to his tuft! The onlookers couldn't contain their laughter.

Then, in a moment, Her mood changed and Her face took on a serious expression. The atmosphere was suddenly very quiet. The silence was broken only by the sound of the Vedic mantras and the crackling of the homa fire, being kept alive with pieces of jackfruit wood. From the expression on everyone's face, it was clear that they were all transported to a mood beyond this world.

Mother gave Her son his new name, Brahmachari Satyatma Chaitanya.[45] After receiving initiation, Satyatma prostrated to Her and went outside to receive bhiksha according to tradition.[46]

A family of Muslim devotees had come to the ashram for Mother's darshan. This was a Muslim holy day, and they had come to spend it with Mother. After the initiation ceremonies, Mother went into the hut with the family. She talked to them for a long time before going to Her room.

Later that afternoon, Mother was sitting on the roof terrace above Her room with some of the brahmacharis. For days, the brahmacharis had been trying to get Mother's permission to take a group photograph with Her, which would be included in Her biography. She had repeatedly refused. Now a brahmachari brought up the request again: "Amma, we have heard of many mahatmas, but there are no pictures of most of them. How sorry we have felt that we do not know what they looked like! If we don't get your picture taken, we'll be cheating the coming generations. Amma, at least for that reason you should allow a photo to be taken."

Mother: "If Amma agrees to this, your attention will only be on such things from now on, and that will hurt

---

[45] Since then Br. Satyatma Chaitanya has received sannyasa initiation, and is today known as Swami Amritagitananda.

[46] Brahmacharis and sannyasis are traditionally supposed to eat only the food they have received as alms. Nowadays they go out and beg for bhiksha on the day of their initiation.

your sadhana. Besides, I can't dress up as you like; that isn't my way. I can't sit for a picture." The serious tone of Her refusal silenced the brahmacharis and made them sad. But for how long could Mother watch Her children being sad? "Go and call everyone," She said finally.

Everyone's face lit up, and they all ran downstairs. All the residents of the ashram gathered together on the roof terrace for the picture. The venerable old Ottoor Unni Namboodiripad, the oldest of Mother's brahmachari children, was also there. When the picture had been taken, Mother asked Ottoor to give a satsang. The *leelas* of Krishna flowed in an unbroken stream from the mouth of this gentle devotee, whose inner self had long been surrendered to the Child of Ambadi.[47] Enraptured, Mother listened with the others to the ever-fresh stories about the antics of Krishna, the little butter-thief. When his talk was over, Ottoor insisted, "Now we want to hear Amma's satsang!"

Mother: "Amma doesn't know how to give satsang. When people ask Her questions, She blurts out whatever craziness comes to mind, that's all."

Ottoor: "It may be craziness, but that is what we like to hear. Amma, we don't have the intensity of devotion you describe. What should we do?"

Mother looked at Ottoor and smiled. He put his head on Her lap. She hugged him with great affection and called him, "Unni Kanna (Baby Krishna)!"

---

[47] Ambadi is the name of the village where Krishna grew up.

DOING SADHANA FOR OUR OWN SAKE
IS NOT ENOUGH

Mother glanced at a brahmachari seated behind Her. The brahmachari lowered his head, avoiding Her gaze. Knowing his thoughts, Mother said, "Children, do you know what expectations Amma has of you? You should be like the sun, not like a firefly. Fireflies make light merely for their own needs. Don't be like that. Selflessness is all you should ever wish for. You should be the ones who raise their hands to help others, even at the moment of your death."

This statement particularly struck the heart of the brahmachari who was sitting behind Her. There had been bhava darshan the day before, with a large crowd of devotees attending. The brahmachari in charge of serving lunch had desperately needed help, and had asked this brahmachari, who shared his hut, if he would help. But the latter had continued meditating without lifting a finger to help him. Mother had heard about this and the brahmachari had avoided Her all morning.

Mother continued, "Children, we should make sure that each of our actions is of help to others and will enhance their happiness. If that isn't possible, we should at least make sure that our actions never cause others any grief or inconvenience. Praying to God that none of our thoughts, words, or deeds will ever harm anyone, but that they will always benefit others—that is real prayer. We should be willing to pray for the upliftment of others, rather than for our own progress. My children, to develop such self-less love is the greatest progress we can make. True worship is seeing the suffering of others as our own suffering, and their happiness as our own happiness. True devotees see themselves in others. Theirs is a world of peace and contentment." Mother stopped talking. Her gaze was resting somewhere far away.

Soon it was time for bhajans. Mother led everyone to the kalari. As She sat down, a brahmachari placed a tambura in front of Her. She began to play the instrument, setting the pitch for the first song. She sang a kirtan that had been written and dedicated to Her by Krishnan Nair, a householder devotee. Everyone sang along with Mother, forgetting all else in Her presence.

Katinnu katayi, kanninnu kannayi...

> *O Mother, who shines as the Ear of the ear,*
> *Mind of the mind,*
> *And Eye of the eye,*
> *You are the Life of life,*
> *The Life of the living.*

> *What the ocean is to the waves,*
> *You are to the soul.*
> *You are the Soul of souls,*
> *You are the Nectar of the nectar of wisdom.*
> *O Mother, you are the Pearl of the immortal Self,*

The Essence of Bliss.
You are the great maya.
You are the Absolute.

The eyes cannot perceive you.
The mind cannot grasp you.
Words are hushed in your presence, O Mother.
Whoever says they have seen you,
Have not seen you—
Because you, O Great Goddess,
Are beyond the intellect.

The sun, the moon, and the stars
Do not shine by themselves,
But are illumined by your brilliance.
Through discrimination,
The courageous one alone can tread
The path to the abode of Eternal Peace,
The Supreme Truth.

After the bhajans, everyone meditated for a short time before dinner. The sweet drone of the tambura beneath Mother's fingers and Her singing still echoed blissfully in their minds:

Through discrimination, the courageous one alone
can tread
The path to the abode of Eternal Peace,
The Supreme Truth...

Wednesday, June 11, 1986

EVER PROTECTING THOSE
WHO TAKE TOTAL REFUGE IN HER

It was just past two in the morning. A brahmachari quietly returned from the beach where he had been meditating. Making his way to the empty kalari, he turned off the light and put his *asana* and shawl down on the verandah. He then awakened Pai, who was sleeping on the kalari verandah, and who had asked to be woken up at two o'clock for meditation. It was also Pai's job to ring the bell at four o'clock to wake everyone up for archana. As the brahmachari walked towards his hut to go to bed, he saw a man and a woman sitting in front of the Vedanta school.

"We have come to see Amma," they said humbly as they stood up.

Br: "Amma went to Her room at midnight. She was climbing the steps to Her room when I went to the beach."

Visitors: "It must have been just after midnight when we arrived."

Suddenly they heard the sound of approaching footsteps. Mother was coming towards them with a smile. The visitors fell at Her feet with a mixture of reverence and delighted surprise.

Mother: "My children, when did you come?"

Devotee: "We came just after you went to your room,

Amma. We were sitting here feeling disappointed because we wouldn't be able to see you tonight."

Mother: "Amma had just closed Her eyes, when suddenly it seemed that you were standing in front of Her. Son, is your daughter all right?"

Devotee: "Her operation is the day after tomorrow. The doctor says it's a complicated case. Our only hope is your blessing, Amma! That's why we came."

Mother: "Why were you so late, children? Did the car break down?"

Devotee: "Yes, Amma. We started at noon but had car trouble on the way. It took hours to get it fixed. That's why we came so late. Otherwise, we would have been here by eight."

Mother: "Don't worry son. Come, let's sit down." Taking their hands, She led them to the kalari verandah, where they all sat down. She talked to them for a long time. She then took some bhasma from the kalari and gave it to them as prasad. "Tell my daughter not to worry. Amma is with her." They both prostrated to Her again as the clock struck four. She instructed a brahmachari to take them across on the ferry, and then went back to Her room. As the visitors were leaving the ashram, they turned and looked back. At that moment, Mother, who was climbing the stairs to Her room, also glanced back and smiled at them— a smile which was an unmistakable sign of protection.

A cool breeze was blowing. Enjoying the external coolness of the early morning and the soothing inner coolness of Mother's grace, the visitors boarded the ferry and departed. The morning star shone brightly, adding a faint glow to the surface of the backwaters.

Friday, June 13, 1986

Mother sat on the front steps of the office, surrounded by a few people. A brahmachari was trying to explain to Her the need to remove the individuals in charge of one of the branch ashrams and to give the responsibility to new people. Mother listened to everything he had to say. Finally She said, "Amma's aim is to turn iron and rust into gold. There is no need to turn gold into gold again!"

The brahmachari tried to reiterate his point.

Mother: "Son, have the patience to listen. It was Amma who put them on the committee, wasn't it? Understand that Amma may have had something in mind. First Amma learned about Herself, then She learned about the whole world; only after that did She take on this role. Amma knows how to guide those people. Amma has seen the suffering and struggles of hundreds of thousands of people, hasn't She? Who else has had such an opportunity? Also, Amma has seen the nature of numerous people undergoing a change. If we remove the members of the committee, they will live their lives without being of any use to anyone. But if we keep them on, then at least they will look after some of the ashram matters; at least they can serve in that small way, and they will earn the merit from it. Isn't that better than letting them sit idle? Amma knows how to make them follow instructions.

"As they do their work, their minds are being purified, and that will lead them to salvation. We can't just discard them along the way. It is our duty to save them. Our purpose is to try to help others to develop devotion for God and to enjoy inner peace. If we sincerely have this wish, we will forgive them for whatever mistakes they make, and try to bring them to the right path.

"We can't expect everyone to be good. Some won't be. But if we throw them out and abandon them, they will commit more mistakes out in the world. So we, who know more than they do, have to come down to their level. Then they will make spiritual progress. Don't think that someone is bad and should be removed just because they have committed one or two mistakes.

"Amma doesn't mean that what you are saying is entirely wrong. Many people collect money in the name of the ashram, but some of them give only a quarter of it to the ashram. Amma knows this, but She acts as if She doesn't know. She gives them another chance to correct their mistakes. If they still don't learn or don't want to change their behavior, they usually leave of their own accord. Amma hasn't had to force anyone to leave. They just leave by themselves.

"Those who err are also our brothers and sisters, aren't they? They may not have gained enough wisdom yet, but we can pray to God that they do. That will benefit us as well, because it will expand our minds."

The brahmachari prostrated and withdrew.

A LESSON IN SHRADDHA

Mother noticed a brahmachari sitting immersed in thought, stroking his mustache.

Mother: "Take your hand away. Such habits aren't good for a brahmachari. When you sit down somewhere, you shouldn't move your body or limbs unnecessarily. Habits like tapping your feet, moving your hands about, and stroking your mustache aren't fit for a sadhak. You should make an effort to be still."

A brahmacharini came to Mother and told Her that many plates and glasses were missing from the ashram. Mother said, "Bring all the plates and glasses here. Don't leave a single one anywhere. Bring everything here."

Each ashram resident had been given a plate and a glass, which they kept in their huts. Mother said to those who were there, "Children, you should all pay more attention to these things. Many plates and glasses were lost because people left them lying everywhere. Then everyone was given a plate and a glass with their names written on them. And now, many of those are also missing. When someone's plate is missing, he just takes a plate from the room next door, without giving a thought to the fact that the person in that room needs it. How will that person manage without a plate? Finally, Amma ends up getting involved to settle the dispute." Mother laughed. "These children are worse than little babies!"

The brahmacharis came with their plates and glasses, and Mother assumed a serious attitude.

Mother: "From now on, no one is to use anyone else's plate. If you've lost your plate, you should admit it. Never tell a lie for your own benefit, even if you lose your life. If you lose your plates and other things due to negligence again, Amma won't eat anything. Remember that, children!"

Within a few minutes, all the plates and glasses were placed in front of Mother, and She counted them. Many were missing.

Mother: "Children, isn't it due to your negligence that we've lost so many plates and glasses? All sorts of people come here. If you leave the utensils lying here and there after you've used them, those who need them will simply take them. Why blame others when you have given them the opportunity to steal? It is you who are to blame. Had you been more careful, those plates wouldn't have been lost. None of you know the value of money, so what difference does it make to you if things are lost?

"Amma grew up knowing hardship. She knows the value of each paisa. She has had to struggle just to get enough firewood to make tea. Because She knows the hardships of poverty, She doesn't let even a speck go to waste. When She sees a piece of wood, She thinks of its value and how it can be used. But if you children saw it lying in your path, you'd just kick it away. Or if you saw it lying in the rain, you'd never think of picking it up, drying it, and saving it. But Amma wouldn't discard it as something worthless. Children, would we throw away a five paisa coin? No, because it's five paisas. But we can't even buy a small piece of firewood for five paisas. Without dry firewood, how can we cook anything? Even if we hold hundreds of rupees in our hands, we still need firewood to light a fire, don't we? We should be aware of the value and possible use of everything. Then we won't allow ourselves to waste anything.

"Look at what is happening in the hospitals. They don't have pure water for injections. It costs one or two rupees to buy it outside. Many patients suffer pain for hours, because they don't have that much money. An injection would alleviate their pain, but they can't afford it, and so they are consumed by pain. To them, two rupees are worth a great deal! Children, Amma has seen so many sick people writhing in pain because they didn't have the money to buy a single pain killer. You should remember those people in all your actions.

"God is in everyone. Those who are suffering unbearable pain are also God's children. They are our brothers and sisters. By thinking about them, you will develop true shraddha. Whenever you casually waste a rupee, remember that someone is suffering ten hours of pain because of you. You are the cause of that poor person's agony. Your carelessness can be compared to throwing dirt into the community's drinking water. Your behavior makes Amma think about those sick people, because with the money you are throwing away, you could instead be buying them medicine. Above all, through your carelessness, you are squandering the chance to give birth to the precious jewel within you."

Mother called the brahmacharini who had told Her about the missing plates.

Mother: "From today, you are in charge of the kitchenware. In the morning, you should give the required number of plates and glasses to those who will serve the food, and in the evening, you should come and collect the same amount of utensils that you distributed in the morning. What has been lost up to now is gone. If we lose anymore, you will have to answer for it.

"The attention we give to each detail can bring us closer to God. The shraddha with which we perform our actions outwardly unveils the treasure hidden within us. So my darling children, pay attention to everything as you move ahead. It is by looking at the little things that Amma knows about the big things."

From the kitchen, Mother walked to the north side of the ashram. At one point She spat to the side, and Her spit happened to fall on a wild spinach plant. She had meant to spit where there were no plants, but the wind caused Her saliva to fall on the spinach leaves. Mother got a mug full of water and carefully washed the leaves.

She then washed Her hands over the same plant, so that no water was wasted.

Mother was always careful not to waste water. Even when a water tap was available, Mother washed Her hands and face with water from a container. She said that when we open a faucet, we tend to use more water than we need. Any unnecessary action is *adharma* (unrighteous). Failing to perform a necessary action is also adharma. If asked what dharma is, Mother would say, "It is doing the required actions at the right time in the proper manner."

The brahmachari walking with Mother was thinking along these lines, appreciating Her example. Yet a doubt arose in his mind and he thought, "But was it really necessary for Mother to wash the leaves of a plant, just because a little spit fell on it?"

As Mother continued walking, She said, as if in reply to the brahmachari's unspoken question, "Those plants are alive, too!"

Mother gazed all around Her for a moment, and then She entered the dining room. Some brahmacharis were peeling and slicing cassava roots for dinner. She sat down among them and joined in the work.

BRAHMACHARIS AND FAMILY TIES

A brahmachari started the conversation: "Several letters have come from home. I haven't replied to any of them. Should I write, Amma?"

Mother: "Son, in the beginning you shouldn't write letters to your family. If you write, they'll reply, and then you'll write again. If you really want to write—for instance, if your parents are ill—then write just a few lines to console them. Surrender your father and mother to the Paramatman, and write to them with that attitude of surrender. Then it won't bind you. When you get letters from home, don't read them again and again. Discard them after grasping the contents. The letters will contain news of your family and friends, and when you read them, your mind will be swayed a little, in spite of yourself. Children, you should always keep in mind why you have come here.

"Suppose you visit a sick person lying in the intensive care unit, and you tell him in detail about the suffering of his family. What will be the result? His health will deteriorate further, and he may even die. Similarly, you are undergoing treatment at present, and a great deal of caution is needed. Once your mind has developed in such a way that you will not weaken or succumb under any circumstances, then there are no more problems. Until then, however, these restrictions are necessary. Now you are all like saplings growing in the shade of a tree. That is why it's necessary for you to abide by certain rules and restrictions.

"If someone in your family has no one to look after them, and if their condition is very bad, then it is all right for you to go and give them the care and assistance they need. You should look upon them as God and serve them.

But if you continue to keep alive your attachment to them in your mind, you won't benefit by living at the ashram—neither you nor your family will benefit from it. If you are unable to break your attachment to the family, it is best that you live at home and take care of your parents.

"Even if you don't visit your home, but through their letters come to know of all their news and problems, all your thoughts will revolve around those things. The thought of the hardships at home will automatically take root in your subconscious. However, your sympathy is of no use to them. Once you attain a certain level through your spiritual practices, you can make a sankalpa which will benefit them. But that isn't possible at this stage. By worrying about them, you only end up losing the strength you have gained.

"If your family writes to you, don't encourage it. A coconut seed cannot sprout before it falls from the mother tree. As a result of your attachment, you only move away from God. You won't advance if you try to do sadhana while maintaining your attachment to your family and friends. If you do sadhana in solitude now, without letting the mind dwell on other things, you can develop the strength to save not only your family, but the whole world."

Br: "But we can't help feeling worried when we hear about the problems at home, can we?"

Mother: "Son, once you have chosen the spiritual path, you should totally surrender everything to the Supreme and go forward. By filling a reservoir, you supply water to all the pipes connected to it. Likewise, by loving God, we love everyone, because He dwells in everyone.

"If your family visits you, you can greet them with a smile, prostrate to them respectfully,[48] and say a few kinds words. That is all right; in fact, you should do that much—but no more than that. Have faith that God will take care of all their needs. You should have that attitude of surrender. After all, are you the one who is actually protecting them? Do you have the power to do so?"

Br: "Why is giving up our ties to our family considered so important?"

Mother: "Son, just as the earth attracts everything to itself, our family will quickly attract our minds. That is the special quality of blood relations. A sadhak should be able to look upon everyone equally. Only by giving up our attachment to everything, can we know our true nature. Our attachment to 'my' father, 'my' mother, 'my' brother or sister is deeply ingrained in us. Without removing it, we cannot expand, and we will fail to receive the expected benefit of our sadhana. If you row a boat that is tied to the shore, you won't get to the other shore."

Br: "Amma, I'm not writing to anyone. I only wanted to know what is proper."

Mother: "If the circumstances are such that you have to write to someone, then write no more than two or three sentences. Make sure that what you write deals with spiritual

---

[48] In India it is customary for young people to prostrate before the elders in their family, and to touch their feet.

matters. Then at least their minds will get a little purity by reading those words. If someone turns to the spiritual path, he can have a great effect on his family, on their way of thinking. Always write only about positive things in your letters to them. Some members of Ramakrishnan's family have begun to favor him staying here. Through their association with him, they have begun to appreciate the need for spirituality in life."

Br: "You said that we shouldn't have the attitude that it's 'my' family, but how can we serve them without that attitude? Isn't it true that we can do something really well only when we do it with the sense of 'my'?"

Mother: "The service of a spiritual person is also his sadhana. His aim is to be free of all bondage. He yearns for complete freedom. He serves others to purify his mind and to become detached, so that he can realize the Supreme Goal. If you love God and surrender to Him, you can perform any action perfectly well without any sense of 'my' or 'mine.' Making the effort and then letting the results be according to His will—this should be our attitude. If we are attached, even serving others will bind us.

"We should serve others without any expectations whatsoever. When others throw thorns at us, we should be able to throw flowers back at them. When they give us poison, we should give them payasam. This is the kind of mind we should have. The purpose of serving the world is to develop that sort of mind. When we serve others we should look upon them as God. Every one of our actions should be a way of worshipping God. Each action will then turn into a divine mantra."

Br: "What is wrong with serving our families in this way?"

Mother: "Once you have developed that sort of mind, it isn't a problem. But at this stage, you are still attached to your family. So it will be hard for you to see the actions you do for them as a way of serving God. In the beginning it will be difficult for you to associate with your family without feeling some attachment, the way you can with others. It's only natural to feel attached to one's home and family. This can be overcome only through a lot of practice. That is why it is recommended that a seeker should detach himself from his family. When he has developed true love and attachment towards God, he won't be able to maintain a bond with anything else.

"The seed has to be completely buried in the soil and its shell has to break before it can sprout. A sadhak must break his identification with the body, and he has to let go of the attitude 'my father and my mother.' He has to see everyone as God Himself."

As She got up, Mother picked up the cassava peels and asked someone to put them in the drink for the cows. Blessed by the nectar of Her words, the brahmacharis also got up and left to do their work.

Sunday, June 15, 1986

Mother was sitting in the darshan hut with some devotees. Because it had rained all morning, the crowd was small.

Mother (laughing): "The ashram children say that we have to change what is written in the *Bhagavad Gita*. The Lord said, 'I am there for those who take refuge in Me forsaking all else.' They say it's just the opposite here, that Amma loves the householders more than the renunciates. But does a shining lamp need light? Those who are in the dark are the ones who need light. It is the one who comes in from the heat that is in need of cold water.

"Amma tells the children who live here, 'The householders are writhing in the heat of worldly life, while you constantly enjoy the coolness here. Because Amma is close by, you can run to Her with whatever problems you have. It's not like that for the others. In the midst of all their affairs, they manage to find a day to come to Amma. If Amma doesn't give them enough attention when they come, they will crumble. Whereas you have renounced worldly life and have come here to realize the Self, they still have to look after their homes, children, and jobs. They are tied to their responsibilities, and yet they seek spirituality in the midst of all that. It isn't possible for them to break all those ties immediately. Only through constant sadhana

will they develop the required detachment. They have to
stand in fire without getting burnt—that is the life of a
householder. Without shoes, they have to walk over thorns
without getting wounded—shoes being freedom from worldly
ties. The householders don't have that freedom. It is therefore our duty to console them.' When the children hear
all this, they keep quiet," Mother concluded, laughing.

A young man named Sudhir was sitting close to Mother.
He had taken an M.S. degree five years ago, but because
there had been no one else to look after his aged mother,
he had cared for her instead of getting a steady job. To
earn a livelihood he tutored the children in the area where
he lived. After his mother's death, he had begun living a
spiritual life, spending his time serving others and engaging in sadhana. Before long, however, he found that he
couldn't continue without a guru to give him the proper
guidance he needed. In fact, he began to feel an aversion
towards spiritual activities. At the same time, his interest
in worldly matters also declined.

Feeling restless, Sudhir had come to the ashram three
days earlier to see Mother for the first time. He had asked
Mother if he could stay at the ashram for some time and
Mother had agreed. By the second day, his sadness had
disappeared. He was taking part in the ashram work with
great enthusiasm and shraddha. Sudhir also sang well, and
had already learned to sing several kirtans.

Sudhir: "Amma, is selfless service possible only if one
believes in God?"

Mother: "Son, only someone with faith in God can truly serve others selflessly. But if a person who has no religious faith is able to really serve others selflessly and forgive others for their mistakes and shortcomings, then it doesn't matter whether or not he has any faith. Those who are able to do real selfless service without believing in God are worthy of our deepest respect."

Sudhir: "What is the purpose of meditation?"

Mother: "Our minds are made impure by the many different thoughts that constantly arise. Meditation directs all those thoughts towards one point of focus.

"We are like pure rain water that has become impure by falling in the gutter. The water in the gutter needs to be cleaned by connecting it to a river; and this is what sadhana does. Even though we are, in reality, the untainted Atman, because we are bound to the gross, physical world, there are impure vasanas present within us. We have to purify our minds by discriminating between the eternal and the ephemeral, and through meditation. And as we are purified by meditating, we grow strong."

Mother asked Sudhir to sing a song. He sang:

Karunya murte, kayampu varna...

> *O Abode of Compassion,*
> *Dark-hued One,*
> *Deign to open your eyes.*
> *O Destroyer of all sorrow,*
> *Please remove my suffering.*

O Luminous One,
With eyes like the petals of a red lotus,
You are my shelter in this world.
O Krishna, I will worship you forever
With the flowers of my tears.

O Gopala, Enchanter of the mind,
I am groping in the dark.
O Shridhara, who permeates all fourteen worlds,
Open your eyes and rid me of my sorrow.

A young woman was meditating near Mother. Pointing at her, Mother said, "This daughter also wants to come and live at the ashram. She refuses to go home, even though she's married. She has gone back to her parents, and her husband's family won't allow her to see her own child. Now she no longer wants her husband or her child. Amma has asked her to wait a little. Her present detachment comes from her disappointment, not from any true understanding. She needs the detachment that comes from true understanding of the spiritual principles; otherwise, she won't be able to stick to ashram life."

A DEVOTEE TESTS DEVI

The lunch bell rang. After giving darshan to the few remaining people, Mother walked to the dining room, accompanied by the devotees. Mother, Herself, served lunch to everyone, and remained in the dining hall until almost everyone had finished eating. She then left the hall, but after just a few steps, She suddenly turned and went back inside. She went up to a man who was still sitting in front of his plate, picked up a ball of rice, which he had kept aside on his plate, and put it in Her mouth. At this, the man was overcome with emotion. With tears streaming down his face he kept chanting, "Kali, Kali, Kali..." Mother sat down beside him and lovingly caressed his head and back. Finally, She got up and went to Her room.

For this man, Mother's unusual behavior held great meaning. He had come from Calcutta to Cochin on a business trip, and had heard about Mother from a friend. Because, like many Bengalis, he worshipped the Divine Mother, his friend's description of Mother's Devi bhava had intrigued him, and he had decided to go and see Her before returning to Calcutta. So that morning he had come to the ashram with his friend and had received Mother's darshan in the hut. A little later, as Mother was serving lunch, he had made a ball of rice and put it aside on his plate, with the thought, "If Mother really is Kali, She will take this ball of rice and eat it. If She does, then I'll stay here tonight to see the Devi bhava. Otherwise, I'll leave right after lunch." When Mother walked out of the dining hall after serving lunch, his heart sank and a feeling of despair came over him. But when She reappeared a moment later and ate the rice ball he had kept aside for Kali, he completely lost control of himself. The clouds that had gathered within him poured out their tears. He stayed for bhava darshan, while his friend returned that afternoon.

INSTRUCTIONS FOR THE DISCIPLES

It was raining in the afternoon. At four o'clock, Mother went to the storeroom and started cleaning it with the help of some brahmacharis. Out in the rain, Neelakantan and Kunjumon were making a fence on the northern side of the ashram.

"Don't stay in the rain, children!" Mother called out to them.

"It's okay, Amma. Our work is almost done!" they replied, and started working faster than before.

Seeing this, Mother said, "Because you are doing your work as an offering to Amma, and because you are doing it with so much joy, sincerity, and dedication, you won't catch a fever. But it is different for those who work half-heartedly for someone else."

A few brahmacharis, who had stayed out of the rain, exchanged glances tinged with shame.

The brahmacharini whose responsibility it was to gather firewood for the kitchen had neglected her duty. One of the residents complained to Mother that the cooking had become difficult because of the lack of firewood.

Mother: "Amma reminded that daughter the other day about the need for firewood, but she still didn't bring any. Where is her respect and devotion? Amma isn't saying that everyone should respect or revere Amma. But when you make a canoe, you heat the wood to make it bend. Only if the wood bends can you shape the canoe. Likewise, we change for the better when we 'bend' out of awe and devotion for the guru. Otherwise, only the ego will grow, and we won't develop spiritually at all. Humility and obedience are essential for a sadhak's development."

When Mother had finished chastising the brahmacharini, another resident began making more complaints about her.

Mother: "Daughter, that child was disobedient, but we shouldn't be angry with her. We should never scold or criticize anyone out of hostility, but only for the sake of that person's progress. If we scold or criticize someone out of anger or jealousy, we are committing an error far greater than theirs, and it will only make our minds more impure. A sadhak should never do this. An important aspect of sadhana is to see only the good in others, for only then will the negativity within us die.

"If we criticize others with love, and with only their betterment in mind, it will lead them from wrong to right. But if we find fault just for the sake of finding fault, it will pollute our own minds, as well as strengthen the hostility in the other person and encourage them to make further mistakes. Children, don't look at the faults of anyone! If someone talks to you about the faults of another person, point out the good qualities in that person, without dwelling on their mistakes. Say to the person who is criticizing,

'You are finding fault with him, but doesn't he have such and such good qualities?' Then he will automatically stop his criticism and won't approach you to talk ill of others again. Thus, we better ourselves and also help the other person to eliminate his habit of fault-finding. Isn't it true that butcher and liquor shops manage to stay in business only because people go there to buy? Fault-finders will change their nature if there is no one to listen to them."

It was time for bhajans. Mother went to the kalari and the singing began. During the bhajans a thunderstorm broke out and it was raining heavily. The thunderclaps sounded like drumbeats accompanying the *tandava* dance of Lord Shiva.

Wednesday, June 18, 1986

THE MOTHER WHO WANTS
TO SEE HER CHILDREN CRY

It was eleven in the morning. Mother was in the meditation room with all the brahmacharis. She was scolding them for their lack of attention to their sadhana. In the end She said, "My dear children, cry out to God! Amma isn't scolding you out of anger. Her heart is full of love for you, but if She shows only Her love, you won't grow. Also, if Amma rebukes you, your sins will be transferred to Her.

"Children, don't get attached to external love. Those

who lead a worldly life have to show their love outwardly, for only then will others come to know of it. In worldly life everyone's peace of mind depends on external love. Without it, there will be discord and no peace. In spiritual life, on the other hand, we find bliss within ourselves.

"If you are attached to the idea of looking only for external love, you won't be able to find the Divine Essence within yourself. Only by realizing That will you find true contentment. If you own your own house, you can live in freedom; otherwise, if you don't pay your rent on time, the landlord and his people will come and bother you. "Amma's happiness is to see you find bliss within yourselves. Amma feels unhappy when She sees you depend on Amma's outward love and on external things, because if you depend on that, you will have to suffer tomorrow.

"If Amma shows too much love, it will be a problem— because, instead of looking within, you will focus only on this external Mother. But if Amma shows some anger, you will turn within thinking, 'O God, what did I do wrong? Give me the strength to act according to Amma's wishes.' And thus you turn towards your own inner Self. Amma listens to the woes of thousands of people who are suffering because they have been fooled by external love. No one loves anyone more than they love themselves.

"Also, Amma has millions of children. If you depend only on Her external love, you will feel jealous whenever She is affectionate towards anyone else. The external Amma you see now is like the reflection of a flower in a vessel filled with water. You can never make that flower your own, because it is only an image. To realize the Truth, you have to seek That which is true. Taking refuge in a reflection isn't enough; you have to take refuge in the real thing. If you love Amma, you should do so with the awareness of the Real Principle. When you fully understand the Real Principle, the mind won't attach itself to anything external. So children, while you are under Amma's protection, try to look within. Only in this way will you be able to enjoy the state of bliss, forever.

"Amma feels sad because Her children aren't trying hard enough to make their minds one-pointed. Cry out for God. Only by crying for Him will your minds become one-pointed. Nothing is possible without devotion for God. A true devotee doesn't even yearn for liberation. Devotion is even higher than liberation. A devotee always experiences the bliss of his love for God. What, then, is the need for liberation? The devotee is in constant bliss while in this world, so why would he want to think about any other world?"

Mother showed the tip of one of Her fingers. "In front of bhakti, *mukti* (liberation) is no more than this."

Mother took a sip from a cup of coffee which had been placed in front of Her by a brahmachari. Getting up with the cup in Her hand, She poured a little coffee into everyone's mouth. As She poured the coffee, She whispered in each person's ear, "My child, call out to God and cry! Cry for God, my child!"

Having given prasad to everyone, Mother sat down again and started giving instructions on meditation: "Children, pray with an aching heart. Bind the mind to the Paramatman without letting it wander. Pray, 'O Supreme Self, remove the coating on the mirror within me! Let me see my real face clearly in that mirror!' Whenever the mind wanders, bring it back and bind it again to the holy feet of your Beloved Deity."

The brahmacharis began to meditate. With Mother's instructions echoing in their minds, meditation came easily. Their minds became still, for they had only to savor with their internal eyes, the form of the Divine Essence whose physical embodiment they had just beheld with their external eyes.

Wednesday, June 25, 1986

MOMENTARY DETACHMENT

A month earlier, a young man came to the ashram with the desire to live there. At first, Mother had withheld Her permission. Then, as the young man's insistence grew stronger, She had told him, "Son, spiritual life isn't that easy. To persevere in spiritual life without true discrimination and detachment is difficult. Only those who never lose sight of the Goal under any circumstances can succeed. Son, in your heart you are still attached to your family, and because of this, Amma isn't sure how long you will be able to stay here. But if you feel so strongly about it, give it a try, son. Amma won't object."

So the young man had begun to live in the ashram. He stole everyone's heart with his adherence to the ashram rules and the intense detachment with which he did his sadhana. When a brahmachari mentioned his detachment to Mother, She said, "When we first plant a cutting from a tree, a few new leaves will appear. Don't assume from this that the new plant has taken root, because those leaves will fall away quickly. You should watch and see whether any new leaves appear after that. If they do, you may assume that the plant has begun to grow. Those leaves appear only after the plant has taken root."

Then one day, the young man's father and brother had come to the ashram. The father had said to him, "Son, your mother is very unhappy about not being able to see you. She isn't eating properly and she talks about you all the time."

The young man's eyes had filled with tears, and he had asked Mother, "May I go home just once and see my mother?"

"As you wish, son," Mother had replied. Then, just like a doctor giving a patient who refuses to stay in the hospital some medicine to take at home, Mother had added, "You should do some japa at home, too, son."

Today, a week later, when the young man still hadn't returned, a brahmachari sitting near Mother asked, "Amma, why do so many people lose their initial detachment?"

Mother: "Most people begin with a rush of enthusiasm. Many of them feel some detachment to begin with, but success lies in maintaining that detachment. Once the initial excitement subsides, the latent vasanas from countless past lives begin to raise their heads, one by one. Then the sadhak's attention turns to external things. It takes intense effort and great sacrifice to transcend the vasanas. Most people become disheartened when they encounter more trouble than they expected. It's also common for the progress in their sadhana to drop off, and this causes disappointment. But those who have true lakshya bodha won't give up. They'll try again and again, ignoring the obstacles and failures. Only those who have such a strong sense of the ultimate goal can maintain their detachment throughout."

Mother got up and walked to the vicinity of the kitchen, where She noticed a foreign devotee trying to wash his clothes. Unaccustomed to washing clothes by hand, he was attempting to first rub a whole bar of soap onto the large washing stone. Mother watched him for a few moments, then went up to him and showed him how to do it. A brahmachari translated Mother's instructions into English. The man was delighted to have Mother teach him the technique of washing clothes.

Next, Mother walked towards the darshan hut. On the way She noticed a brahmachari wearing ochre colored clothes.

Mother: "Son, you shouldn't wear that. You are not ready for that yet. Show reverence for the ochre color

wherever you see it, but don't wear it. Ochre is the symbol of having burned one's body in the fire![49] When we
see that color, we should remember the lineage of the
rishis. When we honor someone wearing ochre, we are
honoring that lineage."

A devotee from abroad was listening to this conversation. When he learned through a brahmachari that Mother
was talking about ochre clothes, he asked Her if he, too,
could be given ochre. Mother simply smiled in response.
But he raised his request again, quite seriously.

Mother: "Son, that's not the type of cloth you buy in a
shop. You first have to earn the maturity required for it."

Still, the devotee wasn't satisfied. "Others are wearing
it, so why can't I have it as well?"

Mother: "Son, will you become a woman just by wearing women's clothes? Will a woman turn into man if she
dresses like a man? Nobody turns into a sannyasi by grab-
bing a piece of ochre cloth and wrapping himself in it.
The first requirement is to dip your mind in ochre. When
you've done that, Amma will give you the ochre cloth."

The devotee was silent.

Br: "Some people run away after a fight with their family
and put on ochre clothes, don't they?"

Mother: "Some people leave home after a fight, and
when they find themselves faced with starvation, they put
on ochre colored clothes just to get something to eat. You

---

[49] This refers to burning one's body-consciousness in the fire of knowledge.

see others wearing ochre out of despair when their wives leave them. The feeling of detachment is good, but one has to grasp its real purpose; otherwise, it's meaningless to wear ochre cloth. These days it's hard to find any real sannyasis. We should find out if they have received the ochre robe from a gurukula according to the established rites. Real gurus don't just give away the ochre; they look at the maturity of the recipient."

EXPECTING TO PASS WITHOUT STUDYING

When Mother reached the darshan hut, everyone prostrated and sat down. A family of devotees had come from Pattambi. Rajendran, the husband, was a teacher, and Sarojam, his wife, a seamstress. They had two children, a son who was in the eighth grade, and a daughter in the third grade.

Rajendran: "Amma, our daughter isn't studying at all!"

Sarojam: "She says she doesn't have to study because Amma will make her pass!"

Mother pulled the girl closer to Her and caressed her affectionately.

Mother: "My daughter, isn't everyone going to blame Amma if you don't learn anything? How can you pass if you don't study?"

In a sweet, innocent voice, the girl said, "But my brother passed without studying!"

Everyone laughed.

Mother: "Who told you that, daughter?"

Girl: "He told me."

Sarojam: "Amma, this is what she says whenever we tell her to study. She says that when her brother sat down to write his examination, you appeared to him. You came and sat next to him and told him all the answers. When he came home he said, 'I didn't study at all. Ammachi told me everything.'"

Rajendran: "What he said is true, Amma. He never studies anything; he's always playing. But he got high marks in the examination. The teacher was amazed at his marks."

Sarojam: "Now this girl says that Ammachi will make her pass as well." Mother laughed and gave the girl an affectionate kiss. "Daughter, if you don't study, Amma won't talk to you. Promise that you'll study!"

The girl promised, and Mother gave her an apple from a packet lying next to Her. The girl's lovely face beamed with joy.

SPIRITUALITY AND WORLDLINESS

Mother's devotee, Damodara Menon, came up and prostrated to Her.

Mother: "Oh, who is this? My son, Damu?" Mr. Menon smiled and lowered his head into Mothers hands.

Mother: "Were you gone for some days, son?"

Damu: "I was traveling, Amma. I have just come back from Bangalore. I haven't even been home yet. I got off the train at Kayamkulam, wanting to see Amma first."

Mother: "Are the little ones doing well, son?"

Damu: "Thanks to Amma's grace, there are no problems at home. But I just saw a friend whom I'm worried about."

Mother: "Why is that, son?"

Damu: "I saw him in Bangalore. We were colleagues once. At one point, he resigned from his job and left home to become a sannyasi. When he came back, five years ago, he was wearing ochre."

Mother: "Where does that son live?"

Damu: "He was staying at an ashram in Rishikesh, but when I saw him this time, he had changed completely. The ochre robe, rudraksha, long hair and beard were all gone. He looked handsome. He gave up sannyasa four years ago. He fell in love with a girl who frequently came to the ashram, and he married her. They live in Bangalore now. He has a job there, but from what he said I understand that he is deeply disappointed."

Mother: "If you leave spiritual life and go back to worldly life, the result will be that you suffer both externally and internally. A mind that has taken to spiritual thoughts cannot find happiness in worldly things again; only restlessness will result. The subtle aura around the body, which is created by one's spiritual practices, will be an obstacle to enjoying physical pleasures. Out of compassion, the sadhak's Beloved Deity and the gods surrounding that Deity will create double the usual amount of obstacles and suffering; for they want him to come back to spiritual life. That struggle is not the result of God's displeasure—it is His blessing! If given more wealth and happiness, the sadhak's ego will get bigger and he will make mistakes. He will have to be born again and again. To prevent this, and to turn his mind away from the world, God gives him suffering.

"The mind that has had a real taste of even a little bit of spirituality cannot find happiness in worldly things. If a man marries someone other than the girl he loves, he'll be unhappy with his wife, because his mind will be on the one he loves. Similarly, the mind that has turned to spirituality can no longer find satisfaction in the material realm.

"Since the marriage has already taken place, your friend should make sure that he continues his sadhana. If a person follows the dharma of a householder properly, he can live a meaningful life. By continuing spiritual practices without interruption, one can taste spiritual bliss in this life. When you truly begin to love God, your mind retracts from physical pleasures; your desires will then diminish, and this will automatically lead to inner peace. Desire means suffering and sorrow. Where there is fire, there is smoke, and where there is desire, there is suffering. But it's impossible to live without any desires. So let all your desires be for God.

"If sadhana is done regularly, the spiritual and worldly aspects of life can be maintained side by side, in perfect harmony. To achieve this, you have to perform your actions with the awareness that the goal of life is to attain liberation. This will save you.

"Still, the greatness of sannyasa is something special. A sannyasi can contemplate God and enjoy bliss, without being burdened by worldly preoccupation. Even if he is engaged in some action as a form of service, he will not feel burdened because he isn't attached to the action.

"Once, a sannyasi was walking along a road when a man caught up with him and asked, 'Swami, what is sannyasa?' The sannyasi didn't even turn to look at him, but the man kept repeating his question. Suddenly, the sannyasi stopped, put down the bundle he was carrying, and continued walking. He hadn't gone ten feet, when the man asked again, 'What is sannyasa?' The sannyasi turned to him and said, 'Didn't you see me putting down my bundle? Sannyasa means giving up the notion of "I" and "mine", and casting away everything you own.'

"The sannyasi walked on, but the man still followed, asking, 'What does one do after that?' Now the sannyasi turned and went back to where the bundle was lying. He lifted it back onto his shoulder and continued forward. The man didn't understand the meaning of this, either, so he repeated his question. As he walked on, the sannyasi said, 'See this? Carry the burden of the world like this. But only by renouncing everything can you put the world on your shoulder.'

"If you are looking after a wild animal, you have to watch it all the time to make sure it doesn't run away. If you let it loose, you have to follow it everywhere, otherwise it could escape. When you feed it, you have to stay with it until it has finished eating. You are never free of toil. But the keeper of a garden has only to stay at the gate and watch to ensure that nobody steals the flowers. He can also enjoy the fragrance. Likewise, if you go after worldly life, your mind will bother you constantly; it will never remain steady. Spirituality, on the other hand, allows you to enjoy the beauty and fragrance of life. There is no turmoil, no botheration. Even if suffering arises from your prarabdha, because of your surrender, it won't be experienced as suffering. Even that suffering is a form of divine grace, which is extending a hand to lift you to a state of peace."

Everyone listened with rapt attention to Mother's detailed description of the nature of spiritual and material life. As they got up, their faces shone with a new understanding of how to mold their lives.

Saturday, June 28, 1986

WAS KRISHNA A THIEF?

Mother was in one of the huts, engaged in a debate with a brahmachari who was a Krishna devotee.

Mother: "Your Krishna is a big thief! Didn't thievery come to the world because He stole butter? Think of all the mischief He did!"

The brahmachari couldn't bear to hear what Mother was saying. Tears were coursing down his cheeks as he protested, "Krishna isn't like that at all, Amma!"

He continued weeping like a small child. Mother wiped his tears and said, "What a baby you are! Amma was just trying to see how strong your attachment is to the Lord. He wasn't a thief. He was the very embodiment of honesty. He stole butter and made mischief to give joy to others. By stealing the butter, He stole their hearts. Only the Lord could do that. He never did anything for Himself. He didn't steal the butter for Himself, but for the poor cowherd children who were His companions, and at the same time, He succeeded in binding the hearts of the gopis to God.

"Previously, the minds of the gopis had been attached to their work. They were immersed in making a living by selling milk, butter, and curd. By stealing those things, the Lord freed their minds from that attachment and focused their minds on Him. Though He stole the butter, He didn't eat it Himself, but gave it to the cowherd boys when they grew hungry while tending the cows. So He achieved two things at the same time: He fed His hungry companions and freed the minds of the gopis from their bondage.

"The Lord was a true revolutionary. The modern day revolutionaries want to take from the haves and give to the have-nots. But they want to eliminate one group of people to achieve this. That is the materialistic way. The spiritual way is different. Lord Krishna taught the way of saving everyone, the rich as well as the poor, the righteous as well as the unrighteous. Today people say we should 'kill the dog if it is rabid.' But the Lord says we should transform the 'rabid' mind. This was His brand of revolution. The solution doesn't lie in killing; what is required is to transform and uplift the person's mind. A change should take place in the individual. The limited, selfish mind should be transformed into an expansive, all-encompassing mind filled with love and compassion. This is what Krishna taught us.

"Even Krishna's marriage wasn't according to His choice. He agreed to marry to make those who were dear to Him happy. His aim was to make everyone enjoy the bliss of the Self, and He used many different methods to achieve this. An ordinary mind cannot understand this. Only a subtle mind engaged in contemplation can understand a little of the inner meaning of His life.

"Now sing a kirtan, son!"

The brahmachari's face broke into a smile, and as he began to sing, the love in his heart took wing:

Nilanjana miri neerada varna...

> *O you, with the complexion of a rain cloud,*
> *Who has blue, collyrium-lined eyes,*
> *You are my sole refuge, throughout eternity.*
> *This is the truth, Krishna,*
> *For there is none but you to protect me.*

O dark, handsome Krishna,
Playful like a child who steals our hearts,
Who is drawn to the sound of Narada's tambura—
O ever-lustrous Krishna,
Who dances to songs of devotion,
Who destroys all greed,
And is the Eternal Witness,
Give me a clear vision of yourself.

O Bestower of liberation,
Who enchants through maya,
Whose Lotus Feet are served by humanity—
O Lord Krishna,
Deliver me from this worldly existence.

As he sang, more brahmacharis arrived with a harmonium, ganjira, bells, and other musical instruments. The hut was soon filled and others sat outside, all singing in response to the brahmachari who was leading the kirtan.

Mother wasn't able to finish the song. Her eyes overflowed with tears. Gradually She closed Her tear-filled eyes and sat quietly, forming a *mudra* with Her hand. Waves of the immeasurable power of the divine state She was in emanated from Her, awakening the hearts of those present. After awhile Her eyes opened, then closed again. It seemed as if Mother was struggling to withdraw from Her elevated state and to come back down. On an earlier occasion, Mother had gone into samadhi during bhajans and had returned to Her normal state only after several hours.

At that time She had said, "If this happens, you children should sing kirtans. Otherwise, Amma could sit like this for months, or She could turn into an *avadhut*." Remembering that incident, the brahmacharis now continued to sing kirtans until Mother emerged from Her bhava. It took a long time for Her to become completely aware of Her surroundings.

BHAVA DARSHAN

That evening, a devotee from Madras named Subrahmanian was sitting near Mother. He asked Her to explain the significance of bhava darshan.

Mother: "Son, people live in a world of names and forms. It is to lead them to Truth that Amma assumes this role.

"Without the mind, there is no world. As long as you have a mind, there are names and forms. Once the mind is gone, there is nothing. Those who have reached that state don't need to pray or do japa. In that state, you know neither sleep nor wakefulness; you aren't aware of any objective existence—there is only perfect stillness, bliss and peace. But one has to advance in order to achieve this state, and so, methods such as bhava darshan are needed."

Subrahmanian: "There are those who criticize Amma for hugging Her children."

Mother: "Son, you should ask them, 'At your age, have you the guts to hug the mother who gave birth to you? Even if you can do so at home, would you give her a hug in the middle of the street?' In fact, they cannot because of their inhibitions.[50] But there are no such feelings in Amma.

"A mother feels great love, tenderness, and affection for her baby, not any physical desire. Amma sees everyone as Her baby. This may be a kind of madness, and you can lock Amma away if you like—but this is Her way. If you ask why She hugs people, the answer is that it's the outward flow of Her inherent compassion. That flow happens spontaneously when you come to Her, just as leaves flutter when the wind arrives. Just as sweetness is the inherent nature of a fruit, the motherly sentiment, the flow of compassion, is Amma's inherent nature. What can She do? It is very real to Her. A cow may be black or white or red, but the milk is always white. Similarly, there is only one Self, not many. It only appears as many to those who think of themselves as the individual soul. That's all there is to it. Amma doesn't feel that distinction, and because of this She doesn't see men and women as being different from each other.

"What is most lacking in the world today is selfless love. The wife has no time to listen to the concerns of her husband or to console him, and the husband doesn't console his wife or listen to her when she needs to tell him about her troubles. People love one another for the sake of their own happiness. No one goes beyond that and loves anyone to the point of sacrificing their own com-

---

[50] In India people rarely hug each other in public.

fort. We don't see in anyone that attitude of sacrifice that makes them ready to die for others. Instead of the attitude, 'I am here for you,' there is only the attitude, 'You are here for me.' But Amma cannot have such an attitude.

"People who are looking at this from their level may think it is strange. But that isn't Amma's fault. They may have their own kind of madness—this is Amma's madness. A cowherd thinks of grass as feed for cattle; a wandering healer looks upon the same grass as medicine. Each sees things according to his samskara.

"A guru and his disciple once went on a pilgrimage. On the way they had to cross a river. A girl was standing on the river bank, crying. She needed to cross the river, but was unable to do so because the water was too deep for her. The guru didn't hesitate. Lifting the girl to his shoulders, he crossed the river and put her down on the opposite bank. The guru and disciple continued their journey. As they sat down for dinner that night, the disciple had a troubled expression on his face. The guru noticed it and asked, 'What happened to you?'

"The disciple said, 'I have a doubt. Was it proper for you to carry a girl on your shoulder like that?'

"The guru laughed and said, 'Well, I put her down on the opposite bank of the river. Are you still carrying her?'"

Subrahmanian: "I have done sadhana for so many years, yet I've had no special experiences. Why is that?"

Mother: "If you mix ten dishes together, can you enjoy

the taste of any of them? Move forward with just one yearning, the yearning to see God. Then you will have experiences."

Several youths came for Mother's darshan. Mother sat with them for some time, talking to them about spiritual matters. Finally, they prostrated to Her and got up. Before leaving, one of the young men said, "Amma, give me your blessing so that my faith in you becomes stronger!"

Mother: "Faith should not be blind, son. You should examine carefully before you decide where to put your faith. You are all young. Don't just start believing instantly. What you see is not Amma's real nature. She's a crazy woman. Don't just blindly believe that She is good!"

Young man: "It is for the child to decide whether the Mother is good!"

His words created ripples of laughter. He had just met Mother, and yet he already felt so close to Her! But then, who could escape the waves of affection rising from Mother, the Ocean of Love?

Tuesday, July 1, 1986

THOSE WHO ERR ARE ALSO HER CHILDREN

Mother and the brahmacharis had gone to Ernakulam. They returned to the ashram at noon. Many of the devotees waiting for Mother prostrated as She walked towards the ashram. Without going to Her room to rest, Mother went and sat on the verandah of the Vedanta school and began giving darshan to the devotees.

During a reception which had been held for Mother in Ernakulam the day before, the organizers had prevented a man from garlanding Mother. Referring to that incident, a brahmachari said, "That man was devastated yesterday. Only when Amma called him and gave him some prasad, did he feel a bit better. He would have gone to pieces if Amma hadn't done that. The organizers felt that people would criticize Amma if a person with such a bad reputation was allowed to come near Her."

Mother: "Until now that son may have committed many mistakes, but yesterday he came to Amma for the first time. How he will be from now on is what we should be looking at. Light doesn't need light; it is darkness that needs light. If Amma rejects that child, what will be his plight? He has made some terrible mistakes because of his ignorance, but as far as Amma is concerned, he is still one of Her sons. Is there anyone here who has never done anything wrong? The biggest mistake is to do what is wrong even though you know what is right. The reason why we practice spirituality is to learn how to forgive others for their mistakes, and to love them—not reject them. Anyone can reject others, but to accept everyone— that is difficult. Only through love can we lead others from wrong to right. If we disown someone for his mistakes, he will only continue to commit them.

"The sage Valmiki was a forest dweller who led a life of robbery and murder. One day he was about to rob and kill some sages who came through the forest. They responded by forgiving him and treating him with great love. If those sages hadn't shown him that compassion, there would have been no Valmiki,[51] and there would be no *Ramayana*, dispelling the darkness in so many people. The compassion of those sages created both Valmiki and the *Ramayana*. Therefore, children, you should forgive the mistakes of others and lovingly show them the right path. Don't refer again and again to the mistakes that someone may have made in the past, because that will only lead that person to commit further errors.

"Yesterday, that son said to Amma, 'Until I met you, I could think of nothing but suicide. But today all that is gone. Now I suddenly feel that I want to live. I even slept well last night! I had thought that my family would always stand by me, no matter what happened; but when I went through hard times, they all abandoned me, one by one. Some of them even disowned me. Now I know that only God is true and everlasting. Had I made friends with God from the very beginning, I wouldn't have had to suffer so much.'

"Children, let us take refuge in God. Anyone—even a

---

[51] Ratnadasan, as Valmiki was called in his early days as a robber, later became the great sage Valmiki, who was the embodiment of love and compassion. He wrote the *Ramayana*, which was the first epic poem in Sanskrit and which continues even today to inspire and influence Indian culture.

businessman with a heavy schedule—can spend an hour a day, focusing his mind on God. God takes care of those who trust in Him. During times of difficulties our Beloved Deity will come to our rescue. God will even change the minds of our enemies in our favor. But who needs God today?"

A devotee: "I've heard it said that eventually the whole world will become Hindu."

Mother: "That doesn't seem likely, but the majority of people will imbibe the principles of *Sanatana Dharma* (the Eternal Religion)."

Another devotee: "That is bound to happen, because people in the West, who never accept anything without having tested it, cannot help but embrace Sanatana Dharma, which is based on the most logical principles."

Mother: "But tests have limits. It's meaningless to say we will believe something only after testing it. Faith and experience are the fundamental requirements."

Devotee: "Nowadays, people generally do not hold mahatmas in high regard. Their faith is confined to temples."

Mother: "That is because there is no appreciation of the scriptures or spiritual principles. Man builds the temple, he makes and installs the icon, and it is also man who worships the icon and bows down to it. The power of any temple comes from the devotees who worship there. And when a mahatma infuses life into a temple, it has even greater power, a much greater power, because the mahatma has fully realized the Divinity within himself. But even so, people have no faith in the divine power in man. What power does a temple have if a mahatma doesn't give it life, or if people don't worship there?"

As the crowd of devotees grew, Mother went inside the darshan hut. A devotee brought a bunch of tender coconuts. He put it down outside the hut and went in and prostrated to Mother.

Devotee: "That's the first bunch from our new coconut tree. Right from the beginning, I was planning to give it to Amma."

Mother: "Didn't people make fun of you when you carried that on the bus, son?"

Devotee: "What if they did? For Ammachi, I am pre-pared to take any amount of ridicule! May I open one of those coconuts for you, Amma?"

Mother agreed. The devotee went to the kitchen with the coconut, and Mother continued Her conversation with the devotees.

THE HOME SHOULD BECOME AN ASHRAM

Devotee: "Can one realize God while remaining a grihasthasrami?" [52]

Mother: "Yes, it is possible. But then you have to be a real grihasthasrami, thinking of your home as an ashram.

---

[52] A grihasthasrami is a householder who lives in the world and carries out his responsibilities, while at the same time living a truly spiritual life.

But how many grihasthasramis exist today? A real grihasthasrami has surrendered his life to God and is not attached to anything. He is not attached to any of his actions. Dharma is the most important thing in his life. Though he lives with his family, his mind is always on God. He never neglects to take care of his wife and children, or to serve the world, for he sees it as a duty entrusted to him by God, and he performs that duty with great attention. But he doesn't cling to his actions as people generally do nowadays.

"If you understand the spiritual principles, you can constantly be engaged in sadhana, even in your home. However, it's not as easy as you may think. If we have the television on in front of us while we're trying to do some work, we'll end up looking at the screen. Our detachment has to be exceptionally strong for us to resist, for us to overcome that vasana. It is a great thing to be able to call out to God in the midst of all the family prarabdha. Many of Amma's householder children meditate and do japa and archana regularly at home. Many of them have taken a vow that they will not eat or sleep before doing archana. Amma's heart overflows with love when She thinks of them."

Turning to the brahmacharis, Mother continued, "You brahmacharis are here to dedicate yourselves totally to the world. You should bind your minds completely to God. Don't leave room for any other thought. Thinking about your family and friends will only create more vasanas. You just have to sit in a room full of coal for your body to be covered with coal dust. Similarly, affection and attachment to the family will pull down a sadhak's mind."

Mother's Devi bhava darshan was in progress. The brahmacharis were sitting in the kalari mandapam singing kirtans. It seemed that even nature had given up sleep and was enraptured by the bhajans. The stream of devotees had not slowed since the darshan began hours ago.

The men entered the little kalari through the left side of the open doorway, and the women through the right. They prostrated to Mother, who was sitting on a peetham, and unburdened their sorrows at Her sacred feet. Each person knelt in front of Mother, rested their head in Her motherly lap, and was embraced by Her. After receiving prasad and holy water from Her hands, they left the temple with a sense of deep fulfillment. At Her feet Mother received the countless heaps of Her devotees' prarabdha. Like the sacred Ganges river that uplifts the fallen, She washed their sins away in the stream of Her Love. Like the all-devouring fire-god, Agni, She cleansed them in Her sacred fire, burning away their vasanas.

As usual, Mother was undaunted by the size of the crowd (In fact, the larger the crowd of devotees, the more radiant Her face became). Through Her shone the invincible presence of the Supreme, which protects the countless cosmic realms, and yet, at the same time, She laughed with the innocence of a child, stirring others to laughter as well.

A devotee came into the kalari with his four-year-old son. The father prostrated to Mother. Just at that moment, the son began making mischief, beating on his father's back and pulling at his shirt. As the father continued to kneel humbly before Mother, the little boy took this as an invitation to hop onto his father's back and ride him like an elephant!

Mother enjoyed the boy's play. She teased him by pouring holy water on his face and body. The child jumped back to avoid the water. Mother pretended to put away the water pot, and the boy came forward again. Once more She poured water on him, and again he jumped back. This sport continued for some time, delighting everyone. By the time he came out of the kalari with his father, the playful child was completely drenched.

EACH ACCORDING TO HIS SAMSKARA

The Devi bhava finished at one in the morning. Most of the devotees went to bed. But Mother, the brahmacharis, and a few devotees stayed up to move the bricks that were to be used for the construction of the main building the next day. Being the rainy season, the backwaters around the ashram were overflowing, and the ashram courtyard was full of water. A young woman from Delhi was among the devotees who were helping. She had come with her mother the day before and had met Mother for the first time. Once the girl started talking to the brahmacharis, she wouldn't stop. The brahmacharis felt uncomfortable about this. Finally, the woman left. When the work was finished, Mother sat down on a dry spot with a few of Her children at the south side of the kalari. The brahmacharis told Mother about the young woman's excessive familiarity.

Br: "She talks too much and she doesn't know how to talk to people. She said that when she saw me, she was reminded of her husband. I felt like slapping her on the face when she said that!"

Mother: "Son, it is a weakness in her that is due to her ignorance. But you should have had the strength of wisdom. In a situation like this, you should look within. At any sign of the mind weakening, move away from there. If you are really mature, you should be able to give people the proper advice. There's no point in feeling angry. That girl was simply expressing her samskara. She doesn't know anything about spirituality. You, in your turn, should have the samskara to give her the advice she needs about the proper way to behave. Before getting ready to punish someone, we should take their culture and the circumstances in which they grew up into consideration. By gently showing people the right path, we can remove their ignorance."

ASSOCIATION WITH WOMEN

Devotee: "Didn't Sri Ramakrishna say that a sadhak shouldn't talk to women or even look at their pictures?"

Mother: "One who has a guru need not fear. It is enough to follow the guru's instructions. Didn't Ramakrishna's own disciple, Vivekananda, go to the United States and accept women as his disciples? In the beginning, however, a seeker should keep as much distance from women as possible. He shouldn't even look at a picture of a woman, and female sadhaks should keep the same distance from men. That is how alert one has to be. During the period of sadhana, it is best to renounce the senses completely and remain in solitude. Later the sadhak has to face different situations in the proximity of the guru. He should consider those situations part of his sadhana. He has to overcome those obstacles. For example, one cannot reach the goal without transcending sexual attraction. A sadhak who has surrendered to the guru will be able to do this. But a person who doesn't have a guru has to follow the external restrictions very strictly, otherwise he could fall at any time.

"A sadhak should be alert when associating with women. But staying away from women out of fear is useless. After all, you have to overcome your fear. How can you reach God without developing the strength of mind to transcend everything? No one will attain Self-realization without learning to see the Supreme Self in everyone. But during the time of sadhana, the seeker should avoid associating closely with women. There should be a certain distance. For example, he shouldn't sit in a room talking to a woman when no one else is present, or be alone with a woman in a solitary place. Without you even being aware of it, the mind will begin to find pleasure in such situations; and if you're not strong enough, you'll succumb. If it's necessary to talk to someone of the opposite sex, invite another person to join you. If a third person is present, you'll be more alert.

"The combination of man and woman is like petrol and fire: petrol will burn if it comes close to fire. So you should always be watchful. When you sense any weakness within you, contemplate and ask yourself, 'What is so attractive about a body full of urine and excrement?' However, in the end you have to overcome that aversion as well, and see everything as a form of the Mother of the Universe. Try to gain strength from seeing the all-pervading Consciousness in everyone. But until you have developed that strength, you have to be very alert. The opposite sex is like a whirlpool that will pull you down. It is hard to overcome these difficult circumstances without constant sadhana, lakshya bodha and, above all, the attitude of surrender towards the guru."

A devotee: "Aren't the brahmacharis getting exhausted with all this brick-carrying, the other work they do, and the trips they make?"

Mother: "Even on bhava darshan nights, the children carry bricks after the darshan is over. They may have gone to bed after singing bhajans throughout darshan, and then they are suddenly called to carry bricks. Amma wants to see how many of them have the spirit of selflessness, or whether they are living just for bodily comforts. On such occasions we can see if their meditation is doing them any good. We have to develop the readiness to help when others are struggling. Otherwise, what is the point of doing tapas?"

Devotee: "Amma, will there come a time when everyone in the world is good?"

Mother: "Son, if there is goodness, evil will exist as well. Suppose a mother has ten children. Nine of them are as good as gold, and only one is bad. That one bad child is enough to ruin all the others. But because he is there, the others will be compelled to call out to God. There can be no world without opposites."

It was now late at night. Being immersed in Mother's words, no one had noticed the passage of time.

Mother: "Children, it's very late. You should go and sleep now. Amma will see you tomorrow."

Mother got up. The devotees bowed to Her and got up as well. Mother went and showed each visitor where to sleep. Seeing Mother wading through the water-covered ground, the devotees said, "You don't have to come, Amma. We can find our rooms."

Mother: "With so much water, it would be hard for you to find the way, children. Amma will come with you."

It was three o'clock by the time Mother had shown them to their rooms and finally went to Her own room. The devotees lay down for a short rest before dawn.

Thursday, July 10, 1986

It was a bhava darshan day. People arrived in a steady stream throughout the morning. At about two in the afternoon, Mother prostrated to Mother Earth and was about to emerge from the hut, when a new group of people arrived. They had come from Nagercoil in a rented bus, hoping to see Mother that afternoon and then leave for home immediately.

With a smile, Mother again sat down on the cot. The devotees who had just arrived came forward and prostrated. Those who had been sitting in the hut for some time got up and gave their places to the new arrivals. Among the newcomers there were three small children who were good at singing, so Mother requested a song. They sang:

Pachai mamalai...

> *O people of Srirangam,*
> *How I enjoy the sweetness of Achyuta,*
> *Whose body is like a lush green mountain,*
> *Whose mouth is like coral*
> *And whose eyes are like lotuses—*
> *The Cowherd Child,*
> *Whom the great souls yearn to see.*
> *I love that sweetness even more than the taste of*
> *heaven.*

At about three o'clock, when Mother had given darshan to the newcomers and had instructed a brahmachari to serve them lunch, She finally went to Her room. There, Mother found a brahmachari waiting for Her. Mother sat down on the floor and Gayatri served Her lunch. A pile of letters from that day's mail lay next to Mother. She held the letters in Her left hand and read them as She ate. Suddenly, without any introduction, She started talking to the brahmachari, answering his question. She knew what was on his mind, without even being told.

MEDITATION SHOULD BE ONE-POINTED

Mother: "Son, when you sit for meditation, keep your mind totally fixed on God, and make sure your attention doesn't drift to other things. Only your Beloved Deity should be on your mind. You need to have that kind of detachment.

"A sannyasi was once sitting in meditation when a man passed by just in front of him, running at great speed. The sannyasi didn't like this at all. A little later, the man came back by the same path holding a child by the hand. The sannyasi asked him angrily, 'Why don't you show some consideration? Can't you see that I am meditating here?' Very respectfully, the man said, 'I'm sorry, I had no idea that you were sitting here.' 'Why, are you blind?' asked the sannyasi. The man replied, 'My son had gone to play with a friend, but didn't return and had been missing for some time. I was afraid he might have fallen into the pond nearby, so I ran there as fast as I could to take a look. That's why I didn't notice you sitting here.'

"The man begged for forgiveness, but the sannyasi was still angry. 'It was extremely impolite of you to disturb me when I was meditating on the Lord!' he said. At this, the man replied, 'You, who were meditating on God, were able to see me running by, but I couldn't see you sitting right in front of me as I ran in search of my son. It seems that your relationship with God isn't nearly as strong as the relationship I have with my child. What sort of meditation is that then? Also, if you don't have any patience or humility, what's the use of meditating?'

"Our meditation shouldn't be like that of the sannyasi in the story. When we sit for meditation, we should be able to focus our minds fully on our Beloved Deity. Whatever happens around us, the mind shouldn't turn to it. And even if it does, we should take care to bring it back immediately and bind it to the object of our meditation. If we practice this constantly, our minds won't wander anywhere.

"When you sit for meditation, make a decision that you won't open your eyes or move your limbs for a certain number of hours. Whatever happens, don't deviate from that decision. That's real vairagya."

Br: "Amma, many thoughts creep in and create a lot of restlessness. Sometimes I feel that all I want is to see God and to love Him with all my heart. At other times I want to learn the secrets of the universe; I want to unravel them by doing sadhana. At other times, I don't want any of this. All I want, then, is to know the Power that is working within me. Because of these different thoughts, there is no stability in my sadhana."

Mother: "When you discover the Self, don't you think you will spontaneously understand all those secrets? What if, in your search to uncover the hidden secrets, you become immersed in them? When you travel in a bus, you see all the sights pass by and disappear. In the same way, all that you see today will disappear. So don't pay any attention to those mysteries or create any attachment to them. Many experts are trying to learn the secrets of the universe, but so far they haven't succeeded, have they? But if you realize God, you will understand the whole universe. So whatever time you have, use it for realizing God. Thinking about anything else is useless."

WORSHIPPING A FORM

Br: "Amma, is God within or without?"

Mother: "It is only because you have body-consciousness that you think in terms of within and without. In reality, there is no inside or outside. Isn't it because of your sense of 'I' that you think of 'I' and 'you' as being separate? However, as long as the sense of 'I' persists, we can't say that the separation is unreal. God is the vital power that pervades everything. When you visualize Him outside of yourself, you should know that you are in fact visualizing what is within you. Nevertheless, it is through such means that the mind is purified."

Br: "There is a special power guiding the universe, but it's hard to believe that it's a God with a certain form."

Mother: "All forms of power are none other than God. He is the all-powerful One who controls everything. If you accept that He is the power behind everything, why can't that power, which controls everything, assume a form that the devotee likes? Why is that difficult to believe?" With great firmness in Her voice Mother continued, "There is a primeval Power in this universe. I look upon that Power as my Mother. That Power is my Mother, and even if I choose to be born again a hundred times, She will continue to be my Mother and I will be Her child. So I cannot make statements such as God has no form.

"It's difficult for most people to keep their minds steady without a chosen deity. You should try to cross to the other side using your Beloved Deity as a bridge. You can't do without it—you can't swim across. What will you do if you lose your strength half way across? You need a bridge. The guru will be with you to show you the way through any struggle or crisis—you should have that faith and surrender. So why struggle unnecessarily? But don't sit idly just because there is someone there to guide you and take you to the other shore. You have to work hard.

"When water is leaking into the boat, it's not enough to just sit there praying to God for the hole to be plugged. While you pray, you have to try to stop the leak yourself.

You have to make the effort and, at the same time, pray for God's grace."

Br: "How long will it take me to get Self-realization?"

Mother: "Son, realization is not that easy to attain, because you have accumulated so many negative tendencies. What happens when we wash our clothes after a long journey? We haven't got down anywhere on the way, we haven't sat in the dirt anywhere, yet there is so much dirt on our clothes when we wash them! In the same way, dirt accumulates in your mind without you being aware of it. You have come here carrying with you not only what you have accumulated in this life, but also in your past lives. You can't possibly realize the Self by simply sitting with your eyes closed for one or two years. That is not enough to purify you within.

"First you have to cut down the forest and clean away the undergrowth; only then can you plant a tree of your own there. If your mind is not yet purified, how can you possibly see the Self? We can't put a coating on a dirty glass and turn it into a mirror. First the mind needs to be cleansed. And as you make that effort, you have to surrender everything to God."

The brahmachari prostrated to Mother and got up. Mother finished eating and, after reading a few more letters, went downstairs for the bhajan program that always preceded the bhava darshan.

A gentle rain began at dusk. The rain grew stronger as the night progressed, and by the time the bhava darshan ended at two in the morning, it was pouring down. The devotees took shelter in the Vedanta school and on the verandah of the kalari. People slept wherever they could. As Mother came out of the kalari after the Devi bhava, She noticed that many of the devotees had been unable to find a place to sleep. She led them to the huts of the brahmacharis, while Gayatri attempted to protect Mother from the rain by holding an umbrella over Her. Mother arranged for three or four people to sleep in each hut. As She assigned each devotee a place, She dried the person's head with a towel. In the flow of Her motherly love, they all turned into little children.

"Amma, where will the brahmacharis sleep? Aren't we causing them a lot of trouble?" a devotee asked.

Mother: "They are here to serve you. Those children have come here to learn selflessness. They will be glad to bear a little inconvenience for you."

The brahmacharis went to the kalari mandapam to sit there until dawn. Three sides of the verandah were open, and gusts of wind blew the rain in, making it impossible to go to sleep. At least they wouldn't have to wait long for dawn.

Mother then spotted four elderly devotees who had yet to find somewhere to sleep. She led them to a room on the north side of the kalari. The door was closed. Mother knocked, and two sleepy-eyed brahmacharis opened the door. They had gone to bed before the end of darshan and had been fast asleep, unaware of everything.

"Children, let these people sleep here." So saying, Mother entrusted the devotees to the two brahmacharis and then She went to Her room. The brahmacharis gave their beds to the devotees and then went to the verandah of the meditation room and sat down close to the door where they were not exposed to the rain, which had abated a little.

All the brahmacharis had come to live in the presence of the One who was the embodiment of selflessness. They had surrendered their lives to Her. And now, at every moment, She was teaching them how to conduct their lives.

Thursday, August 7, 1986

VAIRAGYA

At about two-thirty in the afternoon, Mother returned from the darshan hut to Her room to find brahmacharini Saumya[53] waiting for Her. For the past several days, Saumya, who was originally from Australia, had been hoping to speak to Mother, and Mother had asked her to come that day. Mother sat on the floor, and Saumya placed Mother's lunch in front of Her.

Saumya: "For some time, I have been wanting to ask

---

[53] Swamini Krishnamritaprana

Mother a number of questions. May I ask them now?"

Mother: "All right, daughter, ask."

Saumya: "When I feel an attachment towards something, I decide not to acquire it or accept it. Is that vairagya (detachment)?"

Mother: "If being attached to that thing would lead to what is unreal, then your attitude is vairagya.

"We need to know the real nature of each object. We need to realize that material things cannot give us true happiness. Even though we may receive temporary satisfaction from them, they will only lead to suffering in the end. When we understand this fully, our passion for sense objects will automatically diminish. Then we can easily disengage the mind from such things.

"A man who had a craving for payasam was invited to a friend's birthday party. The main item of the feast was, in fact, payasam. So he was very happy. He got a bowl full of the sweet rice pudding and tasted a little. It was excellent. The rice was cooked with just the right amount of milk and sugar, and with cardamom, raisins, and cashew nuts added. As he was about to take another spoonful, a gecko fell from the ceiling into his bowl! Although he dearly loved payasam, he threw it all out. The instant he knew that the gecko had fallen into it, making it unfit to eat, he lost all interest in the pudding. In the same way, once we understand that being dependent on the senses will only bring us suffering, we'll be able to avoid even those things that normally hold great appeal for us. We'll find it easy to control the mind. That is vairagya. Seeing a cobra, a child who is unaware of how poisonous it is may try to catch it, but we wouldn't do that, would we?

"Daughter, it is better to develop detachment towards things by learning about their good and bad qualities, rather than turning the mind away from them by force. Then control of the mind will come naturally."

Saumya: "It seems to me that real happiness comes from detachment, and not from depending on objects, accumulating or enjoying them."

Mother: "Do you think happiness comes from detachment? No, it doesn't. Happiness is born out of supreme love. What you need in order to realize the Self, or God, is love. Only through love will you experience complete detachment."

Saumya: "Then we don't have to renounce anything?"

Mother: "Tyaga (renunciation) isn't enough. Do you feel any peace of mind when you are angry with someone? Isn't it true that you feel totally at peace only when you love? You feel happy when you enjoy the fragrance of a flower. Would you experience that same joy if you closed your nostrils? Don't you enjoy the taste of sugar most when you let it linger in the mouth? Does that happiness come from vairagya towards sugar? No, it comes from love.

"When you see excrement, you hold your nose. That is aversion. There's no love in that, nor is there any happiness. You can call it vairagya when you renounce worldly things, thinking, 'All the joy I get from outside of myself is transitory and will later cause me suffering. The happiness I get from worldly objects isn't permanent, it's momentary and therefore unreal.' To experience real happiness, however, it isn't enough to renounce the illusory things of the world with vairagya; you also have to attain what is real, through love. This is the way to eternal bliss.

"You don't have to hate the illusory world. You can learn from the unreal world how to reach the real, eternal world. What we want is the everlasting world, and only through love can we expand towards that state. When the moon rises, all the waters of the lakes and oceans on earth rise towards it out of love. The flower blooms to enjoy the touch of the wind, and this, too, is out of love. So what gives us bliss? Not detachment, but love."

Saumya (with some uneasiness): "I don't want the happiness that comes from loving something."

Mother: "What a seeker loves is not something that is separate from himself. He loves his own Self, which pervades everything around him. The more his love for the eternal grows, the stronger becomes his urge to know the eternal. Thus, when we love the eternal, real vairagya develops.

"Suppose we come to know that a friend who lives far away is on his way to see us. From the moment we learn that he is coming and that we can expect him at any moment, we wait for him, forgoing both food and sleep. Isn't it out of our love for him that we wait without bothering to eat or sleep?"

Saumya: "What should come first, restraint or love?"

Mother: "Real restraint arises out of love. Without love, that restraint cannot come into being. Restraint without love will never last for long, because the mind will tire and revert to its original state. As soon as we heard that our friend was on his way, we gave up food and sleep in our eagerness to see him. This came out of our love for him; our restraint came naturally, and because of our love, it didn't seem like a hardship or sacrifice at all. But if there is no love, the restraint will feel like a terrible hardship. If we forgo a meal because of some restrictions we. have imposed upon ourselves, we will think of nothing but food.

"To be detached towards something, you need to love something else. Daughter, it is only because you have a feeling of love for the goal of Self-realization that you are able to live here with an attitude of patience and acceptance. People have desires, anger, greed, jealousy, and pride within them. How, then, is it possible for a few people to control those negative qualities and live here with an attitude of forgiveness and forbearance? You do it only out of your love for Self-realization. Otherwise, all of those negative traits would come out. But because of that love, those traits cannot live and thrive in your mind. Your love for the Goal restrains all such traits."

Saumya: "If so, why do you have to be so strict about keeping the ashram rules? Wouldn't that happen spontaneously?"

Mother: "Amma didn't say that you don't need vairagya. You should practice vairagya, but only through love is it made complete. In the beginning, restrictions are absolutely essential. There are about thirty renunciates here now. Each one desires realization, but their minds are the slaves of their bodies. They want knowledge of the Self, but they find it difficult to forgo the comforts of the body. So it becomes necessary to impose some rules.

"If someone has to go somewhere early in the morning but can't wake up, we have to wake them up, don't we? Say that a child wants to see the sunrise, but being under the spell of bodily comfort it can't get up in the morning. The mother will wake the child up.

"You should be up and alert, ready to meet the Divine Dawn. Time won't wait for you. But my children are not doing their duty. If they are not alert, Mother has to awaken them. Otherwise, She would be seriously deceiving them. Amma feels that Her strictness in this regard is Her greatest act of love toward Her children at the ashram."

RULES ARE IMPORTANT IN AN ASHRAM

Saumya: "Sometimes the rules of the ashram appear to be very strict."

Mother: "Rules are necessary in an ashram where many people live and where there is a large number of visitors. For instance, the boys and girls shouldn't talk to each other too freely. Those who live in the ashram have to set an

example for others. Also, all those living here are not of
the same nature. The children who have just arrived don't
have that much self-control yet. They have just begun
their sadhana. But the children who have been here from
the beginning have gained a certain amount of control
over their minds. The newcomers can bring their doubts
to them, there's nothing wrong with that. But Amma is
saying that there should be some limits. Talk only when
needed, no more than that."

Saumya: "We feel very alert on the days when you wake
us up, Amma!"

Mother: "Those children who love Amma and yearn
for realization will get up in the morning without waiting
for anyone to wake them up. When Amma returns to
Her room at night, She has to read many letters. Even
after that, She can't go to bed before inquiring whether
there are enough vegetables, rice, money, and so on, for
the next day. If there is a shortage of anything, She has
to give instructions regarding what to buy or what to do.
Also, She has to take care of the visitors, as well as consider the routine of the children here and take care of
their needs. After all this, how can She be expected to
come to the room of each of you and wake you up?

"If you love Amma, it is enough to follow Her words
carefully. To love Amma is to obey Her words. You must
feel a thirst. When you have a guru, your love for the
guru and his institution, and your relationship with your
guru will help you to forget all other things and to grow

towards the Infinite. Only when the seed merges with the soil, can it grow into a tree."

Saumya: "Amma, you don't usually scold me. Why is that?"

Mother: "Don't I? Don't I scold you in the kalari during Devi bhava?"[54]

Saumya: "Only a little."

Mother (laughing): "Daughter, in you Amma sees only the fault of not getting up early in the morning. You go to bed after working hard at night. And don't you also spend the whole Devi bhava standing on your feet in the kalari? Also, you're trying very hard to reach the goal of realization. You have the desire to follow the ashram routine regularly, and you never try to escape from it by hiding or slipping away. So there's no need to take you to task."

ELIMINATING FAULTS

Saumya: "There are both boys and girls living here. Isn't it your wish that we should be loving towards everyone?"

Mother: "It is not necessary to go up to everyone and show them your love; it's enough not to have any negative feelings—none whatsoever. Real love is the complete absence of any negative feelings towards anyone. By removing all such negative feelings, the love, which is ever

---

[54] Swamini Krishnamritaprana usually serves Mother during Devi bhava.

present within you, will shine forth. Then there are no distinctions, no sense of difference. Haven't you seen how those who loved each other yesterday, despise each other today? So their love was never real. Where there is attachment, there is also anger. Our aim is to have neither attachment nor anger. That is real love. Besides, we're doing selfless service, and that is the greatest love."

Saumya: "I'm trying not to have any negative feelings towards anyone."

Mother: "Attachment and aversion are not things that we can just pick up and discard. The bubbles in the water will break if we try to pick them up. We can't catch them. In the same way, it's not possible to just throw our thoughts and emotions out of our minds. If we try to suppress them, they'll grow twice as strong and create difficulties. It is only through contemplation that we can eliminate our negative emotions. We should examine our own negative tendencies and weaken them through good thoughts. They can't be eliminated by force.

"If we pour fresh water into a tumbler of saltwater, and continue to pour even after it is full, the saltiness will decrease, and finally we'll end up with a glass full of fresh water. Similarly, we can eliminate bad thoughts only by filling the mind with good thoughts. Emotions such as desire and anger cannot be uprooted, but we can take care not to give them any room in our minds. We should recognize that we are God's instruments, and develop the attitude of a servant.

"In fact, we should think of ourselves as beggars. A beggar comes to a house seeking bhiksha. The people in the house may say, 'There's no bhiksha here. Go away! What did you come to us for?' But no matter what they say, he doesn't open his mouth. He thinks, 'I am only a beggar. There is no one on this earth with whom I can share my sorrows. Only God knows my heart.' If he were to try to explain this to that family, they wouldn't understand—he knows that. So if someone gets angry with him, he walks away in silence and goes to the next house. If they, too, are angry, he again continues on to the next house, without complaint. This is what we should be like. As soon as we take on the attitude of a beggar, the ego greatly disappears. We will feel that we have no refuge other than God, and then the negative vasanas will fall off by themselves. Only by trying to become smaller than the smallest, does one become greater than the greatest. By developing the attitude of being everyone's servant, one becomes the master of the world. Only he who bows down even to a *shava* (corpse), becomes Shiva."

Saumya: "If we have something that someone here needs, is there anything wrong with giving it to them?"

Mother: "You shouldn't do that, daughter. You are a brahmacharini. You have come here to do sadhana. If you want to give something to someone, give it to the office, or give it to Amma, and Amma will give it to the person who needs it. If you give it directly, you'll have the attitude, 'I am giving,' and you'll develop some attachment to

that person. So don't give it yourself. When you reach the
stage of a guru, there is no longer a problem because no
other thoughts about the person to whom you are giving
will arise. At this stage, however, your love doesn't have
to be shown externally—it should be nurtured within you.
When there is no more aversion or hostility—that is love.
When every trace of aversion disappears from the mind,
the mind becomes Love itself. It becomes like sugar: anyone can come and take from it and enjoy its sweetness,
without you having to give anything.

"If a fly falls into syrup, it will die. At this stage, those
who come to you wanting something from you, with an
impure motive in mind, of which you are unaware, are
like flies. Approaching you won't benefit them at all. They
are only ruining themselves and it is harmful for you as
well.

"When a moth approaches a lamp, it is searching for
food. The lamp is meant to give light, but the moths come
to it wanting to eat it. They perish in the attempt, and
the lamp may be extinguished as well. So we shouldn't
give others the chance to ruin themselves and us. We are
full of compassion, but those who come to us may be very
different. In the future, when you're in a responsible position in an ashram or gurukula, some people may approach you with intentions that are not quite pure. If you
have made enough progress by then, their impure thoughts
will be destroyed by your love. A forest fire won't be af-

fected even if an elephant falls into it.[55] At this stage, however, your love will only cause the weaknesses of others to increase."

Saumya: "So we should have a lot of love within us, but not show it?"

Mother: "Amma isn't saying that you shouldn't show it, but that you should behave according to the ashram dharma. Always pay attention to the circumstances. If visitors see the brahmacharis and brahmacharinis talking to each other, they'll start imitating that. They are not aware of how pure your heart is. Besides, you don't have to talk to each other—love doesn't mean such things. Real love is not having any negative feelings within you, none whatsoever."

Saumya: "When we talk to each other here, it's about spiritual matters, about questions we have about the teachings."

Mother: "But people don't know that, daughter. What the onlookers see is a conversation taking place between a brahmachari and a brahmacharini. Whenever people see a man and a woman talking, they misinterpret it. That's what the world is like today."

(Because of her compassion, Saumya used to give everyone whatever they asked for. Many people visiting the ashram had begun asking her for money for the return bus fare. Mother had forbidden Saumya to continue giv-

---

[55] Here, the fire symbolizes the advanced sadhak, while the elephant represents the impure thoughts of others.

ing in this way because some people tried to exploit her. Asking residents for money was also against the ashram rules. Though this had upset Saumya at first, she was now satisfied with Mother's explanation.)

HOW TO DISCRIMINATE BETWEEN RIGHT AND WRONG

Saumya continued her questions:

"I have done some things thinking they were right, but it turned out that they were wrong, and I had no idea of this at the time. How can I tell right from wrong and act properly?"

Mother: "Follow Amma's words for now. Write down your feelings such as, 'I had this bad thought,' or 'I felt angry with so and so.' Then ask Amma to help you, and correct yourself.

"Amma tells the children here that in the beginning there shouldn't be any talking between brahmacharis and brahmacharinis. After a certain period of sadhana, however, it is no longer a problem. Amma isn't so strict in prohibiting Her western children from talking to each other, because they have come from a different world. In their culture, the same distinction between male and female doesn't exist."

Saumya: "When we get the right results from our actions, is it because we have the right mental attitude, or does it simply arise from the external action itself?"

Mother: "We get the right results because of the purity of our mental resolve. Still, we have to pay attention to the action itself and observe the result. Performing actions with a pure mental attitude requires practice."

Saumya: "Will God forgive us for the mistakes we have made?"

Mother: "He will forgive us up to a point, but not beyond that. He will forgive us for whatever mistakes we make unknowingly, because, after all, we aren't aware of those mistakes. But if we knowingly do what is wrong, He won't tolerate it beyond a certain point. Then He will punish us. The little baby calls its father 'da da.' The father knows that the baby is calling him, and he laughs. But if the child continues to call his father 'da da' when he is old enough to know better, his father won't laugh anymore; he'll spank him. In the same way, if we act erroneously, knowing full well that what we are doing is wrong, then God will certainly punish us. But even that punishment is a form of grace. God may punish a devotee even for a small mistake, so that he will never again commit a similar error. That punishment comes from God's boundless compassion for the devotee and is meant to save him. It's like a light in the dark.

"A boy was in the habit of jumping over a barbed wire fence to go to the neighbor's house. His mother said to him, 'Son, don't climb over the fence, because if you slip, you'll cut yourself. Go the normal way, even if it takes a little longer.' 'But nothing has happened to me so far!' the boy protested, and he continued to go the same way. Then one day, as he jumped over the fence, he fell and cut his foot. He cried and ran to his mother. She consoled him with great love, dressed his wound, and told him not to jump over the fence again. But the boy disobeyed her, and again he slipped, fell on the fence, and cut himself. Again, he ran crying to his mother. But this time she spanked him before putting medicine on his wounds.

"If the boy had felt some real pain the first time he fell, he wouldn't have repeated his mistake. The mother spanked him the second time he came crying to her, not out of anger, but out of love. Similarly, the punishment God gives us is His compassion and is meant to turn us away from any further wrongdoing.

"Many pencils have an eraser on one end, so that we can erase our mistakes right away. But if we keep making errors on the same spot and try to erase them, again and again, we'll end up tearing the paper."

Mother finished eating. She washed Her hands and sat down again.

Saumya: "When I'm thinking of something, it seems right at one moment, and then soon afterwards I think it may be wrong. I can't make a decision to do anything. I always have a doubt about what is right and what is wrong."

Mother: "If one can't distinguish between right and wrong, one should seek the advice of the guru or some other wise person. Then the right path will become clear. It's hard to make progress without surrendering to or having faith in a person who can lead us to the Goal. When we find such a soul, who can show us the right course of action, we should develop an attitude of surrender towards him and follow his advice. If we can't find such a person, we should try to learn about the goal of life and the path to be followed by reading spiritual books. If our yearning is sincere, we will certainly find a guru. But it isn't enough to have found a guru; if we are to progress, we must surrender to the guru completely. No progress can be made if we find fault with the guru when he points out our mistakes or reprimands us."

Saumya: "How do desires become obstacles to our spiritual practices?"

Mother: "Suppose a pipe leading to a faucet has many holes in it. The flow of water from the faucet will be weak. Similarly, if there are selfish desires in our minds, we won't get total concentration on God, and we will fail to come closer to Him. How can someone who can't even swim across a small river, swim across the ocean? It isn't possible to reach the supreme state without abandoning all selfishness."

Saumya: "Japa, meditation, and prayer—which of these practices removes vasanas most effectively?"

Mother: "All of these methods help us to overcome our vasanas. If we pray with total concentration, that alone is enough. But few people pray all the time, and they don't have one-pointedness of mind. This is why we use other methods such as japa, meditation, and devotional singing.

In this way we can keep the remembrance of God constantly alive. When we plant some seeds, we have to fertilize them, give them water regularly, protect them from animals, and destroy the worms and insects that attack them. All those actions are done to enhance the crop. Similarly, the different spiritual practices we do all serve to hasten our progress towards the Goal."

Saumya: "Amma asked me to chant 'Om Namah Shivaya' from seven o'clock till eight, so I can't take part in the bhajans."

Mother: "Don't worry, daughter. Amma will ask someone else to take that time-slot."

Mother looked at the clock on the wall. It was a quarter to five. She said, "It's soon time for bhajans. Let Amma take a bath now. Daughter, whenever you have any problems, you should come and tell Amma about it."

Saumya prostrated to Mother, her face aglow with the joy of having talked to Mother for so long, and having had her doubts cleared.

Shortly thereafter Mother went to the kalari, and the bhajans that always preceded the Devi bhava darshan began. The same Mother who, in the form of the Guru, had patiently sat for so long to answer the questions of Her disciple, now assumed the mood of a devotee pouring out the longing of Her heart into song. She sang with Her whole being, forgetting all else in the rapture of devotion.

Wednesday, August 20, 1986

CONQUER YOUR ANGER

At the ashram everyone had worked since morning without rest. It was now late afternoon. The work involved tidying up the ashram grounds and moving building material which was used for pouring concrete for the new building. Mother was helping to move some steel rods. Her white sari was covered with green algae from the damp rods.

A devotee who worked in Rajasthan had arrived the previous night. He had a bad temper and had been praying for Mother's help in overcoming his anger. Mother, who dwells within everyone, knew this. She turned to him with a smile and said, "My son, Amma feels that you have a little too much anger in you. When you get angry again, you should place a picture of Amma in front of you and scold Her. Say to Her, 'Is this anger what I get from worshipping you? You've got to remove it right away! If not, I will...' Then take a pillow and punch it, imagining it is Amma. If you wish, you can even throw dirt at Amma. But, son, don't get angry with others."

Mother's love brought tears to the man's eyes.

By dusk the work was almost done. Now Mother took part in carrying stones. When they saw Her lifting the biggest stone to Her head, Her children protested and tried to dissuade Her, asking Her to only take the smaller ones. But it pained Her to see Her children lifting the heavier stones. She said to them, "No physical pain is as terrible as mental pain."

Hard work turned into a form of worship. Each person tried to carry bigger loads than they could lift. Their sweat fell like flowers of worship at the feet of the Mother of the Universe—flowers that contained the golden seeds of a new age.

Saturday, August 23, 1986

Mother was sitting in the kalari mandapam with some householder devotees. Vijayalakshmi, a woman who had been married for about a year, was among them. A friend had recently brought her to meet Mother. She adored Mother from the first moment she met Her and had complete faith in Her. Though she had come regularly to see Mother ever since, her husband didn't have much faith in Mother. He had no interest in spiritual matters, but he didn't object to his wife visiting Mother. After meeting Mother, Vijayalakshmi stopped paying attention to her external appearance. She put away her ornaments and expensive saris, and wore only white clothes. Her husband objected to this, however, as he was a successful engineer and had a large circle of friends.

Mother: "Daughter, if you wear only white, will my son like it?"

Vijayalakshmi: "It doesn't matter, Amma. I have put

away all my other saris and blouses. I want to give them away to people in need. I have a lot of clothes that I don't need."

Mother: "Don't do anything like that right now, daughter! Don't do anything that will hurt your husband. You have a certain dharma, don't neglect it. Anyway, my son doesn't object to your coming here. Isn't that a great thing?"

Vijayalakshmi: "Amma, he has time for a hundred things, but he doesn't have time to come and see you even once. For years, I dressed up and went everywhere with him, but no more. I'm tired of all the pomp and show. This cotton sari and blouse are plenty for me."

Mother: "Don't talk like that, daughter. It's true that he doesn't come to Amma, but he nevertheless has a lot of devotion."

Vijayalakshmi: "What do you mean? He won't even go to a single temple. When I asked him to come with me to the Guruvayoor temple, he said, 'I decided when I was in college that I'd never put my foot in a temple. But because of you, I once had to break that vow. Because your family is so pious, I had to go against my own word.' Amma, I still have to listen to his complaint about the fact that we got married in a temple."

Mother laughed and said, "Daughter, he may not come here or go to any temple, but he has a good heart. He is compassionate towards the suffering, and that alone is enough. Daughter, don't do anything that he doesn't like."

Vijayalakshmi's face showed disappointment.

Mother: "Don't worry. Isn't it Amma who is telling you this? If you wear only white, he'll be upset. What will he tell his friends? So wear white when you come here, but when you are at home or go traveling with him, wear your usual clothes and ornaments. Otherwise people will blame Amma, won't they? Your husband is also Amma's son. Don't worry, daughter."

Vijayalakshmi had nothing to say in reply to this, but her expression showed that she accepted Mother's words.

PERFORMING ACTIONS

Now another devotee, Ramachandran, raised a question: "Many books say that in the ancient gurukulas, performing actions was given more importance than doing sadhana. Even though the *Upanishads* say that karma yoga alone will not lead to Self-realization, the gurus used to assign new disciples the task of tending cattle or cutting firewood for the first ten or twelve years. Why did they do that?"

Mother: "It is not possible to purify the mind without engaging in selfless action. What a spiritual person needs first of all is selflessness. The disciple was assigned certain duties to test how selfless he was. If he did the work with an attitude of selflessness and sacrifice, it showed the firmness of his resolve to reach the Goal.

"The disciple's attitude of surrendering to the guru's every word makes him the King of kings; it makes him the sovereign of all the three worlds.

"An aspirant needs to be tested properly before being accepted as a disciple in the true sense. A real master will accept a new disciple only after such tests.

"After all, someone who has gone around selling pea-nuts is about to be put in charge of the diamond store. It was all right if he lost a peanut, but a diamond is far more valuable. A spiritual person is meant to give peace and happiness to the world. It is the guru's duty to test and see whether the disciple has the shraddha and maturity re-quired for that; otherwise, the disciple will only cause harm.

"A young man once went to an ashram hoping to be-come a resident. The guru tried to dissuade him, telling him that the time had not yet come for him to join. But the young man refused to go home. Finally, the guru yielded. He assigned the new disciple the task of guarding an or-chard a short distance from the ashram.

"When the young man returned to the ashram at night after doing his duty all day, the guru asked him, 'What did you eat today?' The disciple replied, 'I ate a few apples from the trees.' The guru scolded him, 'Who told you to eat that!' The disciple kept quiet.

"Again, the disciple went to work the next day. This time he didn't pick any fruit from the trees, but ate only what had already fallen to the ground. In the evening, the guru scolded him again. The next day he ate no fruit at all. When he felt famished, he ate the berries from a wild plant. As it turned out, the berries were poisonous. He collapsed and lay in the orchard, unable to get up.

"As he lay there, he begged aloud for his guru's forgiveness. Hearing his cries, some disciples came and found
him. They offered him some water to drink, but he refused, saying that he wouldn't eat or drink anything without the guru's permission. At that point, God appeared
before him and said, 'I will give you your strength back
and take you to your guru.' The disciple replied, 'No, God!
I want you to give me strength only if my guru gives his
consent.' Because the disciple had reached that level of
surrender, the guru, himself, came to him and blessed him.
The disciple immediately regained his strength. He prostrated to the guru and stood up.

"This is the kind of test the gurus of old would give in
order to judge the qualifications of aspiring disciples."

PATIENCE

Ramachandran: "Amma, observing how you behave with
your children, one feels that your reprimand is more helpful
to their growth than your praise."

Mother: "To develop proper discipline and humility,
the disciple should feel both awe and devotion towards
the guru. In the beginning, small children learn their lessons out of fear of the teacher. By the time they reach
college, they study on their own initiative because they
have a goal in life.

"Patience is the one quality that is needed from beginning to end in spiritual life. The shell around the seed has

to break before the tree can emerge. Similarly, you have to get rid of the ego before you can know Reality. The guru will devise many tests to see whether the disciple has come to him out of a temporary surge of enthusiasm or out of real love for the Goal. Like surprise tests in school, the guru's tests will be given without any advance notice. It is the guru's duty to determine the extent of the disciple's patience, selflessness, and compassion. He will observe whether the disciple becomes powerless in certain situations, or whether he has the strength to survive various ordeals. Tomorrow the disciple is destined to lead the world. Thousands of people may come to him and put their trust in him. If those people are not to be deceived, the disciple must possess a certain amount of strength, maturity, and compassion. If he goes out into the world lacking these qualities, he will seriously betray the world.

"The guru puts the disciple through many trials to mold him. A guru once gave his disciple a big stone and asked him to sculpt an icon out of it. The disciple gave up food and sleep and within a short time he had created a statue. He placed it at the guru's feet, bowed with joined palms, and stood aside.

"The guru took one look at the statue and flung it away, breaking it into pieces. 'Is this how to make a statue?' he asked angrily. The disciple looked at the broken statue and thought, 'I worked on that statue for many days, without stopping to eat or sleep, and yet he didn't utter even a single word of praise.' Knowing his thoughts, the guru gave him another rock and asked him to try again.

"Very carefully the disciple made an even more beautiful statue than the last one and took it to the guru. This time he was certain that the guru would be pleased. But the guru's face turned red with rage the instant he saw the statue. 'Are you making fun of me? This one is even worse than the last one!' So saying, the guru threw the statue to the ground, and again it broke into pieces. The guru studied the disciple's face. The disciple stood with his head bowed in humility. He didn't feel angry; he felt sad. The guru gave him another rock and told him to make a new statue.

"Obediently, the disciple made a new statue with great care. It was very beautiful. Again he offered it at the guru's feet. The moment he put it down, the guru picked it up and flung it away, harshly berating the disciple. This time, however, the disciple felt neither resentful nor sad at the guru's response, because he had developed the attitude of total surrender. He thought, 'If this is my guru's will, that is fine; every one of my guru's actions is for my own good.' The guru gave him another rock, and the disciple received it with joy. He came back with another beautiful statue, and again the guru smashed it to pieces. But there was no change of emotion in the disciple whatsoever. The guru was pleased. He embraced the disciple, placed his hands on the disciple's head, and blessed him.

"A third person watching the guru's actions might have

wondered at how cruel the guru was, or he might have thought the guru was crazy. Only the guru and the disciple, who surrendered to him, could know what was really happening. Each time he broke the statue, the guru was actually sculpting a true image of God in the disciple's heart. What broke was the disciple's ego. Only a satguru can do this, and only a true disciple can taste the joy from it.

"The disciple should understand that the guru knows better than he what is good and bad for the disciple, and what is good and bad in general. One should never approach a guru for name and fame, but only with the purpose of surrendering the self. If we feel angry with the guru for not praising us or our actions, then we need to recognize that we are not yet qualified to be disciples. We should pray to the guru to remove that anger. We should understand that the guru's every action is for our own good.

"If the disciple in this story had left the guru, feeling that his work was not receiving the praise it deserved, the door to eternal bliss would have remained closed to him. The gurus assign their disciples different tasks to perform because they know that the disciples cannot gain patience and maturity through meditation alone. The qualities gained from meditation should be evident in one's actions. To experience peace only while meditating, and not at other times, is not a sign of true spirituality. We should be able to see every action as a form of meditation. Then *karma* (action) truly becomes *dhyana* (meditation)."

Vijayalakshmi: "A friend of mine recently received *mantra diksha* (mantra initiation) from the Ramakrishna ashram. Amma, what is the purpose of mantra diksha?"

Mother: "Milk doesn't turn into curd by itself. We have to put a small amount of curd into the milk to start the process. Only then will we get curd. Similarly, the mantra given by a guru awakens the spiritual power in the disciple.

"In fact, just as a son is given life from the seed of the father, the disciple lives by the prana of the guru. The prana that the guru infuses into the disciple and the resolve that he makes at the time of initiation help the disciple to attain perfection. During the initiation, the guru joins the disciple to the thread within him."

Vijayalakshmi: "Will you give me a mantra, Amma?"

Mother: "Next time you come, daughter."

Now a group of devotees came and joined the group and sat down around Mother. One of them mentioned a sannyasi who had recently attained *mahasamadhi* (left his body).

Devotee: "I went to see him being interred in a tomb. A cell was built, filled with salt, camphor, and sacred ash, and the body was interred in it."

Ramachandran: "Won't the body be eaten by worms even if it's put in salt and camphor?"

Another devotee: "I heard that Jnanadeva gave darshan to a devotee in a dream many years after he had attained mahasamadhi. In the dream Jnanadeva instructed the devotee to open the tomb containing his body. When he did so it was discovered that the roots of a tree had enveloped the body and were pressing against it. There was no sign of decay in the body. The tree roots were removed and the samadhi tomb was closed again."

Mother: "Once life is gone, what difference does it make? Do we feel sorry if worms grow in the excrement we discard? The body is just like that; it's perishable. Only the soul is permanent."

Now a devotee told Mother about a story he had read in a newspaper concerning the ashram. It was about the case of Shakti Prasad, a young man who had come to the ashram to become a brahmachari. Trying to force him to go back home, his Muslim father had filed a lawsuit in the High Court to prevent him from joining the ashram.

Mother whispered, "Shiva!" and then sat in silence for a little while. Finally, She continued with a laugh, "Let us tell the Ancient One. But He is in deep meditation and isn't touched by any of this. He has one more eye than everyone else, yet He doesn't seem to be looking at this. He doesn't come down to us, so we are the ones who have to struggle."

Devotee: "Amma, what do you mean by this?"

Mother: "Shiva's third eye is the eye of jnana, supreme knowledge. He is in jnana bhava. Nothing affects Him. Amma, on the other hand, is the Mother. She looks upon all beings as Her own children, and is moved by compassion."[56]

As Mother was talking, a brahmachari sat close to Her with tears streaming down his face. He was distressed because he had heard the news that Mother was leaving on a tour of the United States. He was not unhappy that Mother was making the visit—he just couldn't bear the thought of being separated from Her for three months. The news of Mother's foreign trip had spread gloom throughout the ashram. This was the first time Mother would be away from the ashram for such a long time. Even though the tour was still months away, many of the ashram residents burst into tears whenever they thought about it.

Mother turned towards the brahmachari and gently wiped his tears. She said to him, "My son, it is on such occasions that Mother will look and see who are the worthy ones among you. She wants to know whether you will maintain your lakshya bodha and discipline, even when She is far away."

It was a moment when Mother's motherly love yielded to Her duty as the Guru who instructs Her disciples. Yet even so, the divine stream of Her love seemed about to break its banks, because Her heart always melted at the sight of Her children's tears. Even Her role as the Guru was softened greatly by Her motherly affection.

---

[56] Shakti Prasad's father eventually lost the case. This was a Supreme Court landmark ruling in India, which now rules in favor of the individual's right to freely choose his religion.

Monday, August 25, 1986

Kuttan Nair from Cheppad was one of Mother's house-holder devotees. When he first met Mother, he had thought, like many others, that during Devi bhava the Divine Mother inhabited Mother's body. But as he watched Mother's actions after each Devi bhava, he gradually became convinced that the Divine Mother's presence always shone in Mother. After his eldest son Srikumar became a permanent resident of the ashram, Mother frequently visited Mr. Nair's home. Whenever She did, it was a festival for the children of that family. A room in the southwest corner of the house was set aside for Mother's use, and She often meditated in there. Whenever they visited, Mother and Her children sang bhajans in the family's puja room, and Mother also performed puja on such occasions.

Mother had agreed to visit the Nair's residence this morning on Her way to Kodungallur. It was already close to noon, however, and Mother and Her children had not yet arrived. Everyone at the Nair's had waited to eat in anticipation of Mother's arrival. Now, with the morning almost over, they concluded that Mother had decided not to visit them. What would they do with all the food that had been made for Mother and Her party?

Kuttan Nair went into the puja room and closed the door. He heard some shouting outside, but ignored it. He looked at Mother's picture and mentally complained, "Why did you raise our hopes in vain?"

Just then, Mother's voice rose outside like the clear peal of a bell.

"How could we have come earlier? Think of how difficult it is to get started on a trip even for a family with just two children! So many arrangements had to be made at the ashram, especially since we'll be gone for two days. Many things needed attention. The workers will be there and sand needed to be sieved. Also, the children who were left behind had to be consoled. So much had to be done…"

A brahmachari explained, "Amma came out of Her room at seven this morning and gave an early darshan to the devotees. She then joined us in carrying two boat loads of sand from the ferry to the ashram. By then it was eleven o'clock, and we were supposed to have left for Kodungallur in the morning. We left in a rush, without eating anything."

Nor was there time to eat now. Mother went directly to the puja room, sang a couple of kirtans, and performed puja. As She came out, the young children surrounded Her.

To them She said simply, "Amma will come again later. There's no time now." The children looked disappointed. These days, there was little chance to play with Amma like before. Mother caressed and consoled everyone and gave them sweets. Breakfast was packed and put in the van. After giving darshan to everyone there, Mother and Her disciples resumed their journey, planning to eat breakfast along the way.

Br. Balu was waiting for Mother at the outskirts of Ernakulam. He had come there the previous day on ashram business. He now told Mother that a devotee in Ernakulam was waiting for Her, hoping that She'd visit him at his home.

Mother: "How can we go there? The children in Kodungallur wanted Amma to come last Friday and Saturday, but we changed it to today because one of my children had to go back to Europe on Sunday. Tomorrow we have to go to Ankamali, so we changed the two-day program to a single day. If we don't reach Kodungallur as soon as possible, we'll be doing the people there an injustice. So we can't go anywhere else. We've already put food in the van, so we can eat somewhere along the way and save the time it would take to visit someone's home."

With the van on its way again, the brahmacharis wasted no time in putting their questions before Mother.

Brahmachari: "Amma, is it possible to reach the Goal solely through sadhana and satsang, without the help of a guru?"

Mother: "You can't learn how to repair a machine by just reading a book. You have to go to a repair shop and be trained under someone who knows the job. You have to learn from someone who is experienced. Similarly, you need a guru who can teach you about the obstacles you'll meet in the course of your sadhana, and the way to overcome those obstacles and reach the Goal."

Br: "The scriptures talk a lot about the obstacles in sadhana. Isn't it enough to read the scriptures and practice on that basis?"

Mother: "The label on a medicine bottle may give instructions about the dosage, but you shouldn't take the medicine without a doctor's direct guidance. The label gives only general instructions, but a doctor decides what particular medicine one should take, in what amounts, and how it should be taken, depending on each patient's constitution and state of health. If you take the medicine incorrectly, it may do more harm than good. Similarly, you can learn about spirituality and sadhana from satsang and from books to a certain extent, but when you are seriously engaged in spiritual practices, it could be dangerous without a guru. You cannot reach the Goal without a satguru."

Br: "Isn't it enough to have a guru? Is it necessary to be in the actual proximity of the guru?"

Mother: "Son, when we transplant a sapling from one place to another, we bring some of the soil from the original place along with it. This makes it easier for the plant to acclimatize to the new conditions; otherwise, it may be difficult for the plant to take root in the new soil. The guru's presence is like the soil from the original site which helps the plant to adapt. In the beginning, the seeker will find it difficult to follow his sadhana regularly, without interruptions. The guru's presence gives him the strength to overcome all obstacles and to stay resolutely on the spiritual path.

"Apple trees need a suitable climate in which to grow. We have to give them water and fertilizer at the right time, and destroy the pests that attack the trees. Similarly, in a gurukula, a sadhak is in the most appropriate environment for spiritual practices, and the guru protects him from all obstacles."

Br: "Isn't it enough if we just do the type of sadhana we like the most?"

Mother: "The guru prescribes the sadhana most suitable for the disciple. He decides whether we should follow contemplation or selfless service, or whether japa and prayer will be enough. Some people don't have the constitution suitable for yogic practices, and others cannot meditate for a long time. What will be the result if a hundred and fifty people board a bus meant to carry only twenty-five people? We cannot run a small blender in the same way as a large-scale grinder, because if we run it continuously for a long time, it will overheat and break down. The guru prescribes the spiritual practices appropriate for each person's physical, mental, and intellectual constitution."

Br: "But isn't it good for everyone to meditate?"

Mother: "The guru knows the state of our body and mind better than we do. He gives advice according to the qualifications of the aspirant. If you don't understand this and start doing sadhana according to some instructions that you've picked up from somewhere, you could lose your mental balance. Too much meditation will cause the head to overheat, and may also cause insomnia. The guru will advise each disciple, according to their nature, which part of the body to focus on during meditation, and for how long they should meditate.

"If we are going somewhere and we travel with a companion who lives there and knows the way, we can easily reach our destination. Otherwise, a trip that should take only an hour may take ten. Even if we have a map, we may lose our way, and we could also fall into the hands of robbers. But if we travel with someone who knows the way, we don't have anything to fear. The role of the guru in our spiritual practices is similar to this. There may be obstacles at any stage of our sadhana, and it will then be difficult to continue without a guru. Being in the presence of a satguru is the real type of satsang."

As Mother was talking to them about spiritual matters, Her children were hardly aware of the passage of time. But Mother knew better than they how hungry they were. "What time is it, children?" She asked.

"Three o'clock, Amma."

"Stop the van when you see a place in the shade."

They stopped for lunch on the roadside and sat under a tree. The brahmacharis recited the fifteenth chapter of the *Gita*. Even while traveling, Mother insists on keeping the custom of reciting the *Gita* before eating. Then She served everyone lunch, consisting of rice and *chamandi* (coconut chutney). Water was fetched from a nearby house.

While they were eating, a couple on a scooter sped past them. Pointing to the couple, Mother asked, "Do you wish to travel like that with someone? Amma isn't saying that you won't have such desires, but if such a desire comes, you should get rid of it immediately through contemplation. You can imagine throwing your fantasy woman into a deep ditch as you drive along. Then she won't come back!" Mother burst out laughing.

DARSHAN ON THE ROADSIDE

Because the road was in very poor condition, some of the brahmacharis suggested that they take an alternate route going through a town called Alwaye. But Mother disagreed. So they stayed on the route She had picked. A little further ahead, they saw some people waiting for Mother on the roadside. Perhaps it was for their sake that Mother had chosen not to go the other way.

"Amma, stop here a little before you go on," the people requested.

"O my darling children, there's no time! But next time," Mother said with great tenderness, and they yielded to Her words. As Mother's van was about to drive on, a woman came running from a distance, pleading for the van to wait.

Woman: "Amma, I made coffee for the brahmacharis at ten o'clock this morning. I have been waiting here the whole time. I just had to go home for a minute. Amma, please step into my house for a moment before you go!"

Mother pointed out that it was very late and therefore She couldn't stop.

Woman: "You must, Amma! Please! You can just come in for a moment!"

Mother: "We promised we'd reach Kodungallur by three o'clock, and it's already four. Another time, daughter. Amma will be going to Kodungallur again."

Woman: "Then please wait here for just a minute. I've kept milk for you in a flask and will send my son to get it. At least drink that before you go!"

Mother yielded to the request which was made with such obvious devotion, and the woman sent the boy running to fetch the milk. Meanwhile, an old woman standing next to the van put a garland around Mother's neck. Taking hold of her hands, Mother blessed her. The old woman's eyes welled with tears of devotion.

By this time, the boy returned with the milk. His mother poured it into a glass and handed it to Mother. Only then did the woman remember the plantains she had cooked for the brahmacharis. Again, she made her son run home. She let Mother leave only after the plantains were put in the van. Devi is indeed the slave of Her devotees!

They reached Kodungallur at five o'clock and the bhajans started at seven. As always, Mother's sweet singing raised tides of devotion in the atmosphere.

Tuesday, September 2, 1986

Mother was in the darshan hut receiving visitors. A doctor and his family had come from Kundara. The doctor's young daughter was sitting next to Mother, meditating.

Mother was talking about the ruckus raised against the brahmacharis the previous day by one of the ashram's neighbors.

Mother: "Yesterday, the children got to hear some real Vedic mantras! Our neighbor didn't spare any words. Not wanting to listen to it, the children here played a bhajan tape very loudly. They couldn't talk back to the neighbor, could they? After all, they are wearing this garb."

Mother turned to the brahmacharis and said, "We are beggars, children! Beggars will bear everything they hear. This is the attitude we need now. If we lose our discrimination when we hear a few words from a neighbor, and we then make a lot of noise ourselves, we will lose our peace of mind. Is the power we have gained from doing sadhana for so long to be squandered on such a trivial matter? If we don't pay any attention to the neighbor, his words will stay with him. His words can affect us only if we take them seriously. God is testing us through his words. God is giving us a chance to judge how well we have assimilated what we have learned—that we are not this body, mind, or intellect. What can that man's words do to us? Does our mental peace and tranquility depend on other people?

"Would he behave like that towards a ruffian? He dared behave so badly towards these children because they really are as gentle as little children. Do you know what they said? They said, 'Amma, even though he made a row and kept calling us names, we didn't feel like answering him back. We felt as if a deranged person were talking, and who would take the words of a madman seriously?'"

The doctor started speaking: "The family living next to our hospital won't even give anyone a drop of water to drink. Even when we say that we ourselves will draw the water from the well with a rope and a bucket, they won't let us. They say we will stir up the mud in the well if we do that. They won't even give the patients in the hospital any water. How sad that there are people with such wicked minds!"

Mother: "Let us pray that they may become better persons."

Doctor: "God turns the water from the ocean into rain for us. It is sad when someone claims ownership of that water."

Mother (looking at the doctor's daughter): "My daughter has been meditating from the moment she sat down. What has happened to her?"

Doctor: "Amma, the first time she saw you, you said to her, 'You should meditate; then God will make you so intelligent that you'll do very well in your studies.' She has been meditating every day since then." Mother smiled and gazed lovingly at the girl.

A woman prostrated and got up. Mother asked, "Daughter, did you come because my son, Satish, told you about Amma?"

The woman's eyes opened wide with wonder. Then she began to cry uncontrollably. Mother wiped her tears. When she had calmed down a little, the woman said, "Yes, Amma. I come from Delhi. I went to Sivagiri and met Satish there. It was from him that I learned about Amma and the way to get here. As I prostrated to you, I was wondering in my mind whether you would be able to tell me his name, and as soon as I got up, you did!"

Mother laughed innocently, like a child, and the woman sat down next to Mother's cot.

MEDITATION BESIDE THE BACKWATERS

A few brahmacharis had gone to Ernakulam to shop for supplies. It was now late at night, and they had not yet returned. Mother sat at the edge of the backwaters waiting for them, and the brahmacharis sat around Her. When someone from the ashram went on a trip and failed to return on time, Mother usually waited for them at the boat jetty, no matter how late it might be. Only after their return would She retire for the night.

A motor-boat sped past them on the backwaters, raising waves that splashed against the shore. The sound soon faded.

Mother: "They may come back very late, so don't sit

idly, children. Meditate." Everyone gathered closer around Mother.

Mother: "Let us first chant Aum a few times. When you chant Aum, imagine that the sound begins at the *muladhara* and rises to the *sahasrara*, and then spreads throughout the body, finally dissolving into silence."

Mother chanted Aum three times. Each time She paused a little before chanting again, so that everyone could respond and chant after Her. The sacred syllable rose like the sound of a conch being blown, echoed in the stillness of the night, and slowly dissolved into silence. Everyone settled into meditation. Everything was quiet except for the rumbling of the nearby sea and the breeze blowing through the palm trees.

About two hours slipped by. Again, they all chanted Aum together. Mother sang a kirtan and the group sang each line after Her.

Adbhuta charitre...

O you, to whom the celestials bow,
Whose tale is full of wonders,
Grant me the strength to be devoted to your Feet.
I offer you all the actions I have done
In the darkness of ignorance.
O Protector of the distressed, forgive me
For all the actions I have done out of ignorance.

O Ruler of the Universe,
O Mother, please shine in my heart
Like the rising sun at dawn.
Let me see everyone as equal—
Free me from any sense of difference.

O Great Goddess,
Cause of all actions, both sinful and virtuous,
O Liberator from all bondage,
Give me your sandals
Which protect the basic virtues
On the path of Liberation,
The path of dharma.

As soon as the song ended, they heard the sound of a car horn from the other shore, and the headlights of a van appeared.

Mother immediately got up. "Children, is that our van?" She asked. Before long, the boat carrying the brahmacharis came gliding through the water and reached the ashram shore. The returning brahmacharis were overjoyed to see Her waiting up for them. They jumped out of the boat and prostrated eagerly as though they hadn't seen Her for weeks.

As they unloaded the boat, Mother asked, "Didn't my son, Ramakrishnan, come back with you?"

"He'll be back shortly. He had to take a man to the hospital. On the way back, a group of people stopped the van and brought a man who had been stabbed in a fight. They wanted us to take him to the hospital. At first, we said we had to ask you, Amma; but no other vehicle was available, so Ramakrishnan drove him to the hospital."

Mother: "In such circumstances, you needn't ask Amma. If anyone comes to you who is sick or injured, you should try to get them to the hospital straight away. There's no need to see whether it's a friend or foe. If we can't help people in such situations, when can we?"

It was two-thirty in the morning when Ramakrishnan finally returned. Only then did Mother go to Her room.

Sunday, September 14, 1986

The ashram premises were in complete disarray because of the ongoing construction of the new building. Bricks and rocks were scattered everywhere. Even if the residents tried to put everything in order, the next day the mess would be as bad as ever. Mother disliked seeing the ashram untidy, so whenever She came out of Her room nowadays, She started tidying up.

Today Mother came down early and asked the brahmacharis to bring shovels and baskets. They started moving a large pile of sand lying in a corner of the courtyard to a distant spot. Mother tied a towel round Her head and began to fill the baskets. She worked with great vigor and Her enthusiasm spread to the others as well.

Noticing that a brahmachari was talking incessantly during the work, Mother said, "Children, don't talk while you work. Chant your mantra! This isn't just work, it's sadhana. Whatever type of work you are doing, keep chanting mentally if possible. Only then will it be karma yoga. It isn't enough to read about living a spiritual life, or to hear about it, or to just talk about it—you have to put it into practice. That is why we need to do this sort of work. The mind shouldn't be away from God even for a minute."

Mother began to sing, and everyone joined in.

> *Nanda Kumara Gopala...*
>
> *O Son of Nanda, Protector of the cows*
> *Beautiful Boy of Vrindavan*
> *O Enchanter of Radha*
> *Dark-hued Gopala*
> *O Gopala, who lifted up the Govardhana Hill*
> *And who plays in the minds of the Gopis...*

The sand pile disappeared in minutes. Next, the tasks of washing the gravel and grading the sand began in two separate corners.

A devotee who had come with his family wanted Mother to conduct the anna prasana of his baby boy. After finishing the work She was doing, Mother walked to the kalari with the family, where preparations for the ceremony had already been completed. Mother placed the baby in Her lap. She put sandalwood paste on his forehead and poured flower petals on his head, and then performed a camphor arati for the baby. She sat holding the little boy, caressing him and feeding him rice. Seeing all this, one might have thought She was Yashoda feeding and playing with Baby Krishna. For Mother, this was not just any baby; it was none other than the Darling Child of Ambadi.

When Mother came out of Her room during meditation time that evening, two brahmacharis were engaged in a heated debate outside the meditation hall. Mother stood listening to them. Being immersed in the debate, they were completely unaware of Her presence.

Br: "The ultimate Truth is advaita (non-duality). There is nothing but Brahman."

Second Br: "If there is nothing but Brahman, what is the basis of the universe that we experience?"

First Br: "Ignorance. The universe is a product of the mind."

Second Br: "If there aren't two entities, who is affected by the ignorance? Brahman?"

"Children!" Mother called. Turning around quickly, they saw Mother and fell silent.

Mother: "Children, it is fine to talk about advaita, but in order to experience it, you have to do sadhana. What's the use of being the keeper of someone else's wealth? Instead of wasting time arguing, you should be meditating at this hour. That is the only wealth you have. You should do japa constantly. That's the only way to achieve anything, to evict the impostor (individual ego) that has taken up residence within you.

"The honeybee looks for honey wherever it goes. Nothing else can attract it. But a common fly prefers to stick to excrement even in a rose garden. Even now our minds are like common flies. That has to change. We have to develop a mind that seeks only the good in everything, just like the honeybee that seeks only the honey wherever it goes. Arguments will never help us to attain this, children! We have to try to put into practice what we have learned.

"Non-duality is the truth, but we have to bring it into our lives. We should be able to stand firm in that truth in any situation."

MOTHER CONSOLES A BLIND YOUTH

Mother walked to the guest house where a young blind man was staying, and entered his room. As soon as he realized Mother was there, he prostrated at Her feet. He had been staying at the ashram for a few days. At this moment he was very upset.

From the day he had arrived at the ashram, the brahmacharis had taken care of him. They had accompanied him to the dining room and helped him with his daily personal needs. On this day, many devotees had arrived for lunch, and the rice was quickly eaten. More rice was cooked. Because of the crowd, the brahmachari who was supposed to assist the blind youth had been unable to go and escort him to the dining room at the beginning of lunch. When the brahmachari finally did go to fetch him, he saw the young man coming down the steps with the aid of a devotee. "Please forgive me," said the brahmachari. "In the rush, I forgot to come and fetch you earlier. There's such a large crowd here today, and there's no rice left. More rice is being cooked and will be ready soon."

But the young man was unable to forgive the brahmachari. "I have money. Why should it be a problem getting rice when I can pay?" Saying this, the young man returned to his room. Though he had spoken so roughly, the brahmachari ascribed this to the young man's hunger. He fetched some fruit and brought it to the young man's room. "The rice will be ready soon," said the brahmachari. "I'll bring it to you. Meanwhile, please eat this fruit." But the young man shouted at him and refused the fruit.

Mother went to the guest house when She heard about this. To the brahmachari She said sternly, "How careless you are! Why didn't you give this son his food on time? Don't you realize that he can't see, and that he can't come to the dining room by himself? If this child wasn't blind, he would have gone to eat as soon as the bell rang. If it would have taken too much time to fetch him because you were busy, you could have brought his food to the room. If you can't be compassionate towards people like him, who will ever receive any compassion from you?

"Children, don't waste a single chance you get to serve the devotees. There may not always be someone to receive your help at your convenience. The service you render to people like this is real worship."

Gently stroking the young man's back, Mother said, "Did it upset you, son? It was only because of his workload that he couldn't come and fetch you when the bell rang for lunch. The brahmachari who normally helps you to the dining hall isn't here today, and the other son to whom he had entrusted the responsibility of looking after you went to help those who were serving lunch, because there was such a big crowd. He forgot about you because he was so absorbed in his work. That is why no one came for you on time. So don't think it was deliberate, son.

"Wherever you are, you have to adapt to the circumstances. We need patience for everything. Here at the ashram we have an opportunity to learn to live with a spirit of sacrifice. Only then can we receive God's grace. Son, you should understand that this is an ashram. If you see any deficiencies in others, you should forgive them; that is an expression of your real bond with Amma and the ashram."

The young man burst into tears. With great tenderness, Mother wiped his tears and asked, "Did you eat anything, my son?" He shook his head. Mother asked a brahmachari to bring some food, which was now ready. She then sat on the floor and, taking the young man's hand, pulled him towards Her and made him sit close to Her. The brahmachari brought a plate full of rice and curries. Mother made balls of rice and fed the young man with Her own hands. Basking in Her love, he turned into a little child. She fed him all the food that was on the plate. She then made him get up, guided him to the water tap and helped him wash his hands. Finally She brought him back to his room.

Each beat of his heart must have been declaring aloud, "Though I have no eyes, today I have seen Mother with the eyes of my heart!"

Monday, September 15, 1986

ONAM FEAST AT THE ASHRAM

The Onam festival is a day of great joy for the people of Kerala. It is a day when family members traditionally come together to celebrate. From all corners of the country, Mother's children had been arriving to spend Onam with Her. Many small children had come with their parents. Mother was playing with the children. The boys and girls held hands and formed a circle around Mother, imprisoning Her. Normally a swing would be set up several days in advance, and Mother would swing on it with the children during Onam. But this time there was no swing. Because of the construction of the new building, there was no place to set it up. But now, seeing all the children together, Mother wanted a swing for them. So brahmacharis Nedumudi and Kunjumon quickly attached a beam between two pillars erected for the new building, and hung a swing from it. The children made Mother sit on it and then pushed Her on the swing, to everyone's delight.

Mother also took part in the preparation of the Onam feast for Her children. She cut vegetables, helped get the cooking fires blazing, and generally oversaw everything. At noon Mother made all the small children sit in the northwest corner of the dining room and, sitting in their midst, She made them chant "Aum." Mother would chant it first and they would respond. For a little while the surroundings reverberated with the sacred sound. Arising from the unblemished hearts of the children, the sound filled the atmosphere with a refreshing sweetness.

Next, Mother asked that banana leaves be spread as plates in front of the children. All the food was ready but had not yet been transferred to the serving vessels, nor had the pappadams been fried. But Mother was in a hurry to feed the young children, so She put the different foods in little containers and started serving them. Not satisfied with that, She bent down in front of each child, made balls from the rice on their banana plates, and fed each child with Her own hands.

By the time Mother finished feeding the little ones, Her grown-up children (the householders and brahmacharis) had taken their seats in the two adjoining rooms. Now Mother served them as well. It was for this moment that Her householder children had left their families behind and had come to Her. By serving them with Her own hands, Annapurneswari[57] delighted them all.

While eating, someone exclaimed, "Ayyo! (Oh no!)" Perhaps he had bit into a chili. Hearing this, Mother said, "No matter what happens to them, small children never say 'ayyo!' They'll only call out, 'Amma!' This 'ayyo!' creeps in as we get older. Whatever our age or circumstances, God's name should be on our tongue before anything else. For this, the mind needs practice, which is why we are told to chant the mantra constantly. You children should train your minds to say, 'Krishna!' or 'Shiva!' instead of 'Ayyo!' when you stub your toe or when anything else happens to you."

A woman devotee: "It is said that when we say, 'Ayyo!' we are calling the god of death."

Mother: "That is true, because whenever we are not uttering God's name, we are getting closer to death. Uttering anything other than God's name is an invitation to death. So if we don't want to die, we just have to chant God's name continuously!" Mother laughed.

After serving Her children payasam, She gave them lemon wedges, making use of even this occasion to sow the seeds of spirituality in their minds: "Children, payasam

---

[57] The Divine Mother in Her aspect as the Giver of food.

and lemon are like devotion and knowledge. The lemon helps you to digest the payasam. In the same way, knowledge helps you to imbibe devotion with the proper understanding of its principles. You have to have wisdom if you want to taste devotion fully. But knowledge without devotion is bitter; it has no sweetness. Those who say, 'I am everything,' rarely have any compassion. Devotion contains compassion."

Mother did not forget to ask everyone individually if they had eaten. Like the matriarch of a large clan, She paid attention to every detail concerning Her children. One family that usually arrived early for Onam came late this year. Mother asked them what had kept them so late and also inquired about their children's studies.

After the meal, the brahmacharis and householder devotees started cleaning up the ashram. Because of the ongoing construction work, the ashram grounds were very cluttered, and the cleanup work continued into the evening. After bhajans Mother also joined the crew. They filled the holes and ditches in front of the construction site with soil and covered the area with clean, white sand. All this was done in preparation for Mother's birthday, which was only a week away. Thousands of devotees were expected that day.

Following dinner, more people came and gathered around Mother. Mother talked to them for a while, and then lay down on the sand with Her head resting in the lap of a woman devotee. Mother looked at Markus, a young man from Germany, and laughed. "Look at his head!" She said.

Markus was quite bald. Only a thin wreath of blond hair surrounded the vast expanse of clear space on his head. "Work, work—always working, whether in rain or shine, night or day." Mother said, referring to Markus.

Markus: "All the land is being used for the birthday celebration. There is no more land left. (Touching his head) Now this is where we'll do our farming." Everyone laughed.

A devotee: "Is it because there's a lot of dirt in there?" At this, Mother joined the others in the laughter. Markus was also laughing.

Another devotee: "That is what is called Chertala!"[58]

A brahmachari returning from visiting his family prostrated and sat down next to Mother. Mother said to him, "Son, didn't Amma tell you when you were about to leave that She would serve you payasam if you came back to-day?"

Br: "But there can't be any payasam left, Amma. All the food that was served at noon must be gone by now."

Mother: "God will bring some. Would He allow Amma's word to be false?"

At that moment, a family from Kollam, who had arrived a little while earlier, came up to Mother and presented Her with a dish of payasam, which they had brought with them. Mother served it to the brahmachari and to

---

[58] Chertala is a coastal town north of the ashram. The word literally means 'dirt-filled head' in Malayalam (*cher*: dirt, *tala*: head).

all the others. She, Herself, ate just a few cashew nuts from the dish. A child picked them out of the payasam and gave them to Mother.

Mother: "Amma doesn't really like cashew nuts that much. There are a lot of them in Her room that the children have brought. Amma doesn't usually eat them, but sometimes Amma likes to taste the cashew nuts in payasam or in certain curries." Mother picked a grape, a cardamom, and a piece of cashew nut out of the payasam and put them in the palm of Her hand. She said, "These add flavor to the payasam, just as spirituality adds sweetness to life."

RENUNCIATES VISITING HOME

Mother said to the brahmachari who had just returned from his family, "My son, you say that you don't have relatives, possessions, and so on, and yet you go home. At the same time, those who claim that they are greatly attached to you hardly ever come here. Think of everything you do with great care. Our Onam is a spiritual occasion. When we assume a role in the world, we should play it well. We came to spiritual life to get rid of the sense of 'I.' 'My parents, my brother and sister, my kith and kin'—all are included in that 'I.' When the 'I' disappears, they all disappear as well. Then all that remains is 'You'—that is, God. We should surrender everything to His will and live accordingly. Only then will we reap the benefit of having embraced spiritual life.

"Whenever you leave the ashram, you lose some of your sadhana time. Each moment of your life is precious. If your father and mother have such a strong wish to have Onam dinner with their son, they can come here. We have made all the preparations for them to come. If you keep going home, you will lose all the samskara which you have nurtured here, and only your attachments will remain.

"In the beginning, sadhaks should stay away from their families. Otherwise, because of their attachment to the family, they won't achieve any progress in their sadhana. Being attached to one's family is like storing sour things in an aluminum vessel: the vessel will develop holes, and then you can't keep anything inside it. Attachment to anything but God eats away our spiritual strength. Attachment is a sadhak's enemy. He should see it as an enemy and stay away from such relations. If you row a boat that is tied to the shore, you won't get anywhere.

"We are children of the Self. We should have the same relationship with our family as we have with any other person. If our parents are old and sick, there is nothing wrong with staying with them and taking care of them. But even in that case, if we have the feeling of '*my* father' or '*my* mother,' all is lost. We should feel compassion for the suffering; we should treat them as God, and that should be our attitude at home as well. If those who talk about 'my son' and 'my daughter' felt true love, wouldn't they come here to see you? If you come to the ashram as a spiritual seeker, you have to live like one; otherwise, you'll be of no benefit either to your family or to the world. And that won't do, children!

"We should pour water at the root of a tree, and not at the top, for only then will the water reach every part of the tree. In the same way, if we really love God, we will love all living beings in the universe because God dwells in the hearts of all beings. God is the foundation of everything. Therefore we should see God in all forms and love and worship Him in all forms."

GOD IS IN THE TEMPLE

One of the devotees began talking about Dayananda Saraswati.[59] He described Dayananda's work against idol worship and told the story of how he had turned in that direction.

"One day Dayananda saw a mouse carrying off a sweet that had been placed in front of an image of Devi as a food offering. He thought, 'What power is there in an image of Devi if it can't even prevent a mouse from stealing the food that has been offered to it? How, then, can we expect such an icon to solve the problems of our lives?'

---

[59] The founder of Arya Samaj, the Hindu reform movement. He tried to revive the Vedic practices, and denounced idol worship.

And from that day on, Dayananda became a staunch opponent of icon worship."

Mother who had quietly listened to all this said, "When a son looks at a picture of his father, is he reminded of the artist who painted the picture, or does he remember his father? The symbols of God help strengthen our focus on Him. We point to a picture of a parrot and tell a child it is a parrot. When the child grows up, he is able to recognize a parrot without the help of the picture. If God is everywhere and everything is God, is He not in that stone image as well? So how can we negate the image? And if the mouse took what was offered to Devi, we can think of it in this way: that when the little creature was hungry, it took what had been given to its own Mother. After all, Devi is the Mother of all beings."

Devotee: "Many Brahmins have been doing japa and puja for years, without realizing the Self."

Mother: "The important thing is detachment and a yearning to know the Truth. You can't attain God by tapas alone. To reach God you have to have a pure heart and you have to love."

Devotee: "The *Gita* says that the body is a *kshetra* (temple)."

Mother: "We make statements like 'God is within us and not without,' because we still have a sense of inside and outside. We should see all bodies as temples, and we should think of all things as our own body."

CASTE DIFFERENCES ARE MEANINGLESS

Devotee: "Amma, people observe caste-based *ayitham*[60] even now. Even learned gurus follow it."

Mother: "Do you know the story of the low-caste sweeper who approached Sri Shankaracharya? Shankaracharya told him to move out of the way. The sweeper asked, 'What should I move, the body or the soul? If you want me to move my soul, where would I move it? The same soul is everywhere. If you want me to move my body, what is the difference between my body and yours? Both are made of the same material. The only difference is the color of the skin.'"

A devotee sang a couplet. "Some boast of their Brahminhood that not even Lord Brahma is their equal!" Mother laughed.

Mother: "A true Brahmin is someone who knows Brahman, someone who has raised the *kundalini* all the way to the sahasrara (the thousand-petalled lotus) in the head. The reason for advising those of highly evolved samskara to avoid mingling with those of unrefined samskara, is that such mingling will affect their own samskara. But where can you find a true Brahmin today? The scriptures say that in the Kali age, Brahmins will become *Sudras*[61]

---

[60] The Malayalam word *ayitham* (from the Sanskrit *asuddham*) refers to the observance of the belief that a person of high caste is defiled by the approach or touch of a person of certain low castes.

[61] Sudra is the lowest of the four principal castes according to the ancient Indian system, while Brahmin is the highest caste.

and Sudras will become Brahmins. So at the present time, caste-based injunctions are meaningless.

"In the olden days people were given the kind of work that best suited their samskara. But that isn't the practice today. In those days, distinguished Brahmins were entrusted with temple duties. Today we can't label a Brahmin's son as a Brahmin, or a *Kshatriya's* son as a Kshatriya. There are many members of the traditional fishermen's caste in this area who are well educated and have good jobs. They are not even familiar with the traditional work of their community."

A young man raised a question: "Hasn't the Lord said in the *Gita*, 'I Myself established the four *varnas* (major castes)'? In that case, isn't He the one who is responsible for all the injustice that is prevalent nowadays in the name of caste and religion?"

Another devotee responded, "Why not quote the next line as well? It says, 'According to the *gunas*.' This means that one becomes a Brahmin or a *Chandala* (outcaste)[62] through one's actions and conduct, and not by birth."

Mother: "One doesn't become a Brahmin until the sacred thread ceremony (*upanayana*), just as one doesn't become a Christian before being baptized. The Muslims also have similar rituals. Until a child undergoes such a ceremony, what is he really? You see, man made all these castes, not

---

[62] A Chandala belongs to the lowest caste, even lower than the Sudras.

God. It is no use blaming God for all the injustice that has been done in the name of caste and religion."

Mother's words put an end to the debate. By now it was quite late, but not even the small children had gone to bed. A crowd had gathered around the swing nearby. A few grownups were trying to persuade a little girl to sing an Onam song. At first she shyly resisted, but finally she sang with her innocent voice:

Maveli nadu vaneedum kalam...

When Maveli[63] ruled the land,
All men were equal.
There was no theft or deceit,
And not a single word of falsehood...

To those who sat near Mother, watching the fleecy autumn clouds drift through the moonlit sky, it seemed that if Onam was the festival to commemorate an ancient time, when the world was beautiful because there was equality everywhere, then, here in Amma's presence it was Onam every day, because here all people of different races, castes, and creeds lived together as the children of one loving Mother.

---

[63] Maveli, or Mahabali, was a demon king who is reputed to have ruled the land with justice and righteousness. The tradition in Kerala holds that he visits the earth annually at the time of Onam to see how his former subjects are faring.

Wednesday, September 17, 1986

A class for the brahmacharis was in progress. Mother came down from Her room and walked over to the cowshed. The tank that had been built behind the cowshed to catch cow dung and urine was full. Mother filled a bucket with the contents of the tank and poured it out under the coconut trees. Soon, the brahmacharis arrived from their class. They took the bucket from Mother and continued the work She had started. Because of their insistence, She stopped what She was doing and walked away.

Her hands, feet, and clothing were smeared and splattered with cow dung. A woman devotee opened the water tap and tried to wash Mother's hands and feet, but Mother wouldn't allow it. "No, my daughter, Amma will do it Herself. Why make your hands dirty as well?"

Devotee: "Amma, why do you do this kind of work? Don't you have your children here for that?"

Mother: "Daughter, if Amma stands aside without doing any of the work, they will imitate Her and become lazy, and they will become a burden to the world. That must not happen. Amma is only glad to work. She feels sorry for Gayatri, though. When Amma does these things, Her clothes get dirty and Gayatri is the one who washes them. Even if Amma tries to wash them, Gayatri won't let Her. But sometimes Amma tricks her and does the washing!" Mother laughed.

Another woman came forward to prostrate.

Mother: "Don't prostrate now, daughter! Amma's clothes are full of cow dung. Let Amma go and take a bath and come back."

Mother went to Her room and returned a few minutes later. The devotees, who had been standing around the kalari, now gathered around Her. The brahmacharis also came.

SATSANG IS IMPORTANT
SADHANA INDISPENSABLE

A brahmachari asked: "Amma, why do you give so much importance to satsang?"

Mother: "Satsang teaches us how to live properly. If we have a map with us when we travel to a distant place, we can get there on time, without losing our way. Similarly, with satsang we can guide our lives on the right course, avoiding all dangers. If you have learned how to cook, you can easily prepare a meal; and if you have studied the science of agriculture, farming will be easy for you. If you understand what the real goal of life is and work in the right way towards realizing it, your life will be filled with joy. Satsang aids us in this way.

"With fire we can burn down our house or we can use the fire to cook our food. With a needle we can pierce our eye, or we can stitch our clothes. So we have to find the right use for each thing. Satsang helps us to understand the true meaning of life, and how to live accordingly. What we gain through satsang is a treasure that lasts throughout our lives."

Br: "Is satsang by itself enough to attain God-realization?"

Mother: "Attending a lecture on the theory of cooking isn't enough to remove hunger. To appease your hunger, you have to cook the food and eat it. If you want to grow fruit, just studying agriculture isn't enough. You have to plant the fruit trees and nurse them.

"It is not enough to know that there is water beneath a particular spot, because that won't give you any water. You have to dig a well there. Nor can you quench your thirst by merely looking at a picture of a well. You have to draw water from a real well and drink it. Is it enough to sit in a parked car, staring at a map? To reach your destination, you have to travel on the road which is shown on the map. In the same way, it's not enough to just take part in satsangs, or to read the scriptures. To experience the Truth, you have to live according to those words.

"Only through sadhana can we avoid being enslaved by circumstances, and incorporate what we have learned into our lives. We should learn the spiritual principles by listening to satsangs, and then live according to those principles. We should free ourselves from all desires and worship God, without any desires or expectations.

"Even though the scriptures say, 'I am Brahman,' 'Thou art That,' etc., the ignorance within us has to be dispelled before the knowledge of Reality can shine forth. Repeating, 'I am Brahman,' without doing any sadhana, is like calling a blind child by the name Prakasham (light).

"There was a man who once gave a speech in which he said, 'We are Brahman, aren't we? So there is no need for sadhana?' After the discourse he was served dinner. The waiter put a plate in front of him on which there were pieces of paper with the words 'rice,' 'sambar,' and 'payasam' written on them. There was no food on the plate. The speaker became angry. 'What do you think you're doing! Are you trying to insult me?' he asked.

"The waiter said, 'I was listening to your speech earlier this evening. I heard you declare that you are Brahman, and that this thought is enough; that there is no need for sadhana. So I thought you'd surely agree that it's enough for you to just think about food to appease your hunger. There's obviously no need to eat.'

"It isn't enough to just talk, children! We have to act. Only through sadhana can we realize the Truth. To someone who doesn't make any effort, satsang is like a coconut given to a jackal: his hunger will never be appeased. A tonic will improve your health, provided you follow the directions written on the bottle and take the right dosage. Satsang is like learning those directions, and sadhana is like drinking the tonic. Satsang teaches us about the eternal and the transitory, but only through sadhana will we be able to experience and realize what we have learned.

"If we put the different parts of a radio together in the prescribed manner and connect it to a battery, we can hear the programs broadcast by a distant station, while remaining in our own home. By conditioning our minds properly through sadhana, and living our lives according to the teachings of the mahatmas, we can enjoy infinite bliss while we are still in our present bodies. If we do sadhana and selfless service, we don't need anything else.

"However much Vedanta we study, without doing sadhana, we cannot experience Reality. That which we seek is within us, but to reach it, we have to do sadhana. To turn the seed into a tree, we have to plant it in the soil, water it, and fertilize it. It's not enough to just hold it in our hands."

No one noticed time slipping by as they sat listening to Mother's nectar-like words. Finally She reminded them, "Go to bed, children. It's very late. Don't you have to get up for archana in the morning?"

They all stood up and walked away half-heartedly. After going a little distance, they stopped to look back and saw Mother's enchanting form bathed in the moonlight. Wasn't it the radiance of that face that was reflected in the moon and the sun and the stars?

Tameva bhantam anubhati sarvam
Tasya bhasa sarvamidam vibhati.

When He shines, everything shines in His wake.
By His light, all things shine.

—Kathopanishad

Glossary

ACHYUTA: "The Imperishable One; The Everlasting One." One of Vishnu's names.

ADHARMA: Unrighteousness, sin, opposed to Divine Harmony.

ADVAITA: Non-dualism. The philosophy which teaches that the Supreme Reality is "One and indivisible."

AHIMSA: Non-injury, non-violence. Refraining from hurting any living creature by thought word or deed.

AMBIKA: "Mother." The Divine Mother.

AMMACHI: Mother.

ANNA PRASANA: The first feeding a baby is given of solid food.

ANNAPURNA: The Goddess of Plenty. A form of Durga.

ARATI: The ritual in which light is offered in the form of burning camphor, and a bell is rung before the Deity in a temple or a holy person, as a consummation of puja (worship). The camphor does not leave behind any residue, which symbolizes the total annihilation of the ego.

ARCHANA: "Offering for worship." A form of worship in which the names of a deity are chanted, usually 108, 300 or 1000 times in one sitting.

ASANA: A small mat which the aspirant sits on during meditation. Yoga posture.

ASHRAM: "Place of striving." A place where spiritual seekers and aspirants live or visit in order to lead a spiritual life and practice sadhana. It is usually the home of a spiritual master, saint or ascetic, who guides the aspirants.

ATMAN: The true Self. The essential nature of our real existence. One of the fundamental tenets of the Sanatana Dharma is that we are not the physical body, feelings, mind, intellect or personality. We are the eternal, pure, unblemishable Self.

AUM: Sacred syllable. The Primordial Sound or Vibration, which represents Brahman and the entire creation. AUM is the primary mantra and is usually found at the beginning of other mantras.

AVADHUT: A Self-realized soul who, seeing only the unity of everything, has transcended all social conventions.

AVATAR: "Descent." An incarnation of the Divine. The aim of a God-incarnation is to protect the good, destroy evil, restore righteousness in the world, and to lead mankind towards the spiritual Goal. It is very rare for an incarnation to be a full descent (Purnavatar).

AYITHAM: The Malayalam word *ayitham* (from the Sanskrit *asuddham*) refers to the observance of the belief that a person of high caste is defiled by the approach or touch of a person of certain low castes.

AYURVEDA: "The science of life." Ancient Indian, holistic, health and medicinal system. Ayurvedic medicines are usually prepared from medicinal herbs and plants.

BHAGAVAD GITA: "God's Song." Bhagavad = of the Lord; Gita = song, referring particularly to advice. The teachings which Krishna gave Arjuna on the Kurukshetra battlefield at the beginning of the Mahabharata war. It is a practical guide for man's daily life and contains the essence of Vedic wisdom.

BHAGAVAN: The Blessed Lord; God. According to Vedanga, a branch of Vedic literature, Bhagavan is He who destroys transmigratory existence and bestows union with the Supreme Spirit.

BHAGAVATA: See Srimad Bhagavatam.

BHAJAN: Devotional singing.

BHAKTI: Devotion.

BHAKTI YOGA: "Union through bhakti." The Path of Devotion. The way of attaining Self-realization through devotion and complete surrender to God.

BHASMA: Sacred ash.

BHAVA: Divine mood.

BHAVA DARSHAN: The occasion when Mother receives devotees in the exalted state of the Divine Mother. In the early days, Mother also appeared in Krishna bhava.

BHIKSHA: Alms.

BIJAKSHARA: A seed letter in a mantra.

BRAHMACHARI(NI): A celibate disciple, who practices spiritual disciplines and is usually being trained by a Guru.

BRAHMACHARYA: "Abidance in Brahman." Celibacy and discipline of the mind and the senses.

BRAHMAN: The Absolute Reality; the Whole; the Supreme Being, which encompasses and pervades everything, and is One and indivisible.

BRAHMA SUTRAS: Aphorisms by Sage Badarayana (Veda Vyasa) that expound Vedantic philosophy.

CHAMMANDI: Coconut chutney.

CHANDALA: Outcast.

CHECHI: (Malayalam) "Older sister." It is more affectionate to call someone "Chechi" than by their name.

DAKSHAYANI: A name of the Divine Mother Parvati.

DARSHAN: An audience with or a vision of the Divine or a holy person.

DEVI: "The Effulgent One." The Goddess

DEVI BHAVA: "The Divine Mood of Devi." The state in which Mother reveals Her oneness and identity with the Divine Mother.

DHARA: A continuous stream of liquid. The term is often used to denote a form of medical treatment by which a medicinal liquid is poured continuously over the patient. It is also a form of ceremonial bathing of the icon of a deity.

DHARMA: "That which upholds the universe." Dharma has many meanings, including, the Divine Law, the law of existence, in accordance with divine harmony, righteousness, religion, duty, responsibility, right conduct, justice, goodness and truth. Dharma signifies the inner principles of religion.

DHYANA: Meditation, contemplation.

DIKSHA: Initiation.

DOSHA: Pancake made of rice flour.

DURGA: A name of Shakti, the Divine Mother. She is often depicted as wielding a number of weapons and riding a lion. She is the destroyer of evil and the protector of that which is good. She destroy the desires and negative tendencies (vasanas) of her children and unveils the Supreme Self.

DWARAKA: The island city where Krishna lived and discharged his kingly responsibilities. After Krishna left his body, Dwaraka was submerged in the ocean. Archeologists have recently discovered the remains of a city in the ocean near Gujarat, which is believed to be Dwaraka.

EKAGRATA: One-pointed concentration.

GAYATRI: The most important mantra in the Vedas, associated with the Goddess Savita. Upon being given upanayana, one is supposed to chant this mantra. Also, the Goddess Gayatri.

GITA: Song. See *Bhagavad Gita*

GOPALA: "Cowherd Boy." One of Krishna's names.

GOPI: The gopis were cowherd girls and milk maids who lived in Vrindavan. They were Krishna's closest devotees and were known for their supreme devotion to the Lord. They exemplify the most intense love for God.

GRIHASTHASHRAMI: A grihasthasrami is someone who is dedicated to a spiritual life, while leading the life of a householder.

GUNA: Primal Nature (Prakriti) consists of three gunas, i. e., fundamental qualities, tendencies or stresses, which underlie all manifestation: sattva (goodness, purity, serenity), rajas (activity, passion) and tamas (darkness, inertia, ignorance). These three gunas continually act and react with each other. The phenomenal world is composed of different combinations of the three gunas.

GURU: "One who removes the darkness of ignorance." Spiritual master/guide.

GURUKULA: An ashram with a living guru, where disciples live and study with the guru.

GURUVAYOOR: Place of pilgrimage in Kerala, near Trissur, where there is a famous Krishna temple.

HAIMAVATI: A name of the Divine Mother Parvati.

HATHA YOGA: A system of physical and mental exercises, developed in ancient times, with the purpose of making the body and its vital functions into perfect instruments, in order to help one attain Self-realization.

HOMA: Sacrificial fire.

HRIDAYASUNYA: Heartless.

HRIDAYESHA: the Lord of one's heart.

JAPA: Repetition of a mantra, a prayer or one of God's Names.

JARASANDHA: The powerful king of Magadha, who fought 18 battles with Lord Krishna, and was killed by Bhima.

JIVATMAN: The individual soul.

JNANA: Spiritual or divine wisdom. True Knowledge is a direct experience, beyond any possible perception of the limited mind, intellect, and senses. It is attained through spiritual practices and the grace of God or the Guru.

KALI: "The Dark One." An aspect of the Divine Mother. From the viewpoint of the ego, She may seem frightening because She destroys the ego. But She destroys the ego and transforms us only out of Her immeasurable compassion. Kali has many forms; in Her benevolent form, She is known as Bhadra Kali. A devotee knows that behind Her fierce facade, the loving Mother is to be found, who protects Her children and bestows the grace of Liberation.

KAMANDALU: A kettle with a handle and bent nozzle, used by monks for collecting water and food.

KAMSA: Lord Krishna's demonic uncle whom he killed.

KANJI: Rice gruel.

KANNA: "He who has beautiful eyes." A nickname of Krishna as a baby. There are many stories about Krishna's childhood and he is sometimes worshipped in the form of a Divine Child.

KAPHA: See "Vata, pitta, kapha."

KARMA: Action, deed.

KARMA YOGA: "Union through action." The spiritual path of detached, selfless service and of dedicating the fruit of all one's actions to God.

KARMA YOGI: A karma yogi follows the path of selfless action.

KARTYAYANI: A name of the Divine Mother Parvati.

KAURAVAS: The one hundred children of Dhritharasthra and Gandhari. The Kauravas were the enemies of the Pandavas, who they fought in the Mahabharata War.

KINDI: A traditional bronze or brass container with a spout, usually used for worship.

KIRTAN: hymn.

KRISHNA: "He who draws us to himself," "the Dark One." The principal incarnation of Vishnu. He was born into a royal family, but grew up with foster parents and lived as a young cowherd in Vrindavan, where he was loved and worshipped by his devoted companions, the gopis and gopas. Krishna later became the ruler of Dwaraka. He was a friend of and adviser to his cousins, the Pandavas, especially Arjuna, to whom he revealed his teachings in the *Bhagavad Gita*.

KRISHNA BHAVA: The state in which Mother reveals Her oneness and identity with Krishna.

KUMKUM: Saffron.

KSHATRIYA: The warrior caste.

KSHETRA: Temple; field; body.

KUNDALINI: "The Serpent Power." The spiritual energy, which rests like a coiled snake at the base of the spine. Through spiritual practices it is made to rise through the sushumna canal, a subtle nerve within the spine, and move up through the chakras (power centers). As the kundalini rises from chakra to chakra, the spiritual aspirant begins to experience finer levels of consciousness. The kundalini finally reaches the highest chakra at the top of the head (the Sahasrara Lotus), which leads to Liberation.

Lakshya bodha: Constant awareness of, and intent on, the Supreme Goal.

Lalita Sahasranama: The thousand names of the Divine Mother in the form of Lalitambika.

Leela: "Play." The movements and activities of the Divine, which by nature are free and not necessarily subject to the laws of nature.

Mahatma: "Great soul." When Mother uses the word "mahatma," She is referring to a Self-realized soul.

Mahasamadhi: When a realized soul passes away, it is known as mahasamadhi, "the great samadhi."

Mala: Rosary, usually made of rudraksha seeds, tulasi wood or sandalwood beads.

Mantra: Sacred formula or prayer which is constantly repeated. This awakens one's dormant spiritual powers and helps one to reach the goal. It is most effective if received from a spiritual master during initiation.

Mantra diksha: Mantra initiation.

Mataji: "Mother." The suffix "ji" denotes respect.

Maya: "Illusion." The Divine Power or veil with which God, in his Divine Play of Creation, conceals himself and gives the impression of the many, thereby creating the illusion of separation. As Maya veils Reality, she deludes us, making us believe that Perfection is to be found outside of ourselves.

MOOKAMBIKA: The Divine Mother, as she is worshipped in a famous Devi temple in Kalloor, South India.

MUKTI: Liberation.

MULADHARA: The lowest of the six chakras, situated at the base of the spine.

MUDRA: Sacred hand sign or gesture, which represents spiritual truths.

NANDA: Krishna's foster father.

NARAYANA: Nara = knowledge, water. "He who is established in Supreme Knowledge." "He who dwells in the causal waters." Name of Vishnu.

NASYAM: A cleansing ayurvedic treatment, which consists of a nasal infusion of medicated oil.

OJAS: Sexual energy transmuted into subtle vital energy through spiritual practices.

OM NAMAH SHIVAYA: The Panchakshara Mantra (mantra consisting of five letters), which means, "Salutations to Shiva, the Auspicious One."

PADA PUJA: The worship of God's, the Guru's or a saint's feet. As the feet support the body, the Guru Principle supports the Supreme Truth. The Guru's feet thus represent the Supreme Truth.

PANDAVAS: The five sons of King Pandu and heroes of the epic Mahabharata.

PARAMATMAN: The Supreme Spirit; Brahman.

PARVATI: "Daughter of the mountain." Shiva's divine consort. A name of the Divine Mother.

PAYASAM: A sweet rice pudding.

PEETHAM: Sacred seat.

PITTA: See "Vata, pitta, kapha."

PRADAKSHINA: A form of worship in which one circumambulates in a clockwise direction a holy place, a temple or a holy person.

PRARABDHA: "Responsibilities, burdens." The fruit of past actions from this and past lives, which will manifest in this life.

PRASAD: The consecrated offerings distributed after puja. And whatever a mahatma gives, as a sign of his blessing, is considered prasad.

PREMA: Supreme love.

PREMA BHAKTI: Supreme love and devotion.

PUJA: Ritualistic worship.

PURNAM: Full, perfect.

RADHA: One of Krishna's gopis. She was closer to Krishna than any other gopi and personifies the highest and purest love for God. In Goloka, the celestial abode of Krishna, Radha is Krishna's Divine Consort.

RAJAS: Activity, passion. One of the three gunas or fundamental qualities of Nature.

RAMA: "The Giver of Joy." The Divine hero in the epic, *Ramayana*. He was an incarnation of Vishnu, and is considered to be the ideal of virtue.

RAMAYANA: "The life of Rama." One of India's greatest epic poems, depicting the life of Rama, written by Valmiki. Rama was an incarnation of Vishnu. A major part of the epic describes how Sita, Rama's wife, was abducted and taken to Sri Lanka by Ravana, the demon king, and how she was rescued by Rama and his devotees.

RASAM: A broth made with tamarind, salt, chilies, onion and spices.

RAVANA: The demon king of Sri Lanka, who is the villain in the Ramayana.

RUDRAKSHA: The seeds of the rudraksha tree, which have both medicinal and spiritual power, and are associated with Lord Shiva.

SADHAK: A spiritual aspirant who practices sadhana for the purpose of attaining Self-realization.

SADHANA: Spiritual disciplines and practices, such as meditation, prayer, japa, the reading of holy scriptures and fasting.

SAHASRARA: "Thousand-spoked" (lotus). The highest chakra, situated at the top of the head, wherein the Kundalini (Shakti) unites with Shiva. It resembles a lotus flower with a thousand petals.

SAMADHI: Sam = with; adhi = the Lord. Oneness with God. A state of deep, one-pointed concentration, in which all thoughts subside, the mind enters into a state of complete stillness in which only Pure Consciousness remains, as one abides in the Atman (Self).

SAMBAR: A broth made of vegetables and spices.

SAMSARA: The world of plurality; the cycle of birth, death and rebirth.

SAMSKARAS: Samskara has two meanings: Culture and the totality of impressions imprinted in the mind by experiences (from this or earlier lives), which influence the life of a human being—his nature, actions, state of mind, etc.

SANATANA DHARMA: "The Eternal Religion." The traditional name for Hinduism.

SANDHYA: Sunrise, midday, or sunset—usually sunset.

SANKALPA: A creative, integral resolve which is manifested. The sankalpa of an ordinary person does not always yield the corresponding fruit, but a sankalpa made by a Self-realized being inevitably manifests its aimed result.

SANNYASI: "A monk or nun who has taken formal vows of renunciation. A sannyasi traditionally wears an ochre colored cloth representing the burning away of all attachments.

SATGURU: Self-realized, spiritual master.

SATSANG: Sat = truth, being; sanga = association with. Being in the company of the wise and virtuous. Also a spiritual discourse by a sage or scholar.

SHAKTI: Power. Shakti is also a name of the Universal Mother, the dynamic aspect of Brahman.

SHASTRI: Religious scholar.

SHIVA: "The Auspicious One; the Gracious One; the Good One." A form of the Supreme Being. The masculine Principle; the static aspect of Brahman. Also the aspect of the Trinity associated with the destruction of the universe, the destruction of that which is not Real.

SHRADDHA: In Sanskrit, Shraddha means faith rooted in wisdom and experience, whereas the same term in Malayalam means dedication to one's work and attentive awareness in every action. Mother often uses the term in the latter sense.

SRI or SHREE: "Luminous, holy." An honorable prefix.

SHRIDARA: "He who holds Lakshmi." A name of Vishnu.

SRIMAD BHAGAVATA: One of the 18 scriptures known as the Puranas, dealing with the incarnations of Vishnu, especially, and in great detail, the life of Krishna. It emphasizes the path of devotion.

TAMAS: Darkness, inertia, apathy, ignorance. Tamas is one of the three gunas or fundamental qualities of Nature.

TANDAVA: Shiva's dance of bliss, especially at dusk.

TAPAS: "Heat." Self-discipline, austerities, penance and self-sacrifice; spiritual practices which burn up the impurities of the mind.

TAPASVI: One engaged in tapas or spiritual austerities.

TENGA: Coconut in Malayalam.

TIRTHAM: Holy water.

TYAGA: Renunciation.

UPANAYANA: The traditional ceremony in which a child born to upper caste parents is given the sacred thread and initiated into sacred studies.

UPANISHADS: "To sit at the feet of the Master." "That which destroys ignorance." The fourth and concluding part of the Vedas, which deals with the philosophy of Vedanta.

VADA: a savory, deep-fried, patty made of lentils.

VAIRAGYA: Detachment.

VANAPRASTHA: The recluse stage of life. In the ancient Indian tradition, there are four stages of life. First the child is sent to a gurukula where he (or she) lives the life of a brahmachari. Then he gets married and lives as a house-holder, dedicated to spiritual life (grihasthashrami). When the couple's children are old enough to take care of them-selves, the parents retreat to a hermitage or an ashram, where they live a purely spiritual life, doing spiritual prac-tices. During the fourth stage of their lives, they renounce the world completely and live the life of sannyasis.

VARNA: Major caste. The four major castes are Brah-min, Kshatriya, Vaishya, and Sudra.

VASANA: From "vas" = living, remaining. Vasanas are the latent tendencies or subtle desires within the mind which have a tendency to manifest into action and habits. Vasanas result from the impressions of experiences (samskaras) which exist in the subconscious.

VATA, PITTA, KAPHA: According to the ancient science of ayurveda, there are three primary life forces or biologi-cal humors, called vata, pitta and kapha, corresponding to the elements of air, fire, and water. These three elements determine the life processes of growth and decay, and are the causative forces in the disease process. The predomi-nance of one or more of these elements in the individual determines his psycho-physical nature.

VEDA: "Knowledge, Wisdom." The ancient, sacred scriptures of Hinduism. A collection of holy texts in Sanskrit, which are divided into four parts: Rig, Yajur, Sama and Atharva. They are among the world's oldest scriptures. The *Vedas* are considered to be the direct revelation of the Supreme Truth which God bestowed upon the Rishis.

VEDANTA: "Veda-end." The philosophy of the *Upanishads*, the concluding part of the Vedas, which holds the Ultimate Truth to be "One without a Second."

VEENA: An Indian string instrument which is associated with the Divine Mother.

VRINDAVAN: The place where the historical Krishna lived as a young shepherd.

VYASA: The Sage who divided the one *Veda* into four parts. He also composed 18 *Puranas* (epics), the *Mahabharata* and the *Brahma Sutras*.

YAGA: Elaborate Vedic sacrificial rite.

YAJNA: Offering.

YAMA AND NIYAMA: The do's and the don'ts on the path of yoga.

YASHODA: Krishna's foster mother.

YOGA: "To unite." A series of methods through which one can attain oneness with the Divine. A Path which leads to Self-realization.

YOGI: Someone who is established in the practice of Yoga, or is established in union with the Supreme Spirit.

Index To Volume 1

C

Company
    influence of bad 15

D

Destiny
    can be changed through tapas   125-126
Detachment
    is essential for Self-realization   41, 44-48, 68, 169-170,
        252
Devotion
    accompanied by love, *prema bhakti*   80
    as protection from sorrows   105
    bhakti yoga   16-18
    in principle (*tattvattile bhakti*)   79
    is indispensable for experiencing Truth   73
    is not just going to temples   79
    is tuning our minds to God   16-18
    signs of true   218
    the greatness of   79-82
Dharma (righteousness)
    not being taught to children or followed by parents   241-
        246

E

Ego
    guru's role in eliminating   34-36

F

Faith in God   223

Index To Volume 2

Forgiveness
>through seeing everything as self   43
>as true sign of spirituality   212-213

G

God
>all His forms are the same   160-162
>constant remembrance of   280
>now is the time to turn to   127-131
>punishes out of compassion   243-244

God realization see Self-realization

Gopis
>saw Krishna in everything   42-43, 161

Grihasthasrami see also householder
>the meaning of a true   215-216

Guru
>advantage of having a woman as   137
>giving one's mind as gift to   48
>greatness of a satguru   15-16
>importance of living in the company of   20-21
>mantra initiation from   14-16
>need for living near the guru   262-264
>need for surrendering to   67-69
>we cannot reach the goal without a   261
>**will test disciple's surrender   250-252, 253-255**

H

Happiness
>is born out of love   232
>is not found in the external world   28, 88-89

Householders
>Mother's advice on bringing up children   86-87
>special challenges faced in spiritual path by   185

Humility
>is not a weakness   65